WILLIAM EMPSON
The Man and His Work

WILLIAM EMPSON

The Man and His Work

Edited by

Roma Gill

Department of English Literature
University of Sheffield

Routledge & Kegan Paul
London and Boston

First published in 1974
by Routledge & Kegan Paul Ltd
Broadway House, 68–74 Carter Lane,
London EC4V 5EL and
9 Park Street Boston, Mass. 02108, USA
Printed in Great Britain by
Richard Clay (The Chaucer Press), Ltd,
Bungay, Suffolk

ISBN 0 7100 7823 4

Contents

Preface

Roma Gill

When I first approached some of William Empson's friends in search of papers for this volume, I asked them to write about the man himself, or his work, or the subjects that interested him. I hoped thereby to achieve some sort of coherence for the series of essays, and also to give some impression of the man, the poet, and the critic who has been such a powerful influence in the twentieth century. The first aim might have been satisfied had I asked for papers only on the Elizabethans for instance; but this would have given a false impression. Empson, as the bibliography of his published works clearly indicates, has no 'period', no narrow specialism. The papers presented here range from the biographical to the academic; but what every one suggests is the impossibility of separating the man from his work and the 'life' from the 'thought'—even on a ski-ing holiday.

My thanks are due to all the contributors to this volume, for their papers and for their enthusiasm.

The poem 'A Toast' by W. H. Auden on p. 1 first appeared in his collection *Epistle to a Godson* (1972) and is printed here by courtesy of Faber & Faber.

On his retirement in 1971 from the Chair of English Literature at the University of Sheffield William Empson founded a prize to be awarded annually for the encouragement of student drama; royalties from the sale of this book will be contributed towards this fund.

Contributors

Janet Adam Smith   Author and critic; sometime Assistant Editor of the *Listener* and Literary Editor of the *New Statesman*. She and her husband Michael Roberts (who died in 1948) were friends of William Empson, whom Roberts had known since the late 1920s.

W. H. Auden   Poet, who met Empson during 1939. Empson admired his poetry, but doubts whether there was any influence.

Francis Berry   Professor of English in the University of London (Royal Holloway College); he was a departmental colleague of Empson's at Sheffield from 1952 to 1970.

Ronald Bottrall   Poet and retired diplomat, who first met Empson in 1927 at Cambridge and continued the friendship thereafter in London, Tokyo, and Singapore.

M. C. Bradbrook   Professor of English at Cambridge University and Mistress of Girton College. She was a contemporary of Empson's as an undergraduate at Cambridge and bracketed with him at the head of the English Tripos Part I in 1929.

George Fraser   Reader in English at the University of Leicester, who began reading Empson in his teens, first met him in 1946, and has since seen him in such varied settings as Hampstead, Tokyo, and Sheffield.

Rintaro Fukuhara   Retired Professor of English; he was head of the English Department at the Bunrika Daigaku in Tokyo when Empson taught there.

Graham Hough   Professor of English in the University of Cambridge, and fellow of Darwin College.

L. C. Knights   King Edward VII Professor of English at Cambridge, who was Empson's predecessor at the University of Sheffield; the two were contemporaries as undergraduates at Cambridge but met in America.

Moira Megaw   Lecturer in English at the University of Bristol.

Karl Miller   Editor of the *Listener* from 1967 to 1973 and formerly literary editor of the *Spectator* and the *New Statesman*.

Kathleen Raine   Poet and scholar; she was a fellow-student with Empson at Cambridge.

I. A. Richards   Professor Emeritus of the University of Harvard, poet and critic; for Empson's fourth year at Cambridge (the only year when he studied English) Professor Richards was his supervisor.

Christopher Ricks   Professor of English at the University of Bristol; one of Empson's greatest admirers, who interviewed him for *the Review* (June 1963).

A. G. Stock   Professor of English at Bangladesh, who has spent most of her working life in India but has maintained a friendship with Empson since 1941.

John Wain   Writer and Professor of Poetry at the University of Oxford; he and Empson met in 1952, became friends, and Empson was best man at Professor Wain's wedding.

A Toast

(To Professor William Empson on the occasion
of his retirement in 1971)

W. H. Auden

As *quid pro quo* for your enchanting verses,
when approached by Sheffield, at first I wondered
if I could manage *Just a Smack at Empson*,
   but nothing occurred.

All I could fault was your conceit that Milton's
God, obtrusive prolix baroque Olympian,
is our Christian one. Who, though, but you has pondered
   so deeply on *Alice*?

Good voices are rare, still rarer singers with
perfect pitch. If Graves was right, if at Cambridge
the tuning's a wee bit sharp, then at Oxford
   it well may be flat.

Our verbal games are separate, thank heaven,
but Time twins us: both learned to person Life in
an open-hearthed, nannied, un-T-V'd world, where
   cars looked peculiar.

To wish you long long years would be heartless (may you
leave when you want to, no earlier): but I gladly,
dear Bill, dear fellow mandarin, smile to your
   future holidays.

The Ambiguity of William Empson

M. C. Bradbrook

If I were asked to choose the greatest passage of criticism in Empson, I would plump for the analysis of Pope on the Duke of Chandos's seat, Canons; especially its conclusion.

When Pope prophesies the destruction of the building his language takes on a grandeur which reflects back and transfigures it:

> Another age shall see the golden ear
> Embrown the slope and nod on the parterre,
> Deep harvest bury all his pride has planned,
> And laughing Ceres reassume the land.

These lines seem to me to convey what is called an intuitive intimacy with nature; one is made to see a cornfield as something superb and old as humanity, and breaking down dykes irresistibly, like the sea. But, of course, it *embrowns* as with further, more universal *gilding* and *nods on the parterre* like a duchess. . . .

This seems to me rather a curious example of the comparison which elevates both parties; in this case, it is the admiration latent in a sneer which becomes available as a source of energy for these subsidiary uses; and also an example of how the Wordsworthian feeling for nature can be called forth not by an isolated and moping interest in nature on her own account, but by a conception of nature in terms of human politics. I hope, at any rate, you agree with me, that the lines convey this sort of sympathy intensely; that there is some sense of the immensity of harvest through a whole country; that the relief with which the cripple for a moment identifies himself with something so strong and generous gives these two couplets an extraordinary scale. *Seven Types of Ambiguity*, pp. 161–2

This is not the sort of writing with which Empson is most often associated; but it shews that his intellectual gymnastics, those analyses of variables by which he displays himself as most mathematically agile, are rooted in a much warmer and richer organic response to complex human situations embodied in Nature. In the passage quoted, he enjoys the transfiguration of the scene as he does in his own poems:

> How much more foliage appears by starlight;
> . . . Hall shelters at night under the trees . . .
> *Sleeping out in college cloister*

> Magnolias, for instance, when in bud,
> Are right in doing anything they can think of;
> Free by predestination in the blood,
> Saved by their own sap, shed for themselves,
> Their texture can impose their architecture,
> Their sapient matter is always already informed.
> Whether they burgeon, massed wax flames, or flare
> Plump spaced-out saints, in their gross prime, at prayer,
> Or leave the sooted branches bare
> To sag at tip from a sole blossom there,
> They know no act that will not make them fair.
> *Doctrinal Point*

Empson is generally thought of, both as poet and critic, as working with a high degree of abstraction, but Nature transfigured by perception becomes very often for him 'nature in terms of human politics'. Conversely, he interprets the painful conflicts of our human nature through a transfigured scene. This is often achieved by an alteration of scale.

Empson once said that poems were written to get rid of a neurosis—no grit, no pearl, was his phrase.[1] Conflict and pain are with immense difficulty contained and resolved in his poems, and in many of the poems about which he writes best. Even a deeply buried human pain may be transformed by 'the inventive':

> This last pain for the damned the Fathers found;
> 'They knew the bliss with which they were not crowned.'
> Such, but on earth . . .
> *This Last Pain*

Yet, 'magic-lanterned on the smoke of hell', the idyllic inventions of man can restore for him 'a dappled shade' of a happier Nature.

The human imagination can build more securely by an accepted
fantasy than could the architect of Chandos.

> Feign then what's by a decent tact believed
> And act that state is only so conceived,
>   And build an edifice of form
>   For house where phantoms may keep warm.

The poems from which I am quoting all belong to Empson's
first volume, which appeared in 1935, by the end of which decade
he had stopped writing poetry. The first stage of his work, represented by these poems, and by *Seven Types of Ambiguity*, seems
to me to have a natural unity, springing from a level deeper than
that of the verbal agility so generally recognized, praised—but
sometimes criticized as over ingenious. As he observes in a note
to the most ingenious 'Bacchus': 'Life involves maintaining oneself between contradictions that can't be solved by analysis.'

The balance or reconciliation of opposite or discordant qualities, of sameness with difference; of the general with the concrete,
the idea with the image . . . a more than usual state of emotion
with more than usual order; judgment ever awake and steady self-
possession, with enthusiasm and feeling profound or vehement—
Coleridge's definition of the poet's activity (*Biographia Literaria*,
ch. XIV) could have been recited by any pupil of Richards as
surely as a Presbyterian could recite the Shorter Catechism. It was
partly this definition of the poet and poetry, I would think, from
which *Seven Types of Ambiguity* originated, although Empson himself in his preface names as 'onlie begetter' I. A. Richards and for
the method, Robert Graves's and Laura Riding's analysis of
Sonnet CXXIX in *A Survey of Modernist Poetry* (1927). Richards
himself gave an account of the book's beginning.

> As he was at Magdalene this made me his Director of Studies.
> He seemed to have read more English Literature and to have
> read it more recently and better, so our rôles were soon in
> danger of being reversed. At about his third visit, he brought
> up the games of interpretation which Laura Riding and Robert
> Graves had been playing with the unpunctuated form of 'The
> expense of spirit in a waste of shame'. Taking the sonnet as a
> conjuror takes his hat he produced an endless stream of lively
> rabbits from it and ended by 'You could do that with any
> poetry, couldn't you?' This was a Godsend to a Director of
> Studies, so I said 'You'd better go and do it, hadn't you?' A

week later he was still slapping away at it on his typewriter. Would I mind if he just went on with that? Not a bit. The following week there he was with a thick wad of very illegible typescript under his arm—the central 30,000 words or so of the book. Quoted from *Furioso* (New Haven, Spring 1940) in Stanley Hyman, *The Armed Vision* (New York, 1948), p. 294

One of the most influential works of modern criticism was therefore produced in a fortnight by an undergraduate—which afterwards, I believe, he submitted in part as his 'Original Composition' for the Tripos, for which he was given a starred first class mark in 1929. An early foretaste of the work was provided in the little magazine *Experiment*, of which Empson was one of the editors. The second number (February 1929, p. 35) carried three pages of analysis of Shakespeare's Sonnet XVI (one of the early and more formal of that series) done in a style close to that of Robert Graves and Laura Riding. It ends:

A literary conundrum is tedious, and these meanings are only worth detaching in so far as they are dissolved into the single mood of the poem.

When a year later the passage appeared as part of *Seven Types of Ambiguity*, Empson attached these same remarks to the far more complex Sonnet LXXXIII; and had for comments on Sonnet XVI: 'The fact is, if analysis gets in your way, it is easy enough to forget it; I do not think that all these meanings should pass through the mind in an appreciative reading of this Sonnet' (*Seven Types*, p. 174).

Some of Empson's creative misquotations in this first version are entertaining; Milton's account of Vulcan's fall from Heaven is transposed into something like a social call:

> Flung by angry Jove
> Sheer o'er the crystal battlements; from dawn
> To noon he fell, from noon to dewy eve,
> A summer's day; and with the setting sun
> Dropped into Lemnos, the Aegean isle.

His revised edition of *Seven Types of Ambiguity*, published in 1948, tidied up the book, adding such cool disclaimers here and there as 'It seems no good trying to improve this paragraph, but I still think the last sentence summing it up is sufficiently true' (p. 21); 'It has much the same effect whether you put these lines in or leave them out' (p. 91); 'I now think this example a mare's nest' (p. 171).

This casual tone, which appears also in the footnotes to his poems, provides Empson with a ready weapon. He can use it to give the brush-off to hostile critics. In the early poems it serves as a means of defence, and is part of his recognition of the latent hostility in any relationship. The feminine body, a microcosmos, but infantile, exasperates.

> The proper scale would pat you on the head . . .
> And though your gulf-sprung mountains I allow
> (Snow-puppy curves, rose-solemn dado band)
> Charming for nurse, I am not nurse just now.
>
> The Scales

The mixture of mood here is not so far from what he ascribes elsewhere to the author of Shakespeare's *Sonnets* or *Troilus and Cressida*. Nearly all the examples in *Seven Types of Ambiguity* come from lyric and dramatic poetry, where very often a complex human situation may be presented in its own terms, not transformed by being embodied in a scene. The truth about relationships is found to be rarely pure and never simple. The key word of praise, 'generosity', implies a conflict overcome, resolved, or suppressed. Paradox is the staple of an inclusively human speech, not the exception.

As a hostile or distanced element is reconciled in his own lyric, so in his criticism Empson adopts towards his reader an attitude at once familiar, and yet simultaneously cool and carefully distanced. I have heard something like Empson's accent from Robert Lowell (who once imitated him in verse) and some echo of his tone in the verse of Thom Gunn. He has founded no school; the book of which he thought most highly (as I have been told) was his study of *The Faces of Buddha*, written in the Far East, and lost in the post on the way to his publishers.

Like other Cambridge critics, Empson makes few explicit dogmatic stands within the field of literary appreciation, not from lack of personal commitment, but because imaginative art is falsified if the language of direct experience is used for it.[2] 'The poet never affirmeth and therefore never lieth', as Philip Sidney knew. If Richards puts 'doctrinal adhesions' under taboo for critics, neither he nor Empson has practised a fugitive and cloistered virtue, and therefore neither is fully represented by his published works.

By turns outrageous, unpretentious, rather grandly supercilious or careless, Empson's flexibility of engagement and withdrawal makes him usable by a wide variety of people who do not share his complexities. In a sense his virtuosity at the language-game serves as camouflage for judgments which, if undogmatic, are not uncommitted. Witty, and balanced between innovation and tradition, his humour is apt to be sardonic. 'Just a Smack at Auden' is balanced by the graver political verse of *The Gathering Storm*, such as 'Courage means Running'; this in turn may expand his remark on Dryden's line 'Charge, charge, 'tis too late to retreat' that 'evidently the thought that it is no good running away is an important ingredient in military enthusiasm' (*Seven Types*, p. 252). The observation is just, yet by his rhythm Dryden makes this statement far from 'evident'.

It is easy to object to Empson's criticism but difficult to refute it, when offered so confidently yet unpretentiously. Yet the moral force of his social nuances, though developed more fully in later criticism, is implicit even in *Seven Types of Ambiguity*, as in the passage on Pope with which I began, and in the praise of his other passage on the dowagers (p. 189). Even trivial subjects may bear weighty implications, while serious poetry may get flippant treatment (George Herbert's is the clearest example). His treatment of Herbert, like his treatment of Milton, led to prolonged disputes revealing alike the strength and the weaknesses of his powers at a *later* date, but these disputes are not relevant to this first period.

While Richards was trained in one of the more humanist of the sciences, and one close to everyday life, so that he brought over some of his scientific language as psychologist into his criticism, Empson as a mathematician was applying a training more remote, yet whose effects are as clearly discernible. Perhaps his work may derive not merely from the views of Richards but, for example, from Bertrand Russell, who told T. S. Eliot that the mathematician deals with objects that directly affect his sensibility. Eliot's essay on 'The Perfect Critic', the opening work in *The Sacred Wood* (1920), which with Richards's work supplied the most influential criticism for Cambridge readers in the twenties, offers a definition of Empson's criticism at its best (I do not know if he actually used it). T. S. Eliot praises the scientific mind, the mind exhibiting 'general intelligence', and he also praises the criticism of the artist, who has 'found an adequate outlet for the creative impulse in his poetry; and none of it [is] forced out and back through his critical prose'. The imperfect critic, on the contrary, finds

> the reading fecundates his emotions to produce something new which is not criticism but is not the expulsion, the ejection, the birth of creativeness . . .
> Some writers are essentially of the type that reacts in excess of the stimulus, making something new out of the impressions, but suffer from a defect of vitality or an obscure obstruction which prevents nature taking its course. Their sensibility alters the object but never transforms it. *The Sacred Wood*, p. 6

This essay of Eliot opens with a quotation from Rémy de Gourmont, 'Ériger en lois ses impressions personnelles, c'est le grand effort d'un homme s'il est sincère', while its final definition runs (p. 15):

> The true generalization is not something superimposed upon an accumulation of perceptions; the perceptions do not, in a really appreciative mind, accumulate in a mass, but form themselves as a structure; and criticism is the statement in language of this structure; it is a development of sensibility. The bad criticism, on the other hand, is that which is nothing but an expression of emotion.

When Empson produced *Seven Types of Ambiguity*, he was both close to his work as a mathematician and engaged in writing poetry. This gives an edge to the critical writing here which produces an effect sharper than that of any of his later critical works. It certainly is not 'an expression of emotion' but, I would maintain, to a larger extent than may appear, it is 'a development of sensibility'. The later criticism changed its form; it became more defined, more explicit, more concerned with general structure and less with local effects as found in lyric verse. *Some Versions of Pastoral* (1936) looks at the way in which the complex may be restated in simple form.[3]

Empson has never neglected the art of elimination; I have already quoted his remark that it is not necessary to keep in the front of the mind all the alternatives that may be extracted from a Shakespearean sonnet. He himself, however, is inclined to present on the surface an excess of theoretical variations; the ambiguity behind all this brilliance lies in the passion and concern that is inseparable from the creation of poetry, and which also informs the subtlety and delicacy of response of the critic. His sardonic coolness is the obverse of penetrating insight and counter-balances the excess. Much of Empson's criticism is highly con-densed. Some devices are patently gratuitous, such as the Seven Types of Ambiguity themselves (which as a frame were perhaps useful to the author).

An analogy may be provided from a poem which decisively shaped Empson's and my generation and which is the subject of one of his best passages in *Seven Types of Ambiguity*. *The Waste Land* has recently been given to the world in its original form, from which it is possible to see how many complex images and scenes have been removed, without their effects being entirely lost. The final structure form replaces a looser structure; but the elimi-nated images are not totally irrelevant to the final effect since, although no longer present, they add to the complexity and rich-ness of what has been distilled. Empson, who originally analysed the opening lines of Section II to bring out their fluid indetermin-ancy, manages in that passage to bring out also the feeling of social instability transformed into physical terms. Though what I have termed 'the moral force of social nuance' may be more explicit in later criticism—in *The Structure of Complex Words*, for instance—Empson's earlier critical work is most easily translated into different critical idioms, to produce the New Criticism of Allen Tate and John Crowe Ransom. There, irony, tension, con-flict, and paradox are given a more explicit centrality than Empson gives them.

The wit and agility of Empson are more immediately striking than his humour and his warmth, and they also figured largely in the Oxford fashion for Empson of the early fifties, which A. Alvarez has described in *The Shaping Spirit* (1967). It went with Oxford's cult of Wittgenstein, and represents a side of Empson that was not perhaps the most prominent in his Cambridge days, at least not to his contemporaries. An ingenious cerebral Empson, the antidote to 'punch-drunk songsters' (the phrase is John Wain's), is the object of this later cult. At present Empson is enjoying a third wave of popularity among the French structural-ists who find his language games much to their taste.

Another Empson who is visible behind his poetry and criticism is an eighteenth-century country gentleman. He practises literature as an amateur, but is learned. He does not make it a mercenary trade and will not take the usual routes. In times of stress he suddenly shews a blend of revolutionary independence in political thought and behaves with a highly traditional loyalty and patriotism. When England went to war he made a bee-line back from China.[4] He wrote a masque for the Queen when she visited Sheffield attributing to her, in Jacobean style, sole responsibility for the invention of modern steel processes; and he was pleased when she said, 'Mr Empson, why don't they laugh?' Empson's historic insights, most often revealed in parody or mockery, derive from the kind of innate stability that in the poem 'To an Old Lady', he attributed to his mother. They come out mainly in his handling of topics in the eighteenth century—the passage on Pope which I have quoted, the analysis of *The Beggar's Opera* in *Some Versions of Pastoral* and the treatment of its key words 'honesty' and 'dog' in *The Structure of Complex Words*.

Tenderness for a countryside he knew, warmth and fullness of response, and the wry wit that defends it are combined in 'Flighting for Duck' from his first volume of poems. It is a casual little piece, set on the Ouse but evoking the archaic beginning of history (but it will be noted that the dykes hold here as they don't for Pope):

> Egyptian banks, an avenue of clay
> Define the drain between constructed marshes
> (Two silted lakes, silver and brown, with grass,
> Without background, far from hills, at evening).

The soft indefinite scene is broken by sharp, mock eighteenth-century couplets, warning of an alert.

> What was that drumming in the sky? What cry
> Squawked from the rustled rushes a reply?

Another cosmic ranging passage (the stars are moving like these duck, but slower) is followed in the moment of action by direct parody in double-barrelled couplets.

> Bang. Bang. Two duck blur 'mid the social crew;
> For man created, to man's larder due.
> With plump or splash on the new nurtured field
> To Reason's arm they proper homage yield.
> The well-taught dogs wait but the voice to run,
> Eager, and conscious of the murd'ring gun.

Starlit, mistcircled, one whole pearl embrowned,
An even dusked silver of earth and sky
Held me dazzled, with cobwebs, staring round.
The black band of my hat leapt to my eye.
Alone in sight not coloured like the ground
It lit, like a struck match, everything by.

In that last flash of observation, balancing the modernity of 'the murd'ring gun', the trained eye, no less than Reason's arm, brings down fancy to earth. He has seen and ordered 'the unreachable chaos' of the alarmed birds, and taken aim; the hint of mourning in the black hat band is absurd, yet the whole scene is lit by it, the evening dusk, the more dangerous social reflections that have been cut down to a 'hint of anti-aircraft'.

In these verses the scene is 'transfigured' (to borrow Empson's own phrase) in the same way as Pope transfigures Chandos. The largest cosmic and historic scale is related to a scene of 'intuitive intimacy with nature', the world, in the evening. If Empson is thought of merely as an analyst, this does less than justice to such latent forces, which prime and focus his intellectual analysis.

The effect of Empson on the teaching of English at Cambridge has been to encourage attention to 'the words on the page' while also demonstrating the need for multiple points of view. He developed Richards's 'Practical Criticism' as it could be practised by the intelligent, while sharing something of that original exercise's elimination of the *directly* historic approach. The indirectly historic is manifestly active in his work; Rosemond Tuve's protest about the medieval roots of Herbert's 'Sacrifice' offers a counterbalance to his Freudian approach, but at this distance of time, what with *Godspell* and Barthes' structuralism, it is not safe to ignore Empson. He would not have said, as recently a Cambridge undergraduate is reported to have done, 'Why should my supervisor make me read Pope when I want to read comics?' (*TLS*, 15 February 1972), because he would have seen the need for both. To confuse literature with sociology would not have occurred to him. But he allowed the reader creative freedom to 'relive' the poem.

The excesses to which he is prone are not the sort of excesses that afflict contemporary undergraduates in any large numbers; and he lived in a society which had not heard of the Two Cultures.[5] His First Class in the English Tripos followed a First Class in

Mathematics; yet his work has the air of saying, 'This is what you ought to be doing whenever you are reading; or at least, something equivalent in concentration and range.' His unity of close concentration and wide-ranging perspectives is perhaps the most applied form of applied mathematics that the university of Bertrand Russell has ever turned out.

NOTES

1 Cf. the poem 'Letter V' lines 11–12.

2 For example his attacks on Milton's God may be set against his views on Bunyan's humanity.

3 The chapter on *Alice in Wonderland*, however, develops from hints latent in Empson's poem 'The Scales', quoted above. The lines I have *not* quoted are:

> The proper scale would pat you on the head
> But Alice showed her pup Ulysses' bough
> Well from behind a thistle, wise with dread.

4
> Besides, you aren't quite good for nowt
> Or clinging wholly as a burr . . .
> Nor is it shameful to aver
> A vague desire to be about
> Where the important things occur.
> 'Autumn on Nan-Yueh', *The Gathering Storm*

5 When I was an undergraduate, the mathematical Fellow at Girton, Evelyn Cave, told me that doing mathematics felt much more like reading Shelley than like doing chemistry. She read a lot of poetry and wrote comic verses herself, in the style of C. S. Calverly.

3

Extracts from Unpublished Memoirs

Kathleen Raine

With her flair for the avant-garde, my friend N— discovered the magazine *Experiment* in whose first number were printed some poems by one of its many editors, William Empson. I claimed to be a poet? Very well, here I must stand trial by my generation. Through *Experiment* I did enter upon my own literary adventure; although not quite according to the pattern I had hoped, of the Ugly Duckling who at last finds birds of a feather. Neither ducks nor swans, of what species were these experimental fowl? I read the Empson poems and found them so extremely difficult as to be in no doubt that their author was far more intelligent than myself; yet to me it seemed strange that what appeared to be a love poem should open with the line

> And now she cleans her teeth into the lake.

This image, with its insistence upon a physical function, seemed to my eighteen-year-old self inappropriate to the theme of love. I was told that Empson was to be compared with Donne, whom we were at that time supposed supremely to admire; and not as the Christian divine, but for the modern mood in which he reduced love to physicalities:

> Marke but this flea, and mark in this
> How little that which thou deny'st me is.

On reflection I presently realized that Empson was concerned less with the charms of love than with those of surface tensions, the behaviour of reflections, galaxies, photons, chemical transmutations; and with man's predicament in our brave new universe. Those who adopt the premises of positivism in one or another of its protean forms (behaviourism and Wittgenstein were already afoot in Cambridge, Marxism soon to follow) must forego such openings lines as

> Had I the heavens' embroider'd cloths

or

> Thou wast all that to me, love,
> For which my soul did pine.

Only good poets are aware of the concealed premises of the culture which nourishes (or starves) their inspiration; and William Empson well understood that when the beloved is no more than a complex formula of surface-tensions and viscosities of a chemical compound of 98 per cent water (of which a textbook we all used at the time alleged even the Archbishop of Canterbury to be composed; which being so, of course, so much for his beliefs, but then why not those of Marx or Bertrand Russell?), so much for that for which the soul pines. The beloved is

> . . . that mud
> I have heard speak, that will not cake or dry.

The scientists of the Cavendish and those other laboratories so near King's College chapel and Trinity Great Court, but in how other a Cambridge, had set the problem poets must resolve as they could: to discover the qualitative implications of their new modelled universe. Of the editors of *Experiment*, J. Bronowski besides (in his first year) William Empson was reading mathematics, and the writing of poetry had in the Cambridge of the late twenties no necessary connection with the English tripos. I. A. Richards's attempt to make his literary criticism a 'science' was perhaps not so much a literary exercise as a response to the scientific ambience in which poetic imagination at that time and in that place found its excitement, illumination, or whatever that quickening of the pulse may be that tells the poet that here is matter for poetry. I was reading natural sciences myself; and in that context could better understand William Empson's attempts to capture that strange inhuman beauty of the *mayas* which in awe-inspiring recession lead away from the world of human perception into distances minute or vast. The anguish of the situation which dissolved the beloved into galaxies held by surface-tensions so fragile was real enough too, God knows. William Empson's tracer-photon plunged into a strange cosmos accessible only to intellect, destroying the heart's ancient orientations. Yet this whirlpool through which the familiar and dear aspect of our world was drawn down into chaos exercised upon our young emotions a terrible negative attraction. 'Intellectual honesty' seemed to demand that we throw ourselves over the brink and the rocket's life-line offered little hope of rescue. Empson's despair contained by intellectual stoicism expressed a more than personal predicament. When later we read the political verses of Auden and the other Oxford poets we felt, with some justification, that their encounter with the poetic implications of the time was superficial in comparison with Empson's.

The one or two poems I had written during my first year at Girton were of an immature and personal kind in no way comparable with William Empson's verses, already mature in many poems written at Winchester. However, I sent him my poems, and in due course, to my intense joy, I was invited to lunch with the poet himself.

When I saw William for the first time, he was reclining upon a window-sill of his rooms in the first court of Magdalene. I remember the impression he made upon me—as upon all of us— of contained mental energy, as of a flame whose outline remains constant while its substance is undergoing continual metamorphosis at a temperature at which only intellectual salamanders could hope to live. This impression of perpetual self-consuming self-generating mental intensity produced a kind of shock; through no intention or will to impress; for William was simply himself at all times. William came down from the window-sill and brought in the College lunch from the window-box where it was keeping cool (or hot). I seem to remember that John Marx was the other guest; but in any company William was the one remembered. Never I think had he any wish to excel, lead, dominate, involve, or otherwise assert power; he was at all times, on the contrary, mild, impersonal, indifferent to the impression he made to the point of absent-mindedness. Nevertheless his presence spellbound us all. His shapely head, his fine features, his eyes, full lustrous poet's eyes but short-sighted behind glasses and nervously evading a direct look (I always mistrust people who look you straight in the face) was the head, in any gathering, that seemed the focus of all eyes. His mannered speech, too, charmed us; those Wykehamical intonations slurred and stressed into a kind of incantation, even when he was not declaiming poetry; which he did with frightening intensity, like one possessed.

He was beardless that year; but on a long vacation grew his first beard (I think on a ski-ing holiday in Switzerland) which added to the daimonic energy of his appearance. His mother (I remember his telling us) had offered him ten pounds to remove the beard; and he had written her that 'since no one had offered him a larger sum to keep it on', he was obliged to accept her offer. So the beard went; but not the instinct for that mandarin form of barbarity, which did assert itself later, as we all know.

Sometimes William invited me to meet him in London during the vacation. He could scarcely have taken me seriously as a poet, but he probably thought I was pretty, for at one moment he tried to arrange an introduction for me to his school friend Anthony Asquith, with the idea that my face might adorn a cinema screen. I think he was, besides, quite simply loyal to all his friends in an undemanding, impersonal, quite uncritical way, just because we were there. So, taking the train from Ilford to Liverpool Street, I would meet William on the steps of the National Gallery, or wherever it might be. He took me to the Noel Coward reviews, and to the Diaghilev ballet; *Le Coq d'Or* I remember, and *L'Après-midi d'un Faun*. We walked together among the oriental gods in the British Museum. Left to myself I would no doubt have strayed among the Elgin Marbles; certainly never paused before Bill's hideous idol, his Oceanic 'supreme god in the Ethnological section'. Even before he left for Japan he had considered the Faces of the Buddha. But it was those flame-like, flame-encompassed bronze Shivas, communicating the sense of the motion in stillness of that perpetual transmutation which seemed to me then (rather than the more earthy and serene Chinese figures) of the very essence of William Empson. I was one of the friends privileged to read his manuscript (lost by John Davenport at the time when the blitz made the tracing of mislaid property more than usually difficult), *The Faces of the Buddha*. If I remember aright, one of the contrasts made between the figures of Christ and those of the Buddha was that, whereas it demanded supreme artistry to capture the Christ-like aspect, the Buddha's face itself (and not some symbol comparable to the Cross) was the icon of the Buddhist world; an aspect capturable in its mysterious vacancy by even some ignorant village wood-carver. That expression, written upon the void itself, exerted its power upon the poet of the new void of our world of photons. The sense of the relative, the impermanence, the unreality of the appearances, opened by the scientific universe, was old in Buddhism before our civilization was born. It seemed to me at that time a perfectly natural extension of Bill's intellectual passion and intellectual subtlety that led him to consider the face of the Buddha. Bill was not religious, but then Buddhism is less a religion than a way of apprehending reality.

By the time William reached China a newer anti-religion was already assuming power; and as the son of generations of soldiers and administrators, William concerned himself with the political realities of the world, and therefore with Marxism; though his intellectual poise and detachment would of course no more have committed him to the brash utopianism which captured so many of our contemporaries than he could have committed himself to Buddhism with its finer subtleties. The only commitment of pure intellect is to remain uncommitted. All the same, it is perhaps necessary to an understanding of his subtle sense of the relative to read his poems in terms not only of scientific relativity but in the flicker of that everlasting bonfire which gives the same subtle fluidity to the dance of Shiva as to the smile of the Buddha. Unreality itself, after all, is itself only relative:

> Not but they die, the teasers and the dreams,
> Not but they die, and tell the careful flood
>   To give them what they clamour for, and why.

William was well aware that the answers, no less than the questions, of our sciences were only that rocket life-line of human knowledge projected into the void; which he knew (as cruder minds do not) no increase of that knowledge would ever lessen.

I wish I had written in a journal at the time all the discerning things William used to say about the Buddhas and the Noel Coward reviews. And did no one go home to begin writing at 2 a.m. about those wonderful parties Bill used to give in strange basement studios; that seem in retrospect not like parties in Fitzrovia so much as parties in a book about Fitzrovia written (probably) by Wyndham Lewis? They seem, in retrospect, all one single party with shadowy people cast by that fitful characteristic flame-like flicker (or am I recalling only the candles stuck in bottles?). Their intoxication too seems in retrospect all of the mind. Who were those shadowy guests? I can recall Arthur Waley;

Edward Wilson (translator of Góngora); Edgell Rickword; George Orwell and his first wife; Nina Hamnett; Janet and Michael Roberts; Hugh Kingsmill; Ronald and Margaret Bottrall; Julian Trevelyan; Humphrey Jennings; John Davenport. Whether Malcolm Lowry ever came—he was a close friend of John Davenport's—I do not remember. Bohemian as these parties were, they yet had a social amplitude which could contain with ease William's brother Charles, the Counsellor, and his beautiful wife Monica; or indeed any person of distinction, of whatever nationality, in any walk of life. Some of the shadows seem dimly oriental, with a faint rustle of mandarin robes.

Later William used to write, from time to time, from Japan, then from China. For me the scene of my life had shifted from a Cambridge to which I had never at heart belonged. Soon after the outbreak of war I found myself, by some chance or miracle, living in a dale in Cumberland where my Aunty Peggy had taught her first school half a century before; to me a homecoming from mental complexity to vital simplicity. At a poetry reading at (I think) Leicester, I found myself, not many years ago, with the two poets who had gone up to Cambridge a year before me: Vernon Watkins and William, who, on that occasion, reproached me with having 'escaped from Cambridge', as though I had been a deserter. Truth to say, that Cambridge of which William was himself, with I. A. Richards, the chief creator, was for me a place of spiritual exile, Martindale vicarage a homecoming. The Girton undergraduate who had sent her poems to *Experiment* seemed like a persona in a dream from which I had awakened. But William's unswerving loyalty, his steadfastness of character, simply turned a blind eye—or was really blind—to my defection, if such it was; for indeed if I wished to escape it was not from my friends but only from my own false self. Once he came, with Michael Roberts, to my remote cottage; and so entirely was he as he would have been anywhere and under any circumstances, entirely and in all simplicity as he had been on his window-sill in Magdalene, or in Marchmont Street where, perched on a three-legged chair whose broken fourth was propped by *The Tale of Genji* while he read to me from *Gentlemen Prefer Blondes* a passage marked by a dry kipper-bone, that the past became present again in his presence. For not only is William himself the same against all backgrounds, he assumes that his friends are too. God knows there was never a time, fly from myself as I might, when I was not glad to see William.

In part it is the birthright of the English gentry which he so totally possesses, of creating a norm in whatever circumstances. Battlefield, mountain-top, desert or Communist 'demo' become peripheral to those Englishmen by a right which must be divine since it establishes itself without any assertion. These *mores*—and the culture of Winchester is after all something more than such outward symbols as the dinner-jacket in the solitude of a desert tent can convey to the neo-barbarians of 'the open society'—are a second nature taking precedence over 'nature'; as William's subtle mental processes and mannered simplicity *was* himself. He would in the fires of Hell have behaved with the same aristocratic disregard of the discomfort of his surroundings as he did in Marchmont Street, and no doubt later on the great students' march across China.

Not that for William to appear in Martindale was so very surprising; he is a countryman born; his cousin and sister-in-law Monica was living at Pooley Bridge with her children, and through William's good offices had kindly suggested that my daughter should share her governess. We always understood that he had ridden to hounds in his native Yorkshire; and only a few years ago he was talking with evident delight of taking his own sons beagling on those same hills. But William's mind was so much its own place that he never perhaps occupied any other; so that, when he visited Martindale, my companioning elementals silently withdrew; and all took, as formerly, its quality from William.

He was wearing, I remember, a strange glossy black waterproof garment he had brought from Hanoi, which enhanced that sense of vivid shock his presence always produced. He was also wearing —though I did not notice it and he never mentioned it—two left shoes on that day, absent-mindedly picked up as he dressed for a weekend of rock-climbing with Michael; they were going on from my Ullswater dale to climb Great Gable. He confessed to the blisters only afterwards when Janet Roberts had solicitously noticed the irregularity of his dress.

Not that he was regardless of others; on that same day I walked with my two old friends along the lake as far as Patterdale; and I remember William offering to carry my woollen jacket, taken off as the sun grew hot; thoughtless as he was thoughtful, I refused;

'You would, of course, refuse to have even your jacket carried', he said; one of the very few personal remarks I ever remember his addressing to me.

And on another occasion, a more touching solicitude. The scene was the Hampstead Parish Church; the occasion, the christening of his first son, Mogador, and William's gesture as he dipped his hand into the baptismal water to see that it was not too cold for the baby. Such things William would always do as a matter of course.

4

Mr William Empson in Japan

Rintaro Fukuhara

Saturday 23 May 1931 was a happy day for me. For on that day I met Mr William Empson for the first time in my life. The meeting place was the lounge of the Imperial Hotel, Russell Square, London, where Dr Sanki Ichikawa was then staying. I was a student at the British Museum. Dr Ichikawa had received from Dr I. A. Richards a letter of recommendation of Mr Empson for the post of Professor of English Literature in Tokyo. Thus Dr Ichikawa and I were brought to a meeting at the hotel with Mr Empson, and after half an hour's talk the young poet was quite ready to come over to Japan.

Mr Empson probably left London in the early part of August of that year, and according to my memory, I shook hands of reunion with him at Tokyo station about the end of the month. Empson came to Japan by the Trans-Siberian Railway, and it took about a fortnight for the overland travel. On the night of his arrival he stayed at Tokyo Station Hotel and then moved to a cosy apartment house not very far from the Imperial Palace.

Tokyo is a town of hills and vales built on the slope of a plain, once an expanse of green fields, which is now all covered with roofs. On a hill behind the Imperial Palace stands the British Embassy, and to the east of the Palace there is another hill with a big dome of St Nicholas looking prominent and beautiful. Farther east on the same hill is situated the old Tokyo Imperial University, a very big cluster of Georgian buildings; and on the top of a neighbouring hill is Tokyo University of Literature and Science, a new national institute, later more familiarly called 'Bunrika' University, to which I belonged.

William Empson was appointed that autumn Professor of English Literature of this new university, but he gave lectures as well at the old university, where Dr Ichikawa was head of the department. Both universities being government schools, such convenient ways were possible in their organization. The appointment was devised simply because the only chair left available for Mr Empson was that of the new university.

Regarding Mr Empson's residences, besides the one mentioned above, I remember a period when Mr Empson for a few weeks was living with Austin William Medley, nephew of Augustine Birrell (1875–1940), then a noted professor of the English language at the Tokyo Foreign Language School. The old scholar came to my mind because I recollected that Empson once revered him with the name of 'the Grand Old Man' among Englishmen in Tokyo. The students trained under Mr Medley in the years of his long service deeply appreciated the appellation because they had long been proud of the old teacher whose scholarship and personality were little known outside Tokyo.

Empson lived for most of his three years' stay in Japan in a villa then in the possession of Admiral Takarabe. One could see a typical upper-class residence there. There was a main house looking over a pond quietly surrounded by numerous plum-trees and flower-gardens; two or three houses are seen standing by the same waterside. Mr Empson lived in one of such houses built in a villa-fashion. The villa was kept by a venerable old woman living there 'since the Dutch settlement' (as said by the young poet), very clever in cooking.

According to an interesting personal reminiscence of Empson's friend, one Mr Nobuo Sato, the house was two-storeyed, standing on a basement-room where the ancient cook lived. The first storey consisted of two rooms: one room used as drawing and sitting room, decorated with a bronze statue, book-cases and gramophone etc., and the other room, which contained a cupboard, bedstead, and on the wall Empson's mother's portrait-photograph. The second storey looked rather like a chaos with bookcases, typewriter, bed, desk, bathing-tub etc. (as Mr Sato describes).

This garden house being in the western part of Tokyo, it was a long journey for Mr Empson to come from there to the universities. It was Empson's good idea that he got a motor-bike by which he was free to run about across the big city; and I am glad there occurred no accident, even if Tokyo of forty years ago may have been a little less crowded in the streets. We sent an applause every time when the explosive sounds of the full-speed wheels told us that the poet was come to his classes.

I do not know who that Mr Sato was, the writer of Empson's private life, above mentioned, but according to his memoir which appeared in a literary little magazine, he seems to have been good friends with Mr Empson and it was their custom in summer, at the least in the first summer, to visit together a swimming pool in the neighbourhood and Empson enjoyed the water in his own strange way of jumping and crawling. Mr Sato may have been a young doctor with a literary taste.

In those good old days foreign professors were treated at government universities as government officials under a contract which was renewed every third year: that was, Empson had to teach twenty-four hours a week at his own place and no outside jobs were permitted except for writing and occasional public lectures, but in reality eight hours' teaching a week was the usual limit; the remaining two-thirds of the contract hours were usually spent in talking, smoking, and personal guidance of the students. Mr Empson was often seen taking his class to a coffee-house in the neighbourhood for freer literary talks. He played tennis, and it was a tireless tennis, as I remember, as he was in his analytic reading of English. Here is a specimen week's work for Mr Empson in the year 1932 done at the two universities:

History of English Literature	4 hours
Elizabethan Playwrights	2 ,,
Seventeenth Century English Poetry	2 ,,
Reading of English Literature (Powys' *Mr Weston's Good Wine*, etc.)	2 ,,
Essay-Writing	2 ,,

In the summer of 1932 Empson was invited to Karuisawa Summer University (Karuisawa is a summer resort like Malvern) and talked on contemporary English poetry.

1932 was the year when *New Signatures* was published and general literary interests were concentrated around the new poets included in the anthology, among whom Empson and William Plomer were familiar to us, as they lived in Japan. In the following year, 1933, *The New Country* was published and on the flap of the jacket was printed 'with the exception of Mr Empson, who is in Japan, and Mr Eberhart, who is in America, most of the contributors to *New Signatures*, a book of verse which appeared last year, are represented here'.

Thus Empson became gradually a famous man even among

plain readers of English Literature in Japan. The *Seven Types of Ambiguity* was not left untouched by Japanese students as well as by English and American people living in Japan, to whom, they said, Empson himself was the eighth type of ambiguity.

He was too high-flown a genius for us, indeed, with delicate feeling and profound thought. I used now and then to ask questions on the meaning of his words and phrases found in his poems, and the usual answer was that he could explain the grammar, but could give no interpretation of his thoughts. But there was once a very fortunate moment in my life: he suddenly took up my pen and gave me notes on his 'Arachne' as follows; it was on a page where the poem was printed, of *Recent Poetry, 1923–33* edited by Alida Monro with her introduction.

1.1. *Man hacks his caves* Man—primitive cavemen on the shore between sea and wild animals in the forest. The jump from woman as soap molecule to woman as female spider (bigger than male and eats it after fertilising) depends on the soap m. being bigger than the water one. This rather weak jump makes the end too personal beside the rest.

1.4. *King Spider* man (1.1).

1.10. *least depth of lands* shallow soil which makes rapid growth of some plants: the bubble has already been compared to the earth: the colour effects from interference of light come when it is two molecules thick.

1.13. *We two suffice* The two molecules of thickness then compared to the sexual pair as basis of society . . .
Bubble = soap and water: the woman is then called soap and the man water.

1.14. *my meagre water saves* soap alone wouldn't make a bubble.
Man can only live on surfaces between opposites each of which would destroy him.
membrane . . . surface of living tissue; life dependent on surface reactions (like osmosis making sap rise).
tribe . . . taken as a unity made by mutual tensions . . . one part removed society would break up helplessly . . . hence like a membrane and like a bubble.

To his students Empson was more of a tutor than he was to me. He gave the following notes to an essay on Gray's *Elegy*, written by his student:

'The poet of the *Elegy* is part of the earth rather than the sky.

How about this curfew—I wonder if you think of Buddhist bells? They are heavier and more vehemently melancholy than English church bells. But that does the poem no harm.

The *horn* is the rousing lively instrument of a huntsman. I don't know of a Japanese horn that corresponds to it. (The horn of the tofu seller is the most melancholy sound I have ever heard.)

I think 'incense' is a sort of conceit, the fresh smells of morning are like incense, because they are Nature's thanks to God for the return of day. What you should *think* of are the fresh smells of morning—the fact that 'incense' doesn't really fit them may even be a good thing—he is not imagining morning very vividly because he is surrounded by night and the graves.

> Oft did the harvest to their sickle yield,
> Their furrow oft the stubborn glebe has broke;
> How jocund did they drive their team afield!
> How bowed the woods beneath their sturdy stroke.

The foreigner is free probably from a feeling that interferes with an Englishman's pleasure in this good verse—that the words *glebe* and specially *jocund*, which neither Gray nor the farmer would use of himself when actually cheerful are rather affectedly old-fashioned, so that you feel he is careful to put a distance between himself and his social inferiors.

> Perhaps in this neglected spot is laid
> Some heart once pregnant with celestial fire;
> Hands, that the rod of empire might have sway'd
> Or wak'd to Extasy the living fire.

It isn't a mere romantic fancy (as the student writes) even if it's not true (that potentially very able men were buried there). It was mere fact that a very able peasant had no chance to develop his powers.'

The student then describes Gray's character as 'genial, modest, reserved, and naturally sympathetic with obscure people', to which Empson added his own opinion: 'No: a dismal old don; sympathetic only in theory.' The note on the stanzas reminds one of

Empson's sharp critical remarks in 'Proletarian Literature' (*Some Versions of Pastoral*) on the next-but-one stanza:

> Full many a gem of purest ray serene,
> The dark unfathom'd caves of ocean bear:
> Full many a flower is born to blush unseen,
> And waste its sweetness on the desert air.

Empson's criticism of the student's paper covers both those stanzas ('Perhaps in this neglected spot' and 'Full many a gem') and concludes it with his social point of view: 'but this stanza ("Full many") is only an allegorical way of saying the first ("this neglected spot"). Didn't you feel, probably, that the first was a bit too political and left-wing, while the second is a harmless way of putting it?'

It may not be unnecessary here to quote Empson's critical remarks from 'Proletarian Literature' above referred to.

> By comparing the social arrangement to Nature he [Gray] makes it seem inevitable, while it was not, and gives it a dignity which was undeserved. Furthermore, a gem does not mind being in a cave and a flower prefers not to be picked; we feel that the man is like the flower, as short-lived, natural, and valuable, and this tricks us into feeling that he is better off without opportunities. The sexual suggestion of *blush* brings in the Christian idea that virginity is good in itself, and so that any renunciation is good; this may trick us into feeling it is lucky for the poor man that society keeps him unspotted from the World. The tone of melancholy claims that the poet understands the considerations opposed to aristocracy, though he judges against them the truism of the reflections in the church yard, the universality and impersonality this gives to the style, claim as if by comparison that we ought to accept the injustice of society as we do the inevitability of death.

But then the student in his essay grows more sympathetic with the poet who suffers from his 'too fine susceptibility', while 'the human society is too coarse and rude for such a rare delicacy'.

Empson comments: 'Well, there are many such people but all people of very rare delicacy are not frustrated like Gray. It would be true probably to say that all people of fine susceptibility have to suffer very much, but many keep their vigour and achieve periods of great happiness.'

Then the much discussed lines of the *Elegy* come:

> For who to dumb Forgetfulness a prey
> This pleasing anxious being e'er resigned.
> Left the warm precincts of the cheerful day,
> Nor cast one longing ling'ring look behind?
>
> On some fond breast the parting soul relies.
> Some pious drops the closing eye requires;
> Ev'n from the tomb the voice of Nature cries,
> Ev'n in our ashes live their wonted fires.

Empson's notes:

'One longing look' seems assuredly too weak for the passions with which people desire life even when they throw it away. I only disagree with you about 'ev'n in our ashes', a wonderful line, though I am not sure of its meaning (does he mean *after death*, a sort of animist idea of the ghost tied to the grave; or when we are wholly exhausted?).

(I should guess he wrote the verse to fit the last line.)

The present writer of this article thanks very much the original author of the essay, the late Kyo Nogawa, for his friendship and good will in leaving me this essay embellished with Mr Empson's very valuable autograph notes.

I quite well remember how he came back from his class with his head and shoulder all covered with chalk-dust. He wrote important points of the lecture on the blackboard, so that students could put them down in their notebooks, as Japanese students are generally weak in catching with their ears what their teacher says. A student of those days told me once how Empson was ecstatic, so to speak, when he read aloud Milton before discussing him as a poet.

As for those linguistic and literary analyses, Empson seems to owe much to Dr I. A. Richards, who was his teacher at King's College, Cambridge. And it was natural that Empson had a fairly deep interest in Basic English. One day when I was talking to him about how I could pass through the difficulty of English speaking or writing, he referred to Basic English in his own experience. He said, 'When I feel what I spoke was not properly understood, I try to repeat the meaning I wanted to express in Basic, and when I find it inexpressible in Basic, I know that my own English was not clear enough'.

'An Essay on the Teaching of Literature' written in *Bungei* (a literary magazine) in February 1934 is noteworthy. The most remarkable point was his opinion that in the teaching of literature fostering of 'independence of judgement' must be aimed at, along with the 'keeping of balance of mind' and 'expansion of emotional experience'. Empson kept up with this attitude all through his life in Japan. Empson had expressed a similar view in an extra-mural lecture 'Consequences of Literature' given in 1933 in the Bunrika University Hall.

Tokyo Imperial University, later, after the Second World War, called Tokyo University, was the place where English literary studies were started in modern Japan. James Main Dixon (a Scot, 1856–1933, editor of *Dictionary of Idiomatic English Phrases*, 1887), first taught how to read English literature. Basil Hall Chamberlain (1850–1935, author of *Things Japanese* (1890) and an eminent philologist), aided in the work. Lafcadio Hearn (1850–1904) succeeded them. Many of Hearn's lectures are preserved in book form in their dictated style: *Interpretation of Literature* (1915), *Appreciations of Poetry* (1916), and *Life and Literature* (1917) being the main parts. Hearn taught English Literature there for seven years, 1896–1903.

In the year 1906 John Lawrence (1850–1916), author of *Chapters on Alliterative Verse* (1893), came from London University to occupy the chair. He was a good scholar and diligent teacher, and several students under his training later became eminent teachers of English Language and Literature.

Lawrence died in 1916. It was his merit that the general level of English studies in Japan was raised. But still even at that time the study of literature remained merely a distant view or a cluster of information, arranged according to an academic order— Victorian, if one may say so—and it was necessary to give them a living voice against the book-form appreciations and interpreta-tions. In the year 1916 we were reading in English classes George Eliot, W. B. Yeats, Thomas Hardy, R. L. Stevenson, Joseph Conrad, G. B. Shaw, G. K. Chesterton, etc. But the students wanted to have newer, fresher breaths of younger English literary people.

Robert Nichols (1893–1944) was the first to come to answer such wishes of the Japanese students. He was given the Eng. Lit. Chair of the Tokyo Imperial University in the year 1921 and kept it until 1924. The dates mean that while he was in Japan his *Guilty Souls*

(1922) was published. His tall figure wrapped in a blue mantle was often gazed at in foreign book-stores with envy and adoration.

Edmund Blunden (1896–) succeeded him. Blunden came to Tokyo in 1924. The town was lying half-destroyed by the Great Earthquake of 1923. He was then known as the Hawthornden Prize poet of *The Shepherd and Other Poems* (1922). We found in him a kind-hearted and painstaking professor, whose disciples are in present-day Japan leading powers in English studies. He stayed in Japan for three years until 1927, and back in England he was literary editor of the *Nation and Athenaeum*; then in 1931, he was Merton College fellow, Oxford. After the War he came again to Japan for about two years as Cultural Attaché to the British Embassy, during which period he delivered more than 600 lectures all over the country. He visited Japan in 1960 for the fifth time with all his family and was warmly received as the best friend of the country. After his return to England he was elected at Oxford as Professor of Poetry, but it was a pity that he had (as I hear) to resign the post on account of his ill-health.

Dr Takeshi Saito, author of *Keats' View of Poetry* (1929), was a Professor of English Literature at the Tokyo Imperial University where he was a colleague of Professor Ichikawa. Saito met Edmund Blunden one winter's day at Ralph Hodgson's house in London, when Saito successfully asked Blunden to come to Japan. Saito lost no chance of inviting one more poet to a Japanese university. There was another university in the north of Japan at Sendai where an English Literature course had just been opened, headed by Professor Doi, another important scholar of literature. Saito and Blunden succeeded in moving Hodgson (1891–1962) to go to that new place, where he stayed for fourteen years, relieved with two periods of leave. He was much revered by Japanese English Literature students even long after he left Sendai to go to the USA where he died in 1962.

Other English poets or critics who contributed much by their scholarship to the university studies were George Barker, successor to Hodgson for a short time, the poet of *Calamiterror* (1937); Arundel del Re, an Italian by birth (1892), one of the promotors of *Georgian Poetry*, and at present Professor of English Literature at Victoria University, Wellington, New Zealand; and Sherard Vines who belonged in his youth to the *Oxford Poetry* group and came to Japan in 1923 by Dr J. Nishiwaki's invitation, and taught at Keio University where Nishiwaki was about that time Professor of English Literature fresh from abroad. Vines was then known as the poet of *The Kaleidoscope* (1921), kept his position for five years, and returned to England as professor at the University of Hull. He left to Japan two important books for Japanese students: *Movements in Modern English Poetry and Prose* (Oxford, 1927) and *A Basic Guide To Composition* (Tokyo, 1928), a book of comparison between familiar and formal expressions in English usage, written with Sir George Sansom as joint editor. Those two books helped the students to get to a higher level in questions of literary style and appreciation. Then comes the period of Peter Quennell and William Empson.

About these times, in 1926, William Charles Plomer was staying in Japan. He was a friend of Edmund Blunden and was a teacher of English at Tokyo High School, and was known as a poet and novelist, who wrote *Paper-Houses* (1929) and *Sado* (1931), based on his experiences in this country. Plomer returned to England in 1929 and in the same year I was fortunate to meet and talk to Harold Monro at his Poetry Bookshop near the British Museum. I was looking for a young English poet and critic for my own university (University of Literature and Science; or Bunrika University, later, after the War, University of Education). Monro recommended Peter Quennell. It was the year when Quennell published his first book of criticism, *Baudelaire and the Symbolists* (1929). The book was well received; Quennell loved French literature so much that he once said to me that he would like to give lectures on the French Symbolists.

I asked him to come to Japan and the proposal was accepted. He left London some time in February 1930. His father, C. B. H. Quennell, an architect, was among the people who gathered at Victoria Station to see Peter off. Just before the train came in, the father said half to himself and half to me, 'How professorial Peter looks!' In that year Peter was a contract teacher at the Tokyo University of Literature and Science. The school-work began in April. I remember when he was still in London he said to me, he would like to keep gold-fish in his Tokyo residence and eat persimmons there, but I don't know if he could live just as he wished in that dingy town. Moreover it was a pity that owing to his wife's ill-health, probably because, as I often hear, Japanese air did not suit English ladies, the poet had to return to England after only one year's teaching in Tokyo.

Mr William Empson came to Japan in his stead. There was

something different between these two personalities but in their preference of John Donne and his school they were both of them quite enthusiastic. Metaphysical poetry was not necessarily new in Japan; before these two poets took it up, Dr Takeshi Saito had given lectures on the school at the Imperial University and I know a doctoral thesis on Donne was being prepared about this time, by a friend of mine, Professor Kaichi Matsuura. But still John Donne in new clothes woven by the younger poets of the twentieth century was an inspiration.

Anyhow, Peter Quennell, when we first met in London at his house, gave me *John Donne's Prose and Poetry* in the beautiful Nonesuch edition; and William Empson while we were talking about his poetry in my study in Tokyo, took up a piece of paper on my desk and drew in pencil a rough sketch of John Donne's portrait, which I decided never to lose. To my mind the sketch seemed to have been done almost unconsciously; the pencil moved as if his mental image directed him to draw.

William Empson left Japan after three years' stay on the very hot afternoon of 8 July 1934. This time he took the sea route on board an NYK liner, *Kashima maru*, from Yokohama, with the intention of visiting on the way Buddhistic remains in India. At three o'clock, the gangway was taken away; we on the pier gathered nearer to the rail where the poet stood, high up on the promenade deck, now irretrievably high, a free man. The steamer began to move, when quite unexpectedly Empson took off his panama hat and threw it down just amidst the group of friends and students. We were surprised, and all tried to catch it before it fell on the pier. But who has got it now nobody knows. If the throwing of the hat was meant as a ritual of transferring a tradition, that is now in the possession of Kazuo Ogawa, once his student for three years at the Imperial University and now an eminent essayist and critic.

After Empson left Japan we had little news even about his public activities, although we were very eager to know what he was doing as a literary man.

Suddenly on a summer's day (1950 or 1951) the British Embassy rang me up and took me to Yokohama pier where a big trans-Pacific liner lay at anchor. We had much ado together with Mr and Mrs George Fraser, who were then in Japan on a cultural mission, in searching for an English passenger called William Empson, deep down in the hot bowels of the steamer, until we were at last rewarded with a thankful discovery of a single vacant bed guarded by a copy of George Eliot's *Middlemarch*. Fresh research was started and this time at last high up on the boat-deck the mysterious poet was found out with streaming beard (which was new to me) and glittering spectacles. The first words I could catch from him were, 'It is cool here.' He was on his way back to China from America.

He was at that time Professor of English Literature at Peking University, and concurrently in summer-time taught at Kenyon University. 'They call me Fellow there,' he said.

In our car back to Tokyo from the pier Mr Empson gave me kind words inquiring after his old students with considerate questions. We had dinner in Tokyo and I am glad to write here that time was left enough for his return that evening to Yokohama pier safe again.

Kenyon University is at Gambier, Ohio, USA. There Professor J. C. Ransom taught Literature, from whom the new school of literary criticism, the 'New Criticism', began to show its strong influences. It was just about the end of the 1930s when the *Kenyon Review* was first published and people gathered round it to join in the new movement. (Allen Tate, Richard Blackmur, Robert Pen Warren, and Cleanth Brooks were all known in Japan.) In the movement Empson's *Seven Types* was respected as the Bible—so a writer in Japan introduces Empson's position in the New Criticism.

The new way of treating literary products by the new method is now taken in the studies and appreciations even of Japanese and Chinese literary research, and it is, after all, a phenomenon to be regarded as the Empsonian influence in America and Japan. The Pacific liner for these several years carried the vogue across the ocean. People began to try to read the *Ambiguity* discourses and *Structure* essays, and his peculiar way of analysis, in spite of his difficult style of writing, was learnt by and by through examples, and examples and explications—that was the rise of the New Criticism in which Empson stood out as the Bible.

The first essay on Empson that appeared in Japan and is worth reading was written as early as 1936 by Shigehisa Narita (Empson's old student) in the author's *Modern English Critical Literature*, pp. 348–65.

Then comes, in chronological order, Ogawa's 'William Empson

and his analysis of poetry' in his book *New Criticism: Its History And Essence* (1959), pp. 108–9.

I have here a newly published *History of English and American Literature*, vol. 12, in which Mr Hiroshi Debuchi writes of the three stages (*Seven Types of Ambiguity*, *Some Versions of Pastoral* and *The Structure of Complex Words*) of William Empson with understanding and appreciation.

As a personality, Mr Empson is to be admired as an honest and original man besides being very much a kind-hearted man to his friends and students as he is now and then referred to in this paper.

Yukio Irie, his old student, owes his scholarship much to Mr Empson, whose words and deeds in leading Irie in his studies can be read in his talk about Empson's home-life printed in vol. V of *Rintaro Fukuhara's Writings* (Tokyo 1968, pp. 562–6). A literary little magazine, published by Bunrika graduates, *Eibungaku-Fukei* (English Literary Scenes, 1934–5) edited a special Empson Number (vol. I, no. 4) followed by vol. II, no. 1, which contains Sato's long reminiscences, quoted earlier.

5

A is B at 8,000 feet

Janet Adam Smith

Michael Roberts and William Empson first met at Cambridge in the late 1920s; then, after Michael came down from Newcastle in 1931 to teach mathematics at Mercer's School, they saw a good deal of each other in London. Michael had read William's poems in *Experiment* and the *Cambridge Review*, and chose six of them for his anthology *New Signatures*, published by the Hogarth Press in 1932. For its successor, *New Country*, which had prose as well as poetry, he was keen to have an essay by William; and the earliest letters of William's I have found are on this matter. The first is from Tokyo, on 12 November 1932:

> I should like to write 3–5,000 words about Richards's pragmatism as opposed to the offensive covert pragmatism of people like Wyndham Lewis and Chesterton; also about Richards's theory of value by addition, and how far it is valuable when you have left out the simpler fallacies in it which Richards now admits. Or rather to boil down my scrabbly notes to that length. Is this the sort of thing you want, and when do you want it?

But the boiling did not go well. Five months later William was writing:

> Sorry not to have finished that little article for you, but I found boiling it down made it grow up, and I don't know my own mind about the thing any longer. Not a simple issue and not obviously an important one. I suppose I didn't inconvenience you, but am sorry if I did.

So there was nothing by him in *New Country*; and the next possibility to be discussed was Michael going out to succeed William in Japan when his contract expired—a rather desperate suggestion, made in the spring of 1934, when Michael was suddenly sacked from Mercer's School (for subversive opinions about miracles) and we wanted to be married. Nothing—I think luckily—came of this, and by the time William returned from Tokyo in 1935 Michael was back in Newcastle, at the Royal Grammar School, and editing the *Faber Book of Modern Verse*. He included seven poems by William; also in that year he reviewed William's first volume of *Poems* for the *London Mercury*, and *Versions of Pastoral* for the *Criterion*. In the next year or two, when William was living at Marchmont Street, Michael usually looked him up when he was passing through London on his way from Newcastle to the Alps. He persuaded William—this time successfully—to contribute an essay to the English number of *Poetry* (Chicago), which Michael and Auden edited in the autumn of 1936.

I begin with all this to show how towny and literary Michael's and William's relations had been when we all three set off on a ski-ing holiday in December 1936. No doubt it was a bit of a risk—friendships that flourish on poetry and philosophy in the Fitzroy do not necessarily take the strain of draughty nights in Alpine huts with the lavatory frozen. When Bill suggested joining us, Michael and I made it very plain what our sort of ski-ing implied. We were rough performers—it was only my second season and I had never had proper lessons—mountaineers, really, who regarded ski-ing not so much as a sport on its own as a way of travelling in the mountains in winter. Not for us the soft pleasures of smart centres with ski-lifts and night-clubs; we believed in touring, and travelling light. We rather suspected Bill, whose ski-ing had been more orthodox, and Michael sent him warning letters that there must be no suitcases or overcoats to be lugged around and clog our plans. William did not seem to mind: 'just exactly what I should enjoy about ski-ing' (and went on to thank Michael for giving him an introduction to the Royal Society Library). So the first joke was against us, when we met William at Victoria. *We* had allowed ourselves a small, cheap attaché case, that could be left in valley inns or jettisoned without remorse. Bill eyed it, and our bulging rucksacks, and asked with no irony whatever: 'What *have* you got in them?' His own sack flapped almost empty on his back, and his only spare clothes seemed to be his Japanese ski-skins and a pair of rabbit-fur ear-muffs which he had bought from a newspaper boy in Tokyo.

We were bound for the Tarentaise, a part of the French Alps

that Michael and I knew well from our summer climbing. On the last stage of our journey a bus took us up the Isère valley to Tignes, not yet flooded. Michael and I looked out eagerly, recognizing our familiar peaks and passes, while Bill drew Buddhas in the squared notebook he had just bought at Bourg St Maurice. From Tignes to the Lac de Tignes, where we were to start our holiday, the only way up was on skis: an hour and a half's climb to the charming chalet-hotel, the only building by the frozen lake, where we proposed to stay for a few days to get into training for our tour.

From this pleasant base, Bill found that ski-ing with the Robertses was not too uncomfortable; and the Robertses found that Bill was far the best skier. It leaked out that he had once passed a Ski Club of Great Britain test (second class), an ordeal regarded with respect as well as amusement by freelances like ourselves. There were no mechanical aids at the Lac—no *téléfériques*, no chair-lifts, no ski-tows—indeed a ski-tow at Val d'Isère was the only thing of the kind in the region. There were no regular *pistes*, except the run down to Tignes. So we spent our first days climbing up on sealskins to the passes and minor summits round the lake, and running down as best we could on powder snow, or windslab, or horrid icy gullies. Nearly always, Bill was down first. Many of the runs ended in the Isère valley, with hot drinks at Tignes or Val d'Isère—which thought it had something to boast of, with four hotels!—before the slog up to the lake by moonlight. One day at Tignes we were having tea at the inn, when Bill came in from a shopping expedition, with a huge cake of pink soap. 'What on earth do you want that for?' asked Michael, startled, 'we've got plenty.' Later I had to explain that, looking at postcards in another corner of the shop, I had heard Bill's request but had not felt able to intervene. With firmness and dignity he had demanded 'savon pour les dents'. The shopkeeper was puzzled, produced a normal-sized cake of soap—'Non, Monsieur, savon *pour les dents*', with increased emphasis. So he had fetched the vast pink cube. Toothpaste was purchased before we started up to the lake, but Bill still maintained that the soap would come in handy.

The chalet-hotel filled up for Christmas, but we could not start on our tour yet because Michael had twisted a knee. The long evenings passed pleasantly with drink, gossip, and bouts of quotations—for Bill and me, that is, Michael insisting that he could not remember poetry in snippets. Then we would piece together poems from our joint memories: I could do the 'Ode to a Nightingale' without any help; but we both had to struggle to put the 'Grecian Urn' together, and even so there was a missing line or two. 'Chatter about words', my diary records for one evening, 'honesty, sensibility etc'. On another, I got William on to *our* ground of complex words, when we talked about the names of mountains. How had they happened? What did they signify? Mont Blanc was straight description; but the Aiguille Verte was not green, nor the Aiguilles Rouges red, as Mont Blanc was white; the names implied an effort of memory or imagination. ('The snows looked green at dawn', 'The rocks will look red when the sun is on them.') And surely there was more than a colour implied in the Aiguille Noire de Peuteret—'black' here had something of the significance of 'fierce' or 'stormy' that it had in 'Black Sea'. Then what about the mountains just above our Lac de Tignes? *Motte* and *casse* were words usually applied to lumps and breakages on a human scale—but in La Grande Motte and La Grande Casse they carried the suggestion that we were looking at the handiwork of Titans. Bill had not heard of Les Dames Anglaises, a group of three pinnacles on the Peuterey ridge of Mont Blanc, and enjoyed our explanation of their name, as told us by a local guide: 'parce qu'elles restaient si longtemps vierges'. Another evening, when it was Michael's turn with our only Arsène Lupin (a strong Roberts addiction at high levels) and I was mending a broken sealskin, Bill tried to remember the theorems connected with the Nine-Point Circle. Firmly he rejected Michael's professional assistance: 'I want to work this out.' I went off to bed, leaving them to finish the after-dinner bottle. Michael told me later that they had gone over the list of their most promising contemporaries at Cambridge, counting up those who had gone off their heads, died, committed suicide, taken to drink, or dullness. Finally Bill and Michael had concluded that it was something for anyone of their generation to be alive, sane enough to be left at large, and sober enough to order another bottle.

Two days after Christmas Michael decided that though he could not walk with comfort, he could ski—you don't have to straighten your leg so much—and we set off on our promised journey, up and down across the passes in a wide circle round the massif of the Grande Motte and the Grande Casse. In five days we saw only one other party of travellers like ourselves, ski-ing from

hut to hut. Our first stage was up 2,500 feet to the Col de la Leisse,
five miles down the valley on the farther side, and then a sideways
traverse across slopes which had avalanched and then frozen,
where the spilt snow had hardened into hollow skulls, broken
auks' eggs, and monstrous white roses. 'What's puzzling me,' said
Bill, when we stopped to eat briefly, 'is what you do if you have to
spend the night out. Richards says that you can dig a hole with
your skis and———'

'We're not going to spend a night out,' said Michael.

'Or there's the igloo technique,' Bill went on.

'There's a man eating my dinner,' said Michael. 'Come on.'

'Yes, to be sure,' Bill answered, fixing his bindings, 'you're the
officer type. Now when the war comes, I shall rush for the ranks.'

There were people eating dinner when we reached our first
haven, the Félix-Faure hut on the Col de la Vanoise above Pra-
lognan, soon after dusk; but there was plenty for us too. With our
wet boots exchanged for clogs, wet gloves and stockings toasting
near the stove, hot soup warming us through, we spent a very
snug evening, and decided to stay the next day and climb a small
peak near by, unencumbered by heavy rucksacks. As we sat
round the stove the second evening, 'Do you know any propositions of the form A is B?' asked Bill suddenly, putting down his
glass.

'God is love, beauty is truth, might is right,' answered Michael
promptly.

'Yes—I want to know what the verb "to be" means there. The
Oxford Dictionary is interesting, but it misses the point. Love is
God, truth is beauty, right is might, are quite different propositions. I want to analyse the A is B form. I think there's a book in
it.'

'What about A is A?' asked Michael. 'Business is business, boys
will be boys. The odd thing is, they aren't tautologies.'

'Yes, that's a new class,' said Bill, getting out his Bourg St
Maurice notebook with the Buddhas in it.

I listened placidly—'time is money' seemed to be giving them a
new kind of difficulty—but the voices grew fainter and fainter.
I yawned my way up to bed; but woke up when they joined me in
the dormitory, to help Bill complete Yeats's 'Byzantium'.

Our next day's journey was the toughest: it involved ski-ing up
a glacier, crossing the steep little Col de la Grande Casse, ski-ing
down another glacier to the Champagny valley. Michael and I had

been over most of the ground in summer, and knew how crevassed the glaciers were, though now smoothly snow-covered. So we put on the rope, no hindrance when we were walking up to the col, but complicating our run down the far side, though we did manage to do some cautious turns in unison. We were in shadow and it was so cold that when we stopped for a bite, we found the water in the bottle was frozen hard. After the glacier we unroped: only one more steepish slope between us and the valley bottom. For once, I was first down: my skis had slipped on a sideways traverse on hard snow and I shot down, a somersaulting tangle of limbs and skis and rucksack. As I picked myself up, wonderfully unhurt, Bill joined me; he had skied down properly almost as quickly as I had fallen: 'I wanted to be in at the finish you know'— as if it had been the Derby!

My shake-up, Michael's still painful knee, and a longer descent than we realized—5,000 feet from the Col—meant that we travelled very slowly down the valley in the dark, and arrived at the inn at Champagny after everyone had gone to bed, though it was only eight o'clock. But they bestirred themselves kindly, and produced a splendid dish of veal cutlets and local wine. We decided the day had earned us a bottle of sparkling Seyssel, and Bill, whose French had made great strides since the toothpaste day, boldly ordered 'café complet'.

Our next day took us over another col to the Nancroit valley, uneventfully but exhaustingly, as skis had to be carried where the wind had blown the slopes clear of snow on the way up. From Nancroit there was a delightful last day, walking across the plateau de la Plagne, a mild stretch of pastures and humpy downs, to our final col, the Col du Palet, and a run back to the Lac de Tignes on beautiful powder-snow.

It had been a splendid journey: much more adventurous than anything Bill had done from a ski-ing centre. He seemed to be impressed by our route-finding; we certainly were by his ski-ing. We were all satisfied; so when the weather turned bad, we cut short the holiday and spent an extra day in Paris on the way home. There Michael and William went off to the Musée de l'Homme, and we had a final celebration dinner in a small restaurant in the rue des Saints-Pères. By this time Bill's French was fluent: 'Garçon', he ordered with a great commanding gesture, 'un canard complet!'

'Thanks for the photographs,' Bill wrote Michael a few

weeks later, 'I have a book on Positivism of yours, and a water-bottle.'

Michael died in 1948; in the early 1950s a great dam was built across the valley and Tignes was flooded; a road now sweeps up to the Lac de Tignes where there are a dozen hotels, and cable-cars and chair-lifts shoot up in all directions; even the remote plateau de la Plagne is being 'developed'. But I know that when I next meet Bill he will be the same, in that his ideas will be there in his talk—just as his voice is there in his writings. What goes into his books is not separate from what goes into his conversation—even in an Alpine hut at 8,000 feet, after a hard day on skis.

6

Empson Agonistes

Karl Miller

William Empson has written reviews at various times for the *New Statesman*, whose literary editor I was for some six years. In the autumn of 1966 I found I was not getting on very well with the new editor who had taken over, and Empson was the subject of what was, for me, our main disagreement. A piece of Empson's, the editor protested in a memorandum, was 'incomprehensible' and 'quite unsuitable for the NS'. If this was meant to drive me away from the paper, it succeeded. I dropped out, and enjoyed a spell of Luciferian free fall.

I would accept that Empson's articles—with their velocity, intricacy, and zealous insistence on detail, and his habit of placing many of his most interesting suggestions in asides and subordinate clauses—must have proved difficult for a fair number of readers ('99·9 per cent' seems a bit on the high side, however), and bitterly hard for those who were uninterested in the subjects he was writing about. But the point is precisely that this ought not to have been treated as a decisive consideration. A literary editor should acknowledge the existence of specialist interests, not least his own, and should actually defer to them, rather than try to muster the kind of consensus reviewing that persuades readers they have equal access to all the subject-matters dealt with in the paper. Life is not like that any more, and a paper which pretends that it is, and which relies on all-purpose interpreters and intermediaries— the common writer, so to speak—is likely to seem untrustworthy. The *New Statesman*'s subsequent choice of a more 'popular' style delivered a smaller circulation, but then other established weeklies also lost circulation at this time, including the paper to which I moved, the *Listener*, and I don't claim that Empson's were circulation-building articles in their own right. But it isn't simply senti-mental to believe that, in this part of the press, loss of authority will eventually bring loss of appeal, unless the process is strongly counteracted by the existence of some sort of captive readership or by factors external to the paper's editorial performance. It was for that reason, as well as for the pleasure of it, that it seemed essential to try to get Empson to write for the *New Statesman* and then for the *Listener*. I am only sorry he did not write more.

I am also sorry to be raking all this up, for I know it will be thought that I am attempting to cut a good figure—in a book few of whose readers would suppose that a weekly could be right not to publish Empson. But then there will be some of its readers who suppose that the weeklies are all so 'trivial', and so little distinguishable from the colour supplements, that he was wrong to contribute to them in the first place. And perhaps these people should be told how his contributions were regarded by one of his editors. A properly conducted weekly need yield nothing in point of authority to any academic periodical, but it can only hope to keep its end up by cherishing difficult writers and by seeking out fresh talent in all its awkwardness—rather than sucking at another paper's oranges, or chasing after names and sages and scolds and pleasers and perennials and dependables. Scarcely anything is more wholesome about a set of book pages than a touch of really disastrous difficulty.

It is not necessary to think that what Empson wrote as a journalist during the sixties is as important as any of his main books—those books of his which went up like great aeroplanes, as he said of one in a letter rebuking a reviewer who had questioned whether he was in earnest. But it is necessary to recognize that his journalism is continuous in manner and intent with what he has written in his books. His patient (and impatient) conversational style does not change from occasion to occasion; it is inflexibly characteristic and distinctive; and it is a style which lends itself excellently to literary journalism. In the *New Statesman* and the *Listener*, as well as other journals, he has written during this time principally about Shakespeare and about the iniquities of the Christian religion. One of the finest things he did was his review of D. P. Walker's *The Decline of Hell*, in which he spoke of a point in history, three hundred years ago, when the notion of damnation, of the sufferings of the damned and of the enjoyment of those sufferings by the blessed, grew to be unbearable. 'It seems very odd,' he concluded, 'that the religion was imposed on the state schools after the Second World War.' Earlier he had reviewed, almost as strikingly, *The Dyer's Hand* by the neo-Christian Auden. His review of Eliot's British Council monograph on George Herbert gave an account of the corrupting effects of the religion on admired adherents (neither Herbert nor Eliot was meant), and showed very beautifully the point then reached in his recoil from Christianity. Rosemond Tuve, he says, 'seemed disposed to treat me as a pagan stumbling towards the light. Clearer now about what the light illuminates, I am keen to stumble away from it.' Often enough, the reaction to such strokes is to be offended, or to condescend as to some gallant freak or *farceur*. There are those who cannot bear him to be in earnest, let alone right. But he is both. And his accounts of his position display an unusual composure and, given the subject, a rare power of understatement.

Another feature of his journalism has been a flow of praise and exegesis on the subject of the poetry and personal character of Dylan Thomas, which had lain for some while under a critical cloud—all the darker for the blaze of glory, or publicity, which followed his death. There is a piety towards a friend and fellow artist here, as there is elsewhere in Empson, which makes him want to take the curse off his best-selling *poète maudit*. I believe I now see resemblances between the two of them (say, between the *Eighteen Poems* and an Empson poem like 'The Scales') which I was not aware of in the forties, my frantic youth, when Thomas seemed a working-class Dionysus come out of the West and Empson seemed like the ancient universities (an impression confirmed when I met him at Cambridge—how cold and public-school this just and kind man appeared at first blush). And it may be that Empson has been conscious of a closeness to Thomas: a closeness which included a rapport resembling that of two bohemian wizards, burners of the midnight oil, companions of the lamp and the glass. But I feel that, above all, he has wished to be fair to Dylan Thomas, and to state his merits. 'Some of the early poems I think are the best, but some of the later ones undoubtedly have his full power.' There was, he remarked, none of the 'infantilism' that critics were affronted by.

An occasion worth remembering during these years was his defence of Yeats. Conor Cruise O'Brien had published in 1965 an essay saying that Yeats was a fascist. Discussing this in an article in the *New Statesman* called 'A Time of Troubles', Empson wrote characteristically: 'Surely the first point to get clear is: so were all the great writers in English in the first half of this century, except Joyce.' He went on, with many wonderfully intelligent words about the poetry and personal character of Yeats, to suggest that it was inadvisable to get worked up about his acceptance of projected violence and bad courses. It is true that few have been worked up. But it is also true that O'Brien was not exactly worked up either, and that Empson did not draw attention to much in the essay that would count as outright misrepresentation. And it is true that the mentality of O'Duffy's Blueshirts has not died out in Ireland, and that, in recent years, a rough beast has slouched towards Belfast and been born. The behaviour of the Provisionals has an O'Duffyite strain which seems to be of more consequence than their professions of socialism, and which Yeats's defenders may find hard to pardon now that the hour of the O'Duffys could be said to have come round at last, after their failure of the early thirties.

Yeats is not to blame for the practical politics of Sean Mac-Stiofáin. All the same, it is possible to feel that O'Brien has now been shown to have been wise before the event: the high distinction of his own record in the current troubles, at any rate, has done nothing to cast doubt on his examination of Yeats's troubling politics, and of a situation where some of the same crucial issues were at stake. It is also possible to feel ironic about the murmurs that were heard originally, to the effect that O'Brien was indulging in far-fetched and somehow alarmist aspersions on a great poet and dear old soul: murmurs that might recall the offence that has been taken at Empson's objections to Christianity. O'Brien and Empson have been, in my view, the outstanding critics in Britain and Ireland in the last two decades, and this of all subjects is one on which we are lucky to have had an encounter between them.

I remember Empson telling me that what he had wanted to do was to offer true explanations, to get things clear for himself and for other people—or words, simple and moving words, to that effect. 'Clear' is a word he uses continually. And his career has been shaped by a tenacious belief in the public usefulness of the critic: a belief one might expect to have flourished peculiarly at a time— during and just after the war—when the welfare of the public meant more than at most other times, and inspired a determination to legislate. The critic could contribute his own sort of national assistance by undertaking to teach, and by respecting the opinions of the less sophisticated—those, for instance, who ask: 'If Falstaff and the Prince are both bad, why is it all supposed to be nice?'

This role could be discharged with equal effectiveness in books or in articles or in the classroom, in academic groves or in journalistic grooves. It could also be discharged in the BBC. During the war, from 1941 to 1946, he was at Bush House as the BBC's Chinese Editor, and I have been looking at scripts that he wrote then. Here was his yellowing war work—Empson agonistes: one of the scripts carries the double imprimatur, 'censored' and 'passed for policy'; another was 'censored by J. Grenfell Williams'—an evocative name. The propaganda of the Second World War is apt to look sweet and quaint now, and his scripts were propaganda of a kind. But this line of talk must have come quite naturally to a man who wanted to explain. It probably is not incongruous that such a man has sometimes been 'incomprehensible': it can, after all, be assumed that his teachings will have a long run, that they will be mediated, and made doctrinal, to a nation that has not yet come into being. In any case, there is nothing incomprehensible in these BBC scripts: if there had been, J. Grenfell Williams would probably have suspected a code.

He speaks here in his own voice, if more plainly and patiently than elsewhere, and every syllable is characteristic: 'It's important, I think, that we should get the Far East into perspective and see the changes there as part of world history.' The propaganda in the scripts is, in fact, refreshing, being the expression of patriotic feelings and so disclosing another of his pieties. His patriotism, of course, is not the sort that refuses to take an interest in other countries: 'We are beside the Russians and the Chinese and the Americans, and that means all the main nations who can make a better world between them, who feel in their bones the kind of thing it ought to be.' He was of use to the BBC, since, having lived in the East, he could explain the Japanese. This he does well, condemning the country's racism and 'present rulers', but managing to be sensible and humane. He was not above offering 'a practical bit of advice' on tactics for victory: 'What the Japanese cannot stand is surprises. The Chinese guerrilla tactics are extremely powerful against the Japanese mind, because they continually give the Japanese subordinate a problem which his superiors had not foreseen. So what we must plan to give them is surprises.'

I hope General Slim was tuned in to that. It turns out that a certain Herr Fritzsche was tuned in, and took offence. Fritzsche was a leading figure in German Radio. Empson said recently that this particular broadcast, which questioned enemy doctrines about the racial purity of the Japanese, 'was one of the events of my life I always look back on with satisfaction. It got under the Nazi skin somehow, and I was answered with some stock insults—called a "curly-headed Jew", I remember—but without any effective defence of the racial purity of the Japanese ally. This was done by Fritzsche himself, the top propagandist, in the peak hour.'

The scripts reveal to perfection Empson's didacticism. This side of him was not very apparent, after the war, to those of us who as students admired or enrolled in the Movement school of poets: while professing a wish to be intelligible and practical, each Emp's son—a frantic contemporary coinage of my own—was more inclined to love him for being oracular, for his tropes and tunes and runes and spells, than for tendering citizens' advice. In one passage he was teaching people not only about the Japanese but about poetry— respecting the attitudes of the less sophisticated, and then converting them into the materials for an improved understanding of A. E. Housman. He is referring to his Japanese students, and to the practical advice they discovered in Housman's verse. The point he makes is developed in *The Structure of Complex Words*, and the fact that it makes a small strut for that great aeroplane is perhaps an indication that, for Empson, these scripts, too, were flights of a kind.

I thought A. E. Housman would be a good English poet to read. The English is very clear, and it is all a bit gloomy, so I thought they would like it all right. And I like it very much myself, so I thought I'd be able to put it over. Several of the class were being drafted for the fighting in Shanghai then, which may have altered their picture of the thing, but I think Housman would have been a good deal shocked by what they made of him. In fact, I am not sure that Housman might not have felt ashamed of himself if he had read those little essays. Because he does literally say what they thought he did; when you come to look at it. And yet, however you explain it as a matter of literary criticism, I don't believe Housman would have said it as practical advice. This is what one of them wrote down, almost literally, and most of them took the same line: 'I think Housman is quite right. We will do no good to anyone by dying for our country, but we will be admired, and we all want to be admired, and anyway, we are better dead.'

On one occasion duty called him to broadcast his reflections on the fact that the birthdays of Hitler and Shakespeare and Stafford Cripps occur in the same week. Hitler and Shakespeare were both famous liars—'a very pretty connection', though not one readily apparent to the unsophisticated. But 'the whole force of Cripps is that he is so very clearly an honest man.' And a man who felt in his bones that better world? Shakespeare's feignings, on the other hand, must be of interest to the nation at war since his world, in which things are falling apart, which is full of hatreds and divisions, is like its own.

It has been said that Shakespeare had 'an ever-present fear of the opening of the floodgates'; he keeps praising the mere order and decency of civilisation as a thing that must be loved all the more because it is so fragile. And indeed the civil war had really come in England before he had seen twenty years. But to us, too, who have seen the agony of Spain and France, there is nothing theoretical in such an anxiety. To Shakespeare, the forces of evil that he describes are so great as to become self-destructive; Iago seems to forget in the excitement of plotting and the delights of hatred even to consider his own safety, and the rebels in *Lear* tear each other to pieces. But we who see the monstrous alliance of hatred between Germany and Japan are at no great distance from the experience of Shakespeare; we too live in an age of violent changes, with a threat at each other for power, and no clear picture of a calm end; and it does not seem to us a forced turn of phrasing when Albany, as he feels certain of the victory of Goneril, says to her:

> It will come,
> Humanity must perforce prey on itself,
> Like monsters of the deep.

These thoughts deserve to be compared with his thoughts about Yeats twenty years later, which I have already mentioned. In 1965 he said that hardly any good writing was being done, probably because of the atom bomb, that the last of the great writers were fascists, though we should not care very much that Yeats was a fascist. Since that time, we seem once again to have entered a world of monstrous hatreds, a world which has shown signs of falling apart. 'The mere order and decency of civilization' has been interrupted, and those responsible for the worst cruelties which have been seen in this country during the past hundred years cannot be prevented from going on with them. The occasion on which members of the Ulster Volunteer Force beat up the wife of the politician Austin Currie, who was alone with her small children, and then cut the initials of their organization on her chest, is of a kind with which Shakespeare was familiar, and which he dramatized in *Macbeth*. A civil war is in progress in Britain, two rival fascist militias are in action, and there are politicians about who are advertising a type of demagogic leadership which is bound to appeal to a country which lacks conviction, and which seems reluctant to use force in order to defend itself. I am not predicting a bad end, but there is no clear picture of a calm one, and what we have is bad enough.

That earlier generation of great writers who were fascists is not to blame for the present troubles. But some of their work, so far from loving the mere order and decency of civilization, contains indefensible incitements to hatred, and their public usefulness is by no means entirely clear. Empson—this socialist, most socialist of all in his role of helper and explainer—should explain whether our literature is in its last days, and whether the last of our great writers have been unable to help us to survive, and whether, in this situation, we can be calm. What do you do if explanation reveals the spectacle of a literature terminating in the praise of cruelty? What happens if the light illuminates something worse than Christianity, and causes you to stumble away? Where are you to stumble to?

7

William Empson

Ronald Bottrall

A genial man, perhaps a genius,
I often met him in our Cambridge days.
Together we appeared in 1929
Sine and cosine
In an anthology of poetry,
I with nine stilted lines
Never reprinted, he
With six masterpieces almost beyond praise.

Betrayed by the head porter, ostracized by dons,
Missing the pros, he was sentenced by the cons,
A lamentable case of academic *mores*
Prompted by puritan envy and trumped-up stories.

Later, during my holidays from Helsinki
I saw him at his Marchmont Street abode,
Hands always inky.
One entered skating on a kipper bone
And heavily collapsed on a commode
Garnished with scraps of egg and bacon.
Refreshed by tepid beer
Served in smeared tooth glasses
One settled down to hear
The youthful sage spinning his paradoxes.

Paul Dirac reached full maturity
When twenty-six, William Empson
Had behind him a fine score
Of poems and *Seven Types of Ambiguity*
At twenty-four.
Dirac alas did little more
But William's genius tenaciously went on.

In Tokyo, teaching at the Bunrika Daigaku,
He became a National Treasure.
His Japanese students were trying to construe
In other words and at their leisure
A few well-known English proverbs:
'Out of sight, out of mind' became
'Invisible, insane.'

Learning to paint with Mrs Nishiwaki's aid
He made a splendid start
But put more pigment on suit and carpet
(Here Lady Sansom cannot be gainsaid)
Than on the canvas, which baulked his art.
He rode to work on a whisky diet
And had his love-play with the parlour-maid
Of the somewhat sinister Swiss Minister.
Ski-ing down the mountain he could not brake
When nearing a precipice
But God and Richard Brown were there
And William didn't turn a hair.

In Singapore we lurched and searched
Among the sailors in every sleazy den
For Nobby Clark, but the man
We found was not his Nobby
Much to his chagrin.
He didn't know, who chose words as his hobby,
That in the Navy Clarks are all called Nobby.

Cracked up to the skies by Margaret and me
We had arranged next day
For him to burgeon
At a literary luncheon.
The ladies, dressed in the most stylish way,
Looked at him in awe.
Before the food appeared the poet stood.
An opening speech? Yes, short and quick:
'I'm going out to be sick.'
And that was all the ladies heard or saw.

During the China Incident
Came the long trek
By the exiled Peking universities,

Of which he was a teaching member;
So William went
To Hunan and Yunnan.
He ran about in hope, on trust,
Happy to have escaped from the pell-mell.
The teachers taught just
What they could remember
In strict rotation,
Having no way to check.
This suited William well,
He being a master of misquotation.

In London he brought handsome Hetta
To lunch with us at the Cafe Royal,
Their first time out together.
He married her for worse or better,
Always loyal.

Able to move from Wonderland to Milton's God
From Folly to Sense and Sensibility,
From Mesopotamia to the English Dog,
Blinking like a Wykehamist hooded owl
Through thick glasses at something odd,
Our William has no peer
In providing meat for the critical soul
Making the difficult look easy
Sighting a new variant or a fence to clear
Or finding some lost cause to cheer.

What I admire most about you, William, I,
Is your indifference to the habits
And conventions of society;
Men should walk and talk like men,
Not hobbits or rabbits,
And likewise women;
By all of which I mean your truth to your own I
And your unalterable honesty.

8

The Man within the Name: William Empson as Poet, Critic, and Friend

George Fraser

I

William Empson has made a major reputation as a poet (I do not quite say, a reputation as a major poet) on a smaller bulk of published verse than any of his contemporaries. I think his *Collected Poems* of 1955 contains, quite apart from some of it being taken up with his fascinating prose notes, fewer pages and fewer poems than the *Collected Poems* of one of the few modern poets whom he really admires, A. E. Housman. His *Collected Poems* contains, also, very few poems written after 1940. His first volume of verse, *Poems*, came out in 1935 and his second, *The Gathering Storm*, in 1940. The *Collected Poems* of 1955 contains only a few more short poems and a masque written largely by Empson's colleagues at Sheffield to greet a visit by the new Queen Elizabeth in the old Elizabethan manner; to this Empson contributed only about half the lines, though the 'better half'.

Empson's productive career as a poet was, of course, not quite such a short one as the five-year gap between his two early volumes might suggest. Quite a number of the best poems in the 1935 volume were, in fact, written during his undergraduate days at Magdalene College, Cambridge, in the 1920s, and nobody who knows him well thinks of him, for all his very great reputation as a critic, except primarily as a poet. I have known a great many poets over a period of close on forty years and, strikingly different as they have been in temperament, there is a kind of loose network of family resemblances (the sort of network of resemblances that Wittgenstein noted as binding together our various uses of the word 'game') between all poets, so that, having known many, one can spot a new one: just, for instance, as one can spot, with sufficient experience of the world, a professional actor, a homosexual, a journalist, a male or female rake, an administrator, a Communist, and so on. People meeting Empson for the first time would say at once, 'This is a poet,' but would be rather surprised to hear, 'This is a Professor of English,' or perhaps even, 'This is a critic.'

The imagination of a poet seems to me to suffuse Empson's criticism. Nothing surprised me more in T. S. Eliot's posthumously published essay, 'To Criticise the Critic', than his description of Empson as primarily a theoretical critic, whose criticism had no obvious connection with his poetry. There is after all a very striking contrast between the tone, the voice, of Eliot's own criticism, and the tone, the voice of his poetry. Eliot, the publisher, and the public personage, seemed again, on the few occasions when one was privileged to meet him, something different from Eliot the poet or the critic. He delighted, I think, perhaps rather mischievously, in not appearing as a reader might have expected him to appear.

Empson, on the other hand, is all of a piece throughout. There is the same directness, bluntness, and lack of assumption or disguise in his writing and in his personal manners. He is what one expects him, from his writings, to be. And I think, in fact, that it is this plain directness of manner that has helped to give him his wide influence. Dr Johnson noted of Donne, Empson's favourite English poet, that though he expresses very difficult thoughts he expresses them in very plain language. I shall be dealing, anyway, in this piece with Empson as an example of something rather rare in modern writing, that wholeness which Yeats called 'unity of being'. I think most, though not all, of the literature of our own time that we think of as typically 'modern' is literature of the divided self.

This may be one reason why Empson, in spite of his very great influence, particularly in the early 1950s, on many younger poets does not genuinely like very much modern poetry very much. Apart from a fascinating practical criticism exercise on a poem of Dylan Thomas's 'A Refusal to Mourn . . .', and a piece written for Eliot's sixtieth birthday, and more concerned, at that, with Eliot's personality than with his writings, Empson has on the whole avoided writing about his contemporaries (though there have been one or two interesting reviews of Dylan Thomas, in the *New Statesman* and more recently in the *Listener* and there was a very appreciative review of a volume of poems by Kathleen Raine in the *New Statesman* also). He knows, of course, what century he is writing in; he loves, and has written appreciatively about, the Joyce of *Ulysses*. But his great achievement as a critic has lain, I think, in making us read a number of writers, dating from the late sixteenth to the late nineteenth century, *as if* they were our contemporaries.

II

Eliot's odd observation, cited above, may have been based on the fact that Empson's first fame was won as a critic. Eliot may have been thinking of Empson's poetry as a by-product of his criticism, just as he thought of his own criticism (which he wrote laboriously, and which he disliked re-reading) as a by-product of his poetry. *Seven Types of Ambiguity* was, in fact, published in 1930, five years before his first volume of verse. It was largely based on a dissertation which Empson had worked on at Cambridge, under the supervision of I. A. Richards, after switching from mathematics in the first part of his Tripos to English in the second part.

It at once made Empson famous. It lies, I think, at the roots of all that is most stimulating, as well as much that is most perverse in the American New Criticism. (Empson, however, is oddly uninterested in his own critical progeny; I was rather struck in a fairly recent conversation with him to discover that he had never heard of Josephine Miles's *Eras and Modes of English Poetry* and had heard of, but never read, Winifred Nowottny's *The Language Poets Use*.) He began, I think, not exactly as a theoretical critic, as Eliot calls him, but, to use an uglier but more precise word, as a methodological one. He was not interested, that is, in theories about what literature is but in new methods of analysing literature: in a sense, the approach was practical or technical, the very opposite of theoretical. As he has grown older, he has, like all good critics, come to trust more to his hunches, to the sense of the lie of the land that comes with the experience and reading of a lifetime, and I can quite see why he should be bored with new methodologies, even if they are refinements of his own pioneer inventions.

I read *Seven Types of Ambiguity* almost as soon as it came out, when I was about sixteen years old, and the sheer cleverness bowled me over, as I suppose it still bowls over most young readers. I. A. Richards's *Practical Criticism*, published two years earlier, in 1928, had a similar revolutionary effect on receptive young readers, but it has not quite to the same degree *le diable au corps*. For youthful vivacity, and its power of shocking the old, *Seven Types* has its place not so much alongside *Practical Criticism* (a book full of grave, sober, and mature wisdom) as alongside A. J. Ayer's *Language, Truth and Logic* with its abolition of all metaphysics and its reduction of ethics to approving or disapproving noises.

Not that Empson's youthful attitude to past poetry was like Ayer's to metaphysics, a sweeping of it away. The effect was, on the contrary, a reassuring one. The young reader of poetry often feels, at the same time as he feels delight and admiration, a certain confusion and bewilderment. Empson suggested that this confusion and bewilderment is not necessarily due to obtuseness or stolidity but may often be a mode of perception, an awareness of something confused and bewildered, but justifiably so, in the poet's own attitudes. It was impossible, of course, and Empson did not expect one, to keep clear in one's mind when one had closed the book, or even in the course of reading it, which type of ambiguity was which. But *Seven Types* was, and remains, an indispensable primer of close reading.

Richards's *Practical Criticism*, still an indispensable text-book for undergraduates, was primarily concerned with teaching us not to be stupid through laziness or self-complacency, not to project irrelevant obsessions or *idées fixes* of our own into poems, not to rush our fences, not to make up our minds till we have really grasped sense, tone, feeling, and (that much more slippery concept) intention. It was essentially a great text-book about the morality of reading, and perhaps about morality in general, for Richards's cautionary tales and dreadful examples apply, of course, not only to the reading of poems but to the kind of sense we can make of our feelings and perceptions in personal relationships. But in so far as he was merely giving technical advice about how to read, Richards, I think, was concerned with making us read poems as wholes, suspending our judgment till we have grasped the whole; if you have grasped a whole, the parts must be the parts that fit into it.

Empson, not always but often in *Seven Types*, was a brilliant reader of *parts* of poems. Temperamentally the opposite of Richards (it is often useful for students to have teachers, as for teachers to have students, temperamentally the opposite of themselves), frank, haughty, rash, the Rupert of debate, but a Rupert who never came but to conquer or to fall. In brilliant wrongheadedness, some of the interpretations in *Seven Types* equal Dr Johnson on Gray's poem about the cat drowned in a bowl of goldfish or on Milton's *Lycidas*: but the wrong-headedness, in Empson's case as in Johnson's, expresses a wonderful quality of mind and spirit, an exultation in the exercise of careless power. Some of the passages, like that on Keats's 'Ode on Melancholy', are still among the most brilliantly exciting short specimens of English criticism and moreover, as in this instance, *right*.

The method of supposing that any possible meaning of a word that historically *might* be there actually *must* be there was, of course, a vulnerable one. R. S. Crane comments on a passage by the American critic Philip Wheelright on a famous couplet in Marvell's 'To His Coy Mistress':

> The grave's a fine and private place,
> But none I think do there embrace.

Wheelright is very much one of Empson's American disciples, though he prefers the word 'plurisignification' to the word 'ambiguity'. (Mistakenly, I believe, for I cannot think of any English word that is *not* plurisignificant. The word 'triangle' *means* a figure with three angles but cannot help also signifying a figure with three sides. The disjunctive conjunction 'or', in ordinary speech though not in the language of logicians, can signify either—as in 'port or madeira?'—the idea that one of the alternatives is excluded, or—as in 'either a knave or a fool'—that both alternatives may possibly apply. I do not think that Empson was concerned with such a very *general* quality of language as this, which is a subject for the philosopher or the linguistic theorist rather than for the literary critic, strictly so called.)

In Marvell's couplet, Wheelright thinks 'fine' must have its ordinary sense of an approval noise (as in Hemingway's novels and stories), but also must suggest finality (from Latin *finis*) and constriction or tightness as when we talk of a 'fine line'. I feel worried about the 'fine line': when I talk of a 'fine line' of verse I think I am usually merely making an approval noise, not neces-

sarily meaning tight, constricted, or condensed: Shakespeare's
lines

> Thy glass will show thee how thy beauties weare,
> Thy dyall how thy precious mynuits pass,
> The vacant leaves thy mindes imprint will beare,
> And of this booke, this learning maist thou taste,

are 'fine lines' but the first three say the same sort of thing three
times over, in different *exempla*, and the fourth line says that this is
the sort of thing that this and many of the other sonnets are
repeatedly saying. The praise of fineness in lines of verse may, in
other words, often be praise of felicitous expansion of a topic
rather than praise of abrupt constriction, the packed or 'strong'
line, something not very common and, where it does exist, rarely
felt as the highest quality of verse composition. But it does, of
course, illustrate what I have been saying about the universality of
plurisignification in English that Wheelright, very probably, may
not have been thinking of lines of verse at all but of fine lines in a
Whistler etching, say, or even of fine thread.

Wheelright goes on to say that for Marvell 'private' means not
merely a place where one is in no danger of 'household spies' but
also what is implied by the Latin epithet *privatus*, a place of priva-
tion or deprivation. R. S. Crane, the genial doyen of the Chicago
critics, sensibly points out that if we pause to work out these five
possible senses of two words we lose the sense of the witty turn of
the second line of the couplet (the thing works better, in fact, if
we stick to the *obvious* senses). Also, there could be no possible
evidence that Marvell *intended* us to have these five possible senses
of two words in mind. Crane remarks on this:[1]

> It is no argument to say that the multiple meanings attributed to
> 'fine' and 'private' are authorised by the O.E.D., except on the
> absurd assumption that particular words in poetry always mean
> in any given use of them all the different things they *may* mean
> in the language (this is pure early William Empsonism).

'Pure early William Empsonism' was obviously a heady brew
but one is glad, in one's time, to have drunk deeply of it. This
Marvell example, from the work of a disciple, perhaps illustrates
more clearly than any example one could take from *Seven Types*
itself both the fascination and the danger of the early method at its
most extreme. It is a useful example, also, in that it leads one back

to Empson in his own person. Marvell is a poet about whom he has written with great relish, and with whom he has affinities. (I remember noting, reviewing *The Gathering Storm* in Tambimuttu's *Poetry London* when it first came out in 1940, a closeness to the tone of Marvell, in his post-Restoration satires, and to that of Rochester: whereas the underlying voices one hears in *Poems* (1935), are earlier and later, a voice sometimes something like Donne's, but also sometimes something like Pope's.) The most famous paragraph about Marvell is not from *Seven Types* but from Empson's second critical book, *Some Versions of Pastoral* (1935), and is about the stanza in Marvell's 'The Garden' beginning,

> Meanwhile the mind, from pleasure less,
> Withdraws into its happiness . . .

Empson sees two possible meanings of 'from pleasure less': [2]

> Either 'from the lessening of pleasure'—'we are quiet in the country but our dullness gives a sober and self-knowing happiness, more intellectual than the over-stimulated pleasures of the town' or 'made less by this pleasure'—'The pleasures of the country give a repose and intellectual release which make me less intellectual, make my mind less worrying and introspective.'

Pierre Legouis, in a sharp and witty piece, 'Marvell and the New Critics', included in the same anthology, has this comment to make: [3]

> *From pleasure less*. Either from 'the lessening of pleasure' . . . or 'made less by pleasure. . . .' Since three meanings, in Mr Empson's theory, are better than two, his omission of the real meaning conclusively shows that he never saw it: 'from a pleasure that is inferior' (see O.E.D. under *Less*, 2), viz. sensuous pleasure, the mind withdraws itself into a pleasure that is specifically its own, viz. contemplation.

This is fine cut-and-thrust stuff, like a sabre duel in Stevenson, but I am not in the least convinced by Legouis's third 'real meaning'. An equation of the sensuous and the contemplative, a 'green thought in a green shade', not a sharp Cartesian dichotomizing of them, is what 'The Garden' is about. The sensuous, the pleasure of a garden, is not only as good as but better than the sensual, the pleasure of sex. Empson's second interpretation, 'made less by this pleasure' seems clearly the correct one. The poem is about 'amorousness'. But it is the mind rather than the phallus that has expanded itself to penetrate and possess the garden: when it retracts, diminishes, is 'from pleasure less', there is no question, as there would be after expansion and penetration of a woman, of *omne animal post coitum triste*, of

> Only the lion and the cock,
> As Galen says, withstand love's shock,

but simply a wonderful relaxation of tension, a withdrawal of the mind into inner easing, Marvell dozing on the grass: as there can be, for that matter, after successful and spontaneous human love-making, for we should not take Galen for gospel. It would be silly to say that Empson had this notion in mind, but if one knows him well, it is hard to know what notion he may not have from time to time in mind. If he did have something like this notion in mind, I think the literary and social conventions of the 1930s would, unlike those of the 1970s, prevent him from expressing it directly. The conventions of the 1970s on the other hand would probably prevent him from making his condensed and I am sure critically relevant contrasts and comparisons between town and country life: though I must confess that I do not think that 'The Garden', except minimally and marginally, is really a Town-and-Country-Mouse sort of poem.

Some Versions of Pastoral is, at first sight, an oddly titled book (even more oddly titled in the American edition, *English Pastoral Poetry*). *The Shepherd's Kalendar*, *Lycidas*, Pope's pastorals, Thomson's *The Seasons*, Goldsmith's *Deserted Village*, Wordsworth's *Michael*, Shelley's *Adonais*, Arnold's *Thyrsis* are among the masterpieces of English pastoral poetry with which it does not deal. The only work it does deal with which its author ironically *called* a pastoral is Gay's 'Newgate Pastoral', *The Beggar's Opera*. But Empson is not merely being whimsical or perverse. Pastoral poetry from the days of Theocritus onwards has not been written by shepherds but about them. Courtiers or men leading a complicated and difficult city life have either romantically idealized the simplicity of rustic existence or, more interestingly, used a simplified picture to express criticisms of their own complex existence, which it might be dangerous to express directly. Both Spenser and Milton, for instance, use pastoral as a vehicle for satirical invective, from a Puritan point of view, against what they regard as the corruptions of church government under the Anglican settlement.

But one of the elements of the pastoral mode in this much wider sense, Empson points out, is that, like the narrower kind of merely verbal ambiguity, this structural mode of translating the complex into the simple, or setting it alongside the simple for contrast, can express mixed feelings, notably a secret hankering after pagan and primitive ways of feeling that are consciously disapproved. Milton, for instance, in his constant reiterations of the idea that the real Eden is much more beautiful than any of the pagan paradises feigned by the classical poets is covertly using these as a touchstone for its beauty and may indeed be suggesting unconsciously to his younger readers, well read in their Rochester and Hobbes, that Milton's Eden is a beautiful fable too. Gay, satirically suggesting that heroes are only highwaymen writ large, makes us feel also that Macheath is a genuine rogue hero. Lewis Carroll's Alice books are an idealization of innocence, but Alice is so genuinely innocent and endearing because her dreams, of falling down wells, of magic potions that make her small or large, of little doors, too small for her to enter (or the key is up on the big table, too far away) leading into unimaginably beautiful gardens, embody, but innocently, every kind of Freudian sexual image. The comic sub-plots of Elizabethan and Jacobean plays similarly mirror, and question, the main plots. Empson is peculiarly fascinating on a certain affinity between the relationship of Falstaff to the coldly self-possessed, the unlovingly tolerant and indulgent Prince Hal and the relationship of the speaker in the sonnets to the Fair Young Gentleman, as expressed in the sonnet

They that have power to hurt and will do none . . .

These two books of criticism coincide roughly with Empson's most productive poetic period. *Some Versions of Pastoral* is to me his most satisfying critical book, and in some ways also his most poetic. I would like therefore to turn now to his poetry before going on to consider his later critical writings, and to give some impressions of Empson the man.

III

One of the last times I saw Kathleen Raine, in a late summer visit to London, we talked about the brilliant Cambridge poets of her youth, Empson, Ronald Bottrall, her own former husband,

Charles Madge. Miss Raine said to me that she now resented very much being thought of as a poet of that Cambridge school, in so far as there was a school. She now saw that the three figures she mentioned were essentially poets of cleverness, of wit, producing the verse equivalent of prize undergraduate essays, whereas she from the first, however hesitantly at first, had been a poet of vision. If there was any poet who had been at Cambridge with whom she felt a deep affinity, it was Vernon Watkins, a religious visionary like herself. Fond as she was of Empson, and dear friend as he had been, she had avoided seeing him in recent years, because she felt he was a captain in an opposite camp. Yet, with her essential fairness of mind, she added that the first volume of Empson's poems, the 1935 one (she has no liking for *The Gathering Storm*) did express memorably, and with the proper poetic equipment, a universal experience, the agony of youth, the agony, perhaps, simply of being young. Empson had turned, she thought, mainly to criticism in his later years because life had never again offered him such a set of provocations to fine poetry as simply being at once very intelligent (he had remained very intelligent) and at the same time very bewildered and unhappy.

It is in fact Empson's second volume, *The Gathering Storm*, a much more straightforward and a much more outward turned volume, one concerned not with private agony but with the public predicaments of the late 1930s, that has been a great influence on younger poets, from about 1948 onwards, when John Wain published a long pioneer essay on Empson's poetry in John Lehmann's *Penguin New Writing*. The bewildering intricacies and contortions of the 1935 volume were, whether one thought them deplorable or wonderful, inimitable; the villanelles, the poems with refrains subtly shifting their meaning, like 'Aubade', which is not in villanelle form, the poems in *terza rima* with a hanging line at the end, the extreme regularity of metrical form of most of the poems in *The Gathering Storm*, the diction, also, plain, direct, and colloquial without being 'low', lent themselves admirably to imitation. The mode of emotional understatement, a certain blunt and humorous stoicism, a dogged Englishness (nobody could be more English than Empson, even when the setting of his poems is China or Japan) all appealed to what, from the date of their earliest volumes and pamphlets, one can call 'the generation of 1953'. In a strange way, Empson found his first poetic contemporaries among poets, like John Wain, about twenty years younger than himself.

I do not know how far he was flattered by such imitations. In a review of an anthology, *Springtime*, edited by Ian Fletcher and myself, Edwin Muir remarked that it was easy enough to imitate some of the surface characteristics of Empson's verse: but that what gave that verse its distinction was not its mannerisms, but its passion.

In at least two other essays,[4] I have dealt in some technical detail with particular poems of Empson's. In a tribute of this sort, it is better to paint with a broad brush, and to try to say what the poems mean to one, after one has lived with them for half a lifetime or so. I think that Empson's immediate contemporaries made, on the whole, very little of them. I remember, in Egypt during the war, that fine neglected poet, Bernard Spencer, telling me that he liked the sound and the gestures of the 1935 volume, but found the sense too intricate and riddling to be worth working out: it was, for all its 'rough magic' or rough music, crossword-puzzle poetry. I said that with the help of Empson's notes I had worked out the sense, but today perhaps I have lost that youthful agility of mind, or eagerness of purpose, that would help me to work it out again.

When I hear Empson read his poems aloud, his earlier poems particularly (I do not find the sense of *most* of the poems in *The Gathering Storm* very difficult) I am reassured, I suppose, by knowing that there *is* a sense, but what captivates me is the mastery of rhythm revealed in Empson's reading, and the absolute confidence of command over the audience revealed in his tone. One of the few contemporary poets for whom Empson has a whole-hearted admiration is Robert Lowell. Lowell's earlier volumes have the same contorted strength as Empson's *Poems* of 1935, and with *Life Studies* he made a transition, rather like the transition in *The Gathering Storm*, to a poetry of sometimes startling informality and deliberate abrupt gaucheness, a poetry, so to say, jettisoning the 'poetic' (though Lowell, of course, does later take up the 'poetic' again, in a publicly eloquent vein). Lowell, on a visit to me at Leicester to give a poetry reading, a visit during which William and Hetta Empson were also my guests, read his audience parts of what is often thought of as his greatest poem of his earlier phase, 'The Quaker Graveyard in Nantuckett'. He explained that, reading this poem over silently to himself, he could still make out what he was intending, when he wrote it, to say; but that reading it aloud, performing it, he had to forget all that, forget the 'deep meanings' and simply ride along with the rhythms. I am sure that Empson still could, though he very sensibly would not, make a prose paraphrase of his earlier poems. But, reading them aloud, as he has done, like Lowell, to a large audience mainly of Leicester students and young people, but on a different occasion, he rides on the rhythms: and he can hold an audience of very young people, the same sort of audience that responds to Brian Patten or Adrian Mitchell, not, certainly, because they are performing the impossible task of doing a practical critical, analytical task while they listen, but because Empson's *broad* semantics in poetry (the planting and repetition of words with a strong emotive charge) enable a listener to stop worrying about the *narrow* semantics, and to be carried on by the authority of tone and the wonderfully effective, usually expressive rather than euphonious rhythms. Empson could make a living on the circuits, if he wanted to. He is the only poet of his generation towards whom I have found, in my students and in young people in my Poetry Workshop evening classes, an unfeigned response.

The whole question that I have been raising, in a rather amateurish way, is really the question of the relationship between what Saussure called *le signifiant* and *le signifié* in poetry. I owe most of the insights in the following two or three pages to conversations with my colleague, Dr Veronica Forrest-Thomson, who is working on a book on the aesthetics of poetry, or on poetics, in which Empson's earlier poems (which have never been adequately critically examined by anybody, certainly not by myself) will provide one of her main areas of examination. Very roughly speaking, *le signifiant* is, in the context of poetry, such elements as rhythm, metre, alliteration, rhyme, grammar, effects got from the handling in a poem both of the grammatical substructure and the rhythmical superstructure (we write poems, mostly, in correct grammatical sentences and we superimpose upon the sentence structure an equally rigorous line and sometimes stanza structure): *le signifié* is the 'meaning', the extractable sense, the content or range of reference of the poem, in so far as we could ever get at that while jettisoning the verbal handling. Words of course refer, poems in the end make some sort of sense, but we are attracted to a poem by *le signifiant*, we can recognize whether it is grammatically correct and rhythmically attractive, whether it 'works' as a poem, long before we are able to attempt to isolate *le signifié*, the paraphrasable prose content, the 'meaning'.

After all, the 'meaning' in poems is often a very odd sort of meaning. Wordsworth *knows* that the cuckoo is a bird and not a wandering voice, Keats knows that nightingales have a very small average life-span as compared to man, Shelley knows that the skylark is not a blithe spirit and not singing to express any emotions comparable to human emotions in any way: and all three poets know that the birds are not listening to them, and cannot be expected to answer back. Conventions like this, which would seem crazy in life, are part of the tradition as a high-level artifice, or a complex convention imposed upon and questionably juxtaposing other conventions, equally rigid but of a simpler kind:

> O cuckoo, shall I call thee bird
> Or but a wandering voice?
> State the alternative preferred
> With reasons for your choice.

This is peculiarly effective, Dr Forrest-Thomson points out, because two equally rigid conventions—the afflatus of the ode, the dry rigour of the examination question—are imposed on each other, making us question each, and yet the result is perfectly adequate in the *signifiant*, in rhyme, rhythm, and correct grammatical structure.

Her example of something very dull and not worth doing in poetry would be the flat imitation in verse of a statement which would be dull and ordinary, and indeed hardly worth making in ordinary life: Kingsley Amis's,

> Shaving this morning, I looked out of the window . . .

I pointed out to Dr Forrest-Thomson, however, in the seminar where this came up, that a reader who took 'this morning' not as an adverbial qualification of the participle 'shaving' but as its direct object, the line would become a very interesting line by her standards. The thought of Kingsley Amis undertaking the awesome and indeed almost unimaginable task of shaving the morning, and yet remaining nonchalant enough to look out of the window at the same time is a poetic thought. Old discussions by myself, Alvarez, F. W. Bateson, of the difficulties, say, of 'The Teasers and the Dreams' back in the early 1950s seem by comparison to belong to the horse-and-buggy age, and I can under-

stand why today bright young Oxford people no longer belong to
the Critical Society or attend, say, Roy Fuller's lectures much, or
get very excited even about the return of Auden. They might be
attracted by somebody like Dr Forrest-Thomson who wants to
insist both that poetry ought to draw attention to its own arbi-
trariness and artifice, and yet seem necessary too: just as it is
arbitrary that 'cat' means cat—the word in sound or printed shape
has no resemblance to the creature—but necessary, and rational,
that 'cat' means cat, *if you are talking the English language*. Her sense
that in a poem as a small system, just as in language as a large
system, every element is and should be seen as arbitrary but that
the *whole* is rational and necessary, ought to throw a dazzling light
on the early poems. Our old way of saying, 'It sounds all right but
I can't get the hang of it', was by comparison very amateurish and
clumsy.

There might, of course, be less flattering explanations. Empson's poems might continue to entrance a new generation, which
has almost nothing in common, for instance, with the generation
that first fell for them, John Wain's, in a big way, because *no*
definite message can be got out of them. Reviewing a volume of
essays of mine, *Vision and Rhetoric*, in Eirene Skilbeck's *Twentieth
Century*, Donald Davie said that my best essay was that on
Empson, because Empson was essentially a poet of tone (in
I. A. Richards's sense, a tactful handling of the imagined reader's
social responses), and that I was good at talking about tone, but
not so good at grasping grand intellectual structures. Empson,
Davie seemed to imply, gave in poetry a wonderful impression
of a man talking intelligently, but you could not carry away in
the end any coherent account of what he had said. At a Critical
Society meeting in Oxford in the early 1950s, Alvarez, then a
research student working on the school of Donne, may have had a
similar point in mind when he described Empson as essentially a
'grammatical' poet. Like many remarks which one fails utterly to
understand, this struck me as probably very profound, if one had
understood it. (The remark has been puzzling me for twenty years
or more but at the moment of writing this it occurs to me that
Alvarez may have had the medieval trivium in mind and have
been asserting that Empson is a *grammatical* rather than a *rhetorical*
or a *logical* poet—let alone, if we bring in the quadrivium, a
musical poet.[5] If we translate these medieval terms into modern
language, Alvarez may have been meaning that Empson's great

gift is to exploit the concessive-aggressive hesitancies and stutters of English syntax—like 'Not but . . .', like, in his prose writing and conversation, 'To be sure . . .' ('I admit that, it's obvious, but it's irrelevant to what we're talking about, though I can see your sly reasons for bringing it up!') or 'Of course . . .' ('I am asserting that everybody accepts this because I know they don't. I am banging down a ten or a jack on the table with the assurance that will make everybody agree it is an ace'). Grammar is partly a game; Empson loves games, and I remember a pleasant morning in a Hampstead pub when he was trying to teach me, abortively I am afraid, to play shove ha'penny.

One is getting far away from the poems, but not so very far away, for the poems are also the person. Briefly I would say that I think Empson is a very splendid poet indeed, and that the ideas, though put forward by such distinguished characters as Alvarez and Davie, that he uses poetry merely as a grammatical trampoline or a tonal sounding board are nonsense. I think there are some bad poems, for instance his long *tour de force* poem, 'Bacchus', is a succession of ingenious Clevelandisms: it is so sharp, it cuts itself. But the early poems do seem to me to express not only the agony, as Kathleen Raine calls it, but the splendour of youth. Anyone who has read them once can never fail to eternally remember these two great stanzas, in Marvell's 'Horatian Ode' metre, from 'This Last Pain', from the 1935 volume:

> All these large dreams by which men long live well
> Are magic-lanterned on the smoke of hell;
> This then is real, I have implied,
> A painted, small transparent slide.

> These the inventive can hand-paint at leisure
> Or most emporia would stock our measure
> And, feasting in their dappled shade
> We should forget how they were made

And there is the other great stanza, which I quote from memory, but I trust not incorrectly:

> Imagine, then, by miracle, with me,
> (Ambiguous gifts, as what gods give must be)
> What could not possibly be there,
> And learn a style from a despair.

This poem was a response to the view of I. A. Richards, Empson's mentor in his later years at Cambridge, that the outer universe is neutral, it neither hates nor loves nor has any real interest in us, and that when the poet says all's well with the world he cannot mean more, in the cash value of his meaning—whatever he *intends* to mean—than that all is well, for the moment, with his nervous system. (But the world is all before me, mine to choose, and my doctor knows much more about my nervous system than I do: he, not I, can distinguish between steady, efficient functioning, and euphoria!) In a very interesting interview in Ian Hamilton's *the Review* Empson, I remember, said he could not now accept the argument of this very fine poem; it was too much an Oscar Wilde argument, a let's-pretend argument, and much as there is to be said for good old Oscar,[6]

> The Duchess she was dressing,
>   Dressing for the ball,
> When there she saw old Oscar
> A-standing by the wall . . .

Empson did not want to be a Wildean, saying that only deliberate pretence and projection of imaginary meanings will give any sense to the meaningless of the universe. Empson, in this great poem, as I think it, mentions Wittgenstein:

> What is conceivable can happen too,
> Said Wittgenstein, who had not dreamt of you . . .

For Wittgenstein, in the *Tractatus*, the world was simply everything that was the case, an endless accumulation of atomic facts, which are facts about inconceivably simple entities. (A blue spot on a white wall cannot, for instance, be a constituent of an atomic fact, since it is both extended and coloured, and exists in an extended and coloured spatial context: Wittgenstein had invented a wonderful slotting machine, into which nothing conceivable, since we cannot imagine an absolutely simple particular, could slot. But the world was this set of slots, anyway, with whatever unimaginable simples they contained. And the meaning of the world, 'the mystical', lay outside the world, and since it could not be conceived clearly ought not to be spoken about. I imagine that Wittgenstein, whose favourite reading was American pulp thriller magazines like *The Black Mask*, never read poetry, and had never considered poetry's round-about way of saying things.)[7]

Empson, I think, dislikes philosophers on the whole, as many poets do: but to have intellectually matured in that extraordinarily distinguished Cambridge of the 1920s, when Richards and Wittgenstein and Moore were around (and the young Leavis, to be sure, but I do not think that Empson ever took much of an impact from Leavis), must have left its mark on him. Most really fine poets know and do not really know what they know, can say things they did not think they were going to say; from quarter of an hour's casual browsing in a library, may have constructed, and forgotten, a whole system of philosophy. Empson's mind is, in a sense, the opposite of philosophical. I think the beautifully tedious prose of G. E. Moore, leaving no possible step in an argument out, fussing and fretting over every even faintly ambiguous concept, sublimely pedestrian, one might say, is the model of what a good philosopher's prose should be: whereas Empson's mind, in prose or verse, moves in seven-league boots, in a giant's elliptical leaps, and there are great Serbonian bogs between his premises and his conclusions. But Cambridge, in his time there, was a great philosophical place, and this must have influenced him: an influence, as Empson himself said of that of T. S. Eliot, bleak and penetrating, like an east wind. I remember, and perhaps retain, the agony of my own youth enough to still feel the impact of the early poems very strongly. The state of youthfulness is a state of soaring aspiration blocked and thwarted by the blockishness of people and things: as Shakespeare's Troilus says:

> This is the monstruositie in love Lady, that the will is infinite, and the execution confined; that the desire is boundless and the act a slave to limit.

That is what the earlier poems seem to me to be about, and love can be love of the divine, a fable, and the lady in a love poem can be a poetic fiction. Marvell's Coy Mistress, all the modern critics seem to agree, never existed (he settled down, after the Restoration, to a very humdrum liaison with his landlady). The poem is in a convention, or it plays brilliantly with a convention: but Marvell's feelings about death, pleasure, and frustration were, I think, like the young Empson's, real enough.

The Gathering Storm of 1940 (it is one of Empson's often repeated but perpetually good jokes to claim that Winston Churchill, for an early volume of his Second World War memoirs, cribbed without acknowledgment Empson's title) is quite different. Empson was teaching in Japan between 1931 and 1934, in Tokyo National University, and between 1937 and 1939 in the National University at Peking. I suppose the intervening period in England may have been largely taken up with arranging for the publication of both *Poems* and *Some Versions of Pastoral* in 1935. And in seeing old friends. There is an astonishing new social maturity of tone, a sense of what history is like, a refusal to be either panicky or utopian: he knew that we were in for a bad time, in these islands, but felt that we would get through it. In China, in the later 1930s, he had been caught up in the Great March, or the Great Retreat, from the invading Japanese and had given his lessons in various remote places, relying on his extraordinary memory for verse he had read (prose is harder to remember, but he does say in one poem that he had memorized a paragraph by Virginia Woolf) and on the blackboard. Far Eastern education does consist very largely of memorialization. There is a system of deference, the Confucian system, and a rather more rigid pecking order between different grades of lecturer than our British universities allow, but on the other hand Japanese and Chinese students will not respect a *sensei* unless they respect him morally, feel that, teaching and embodying order, he has created order in himself. I have taught in Japan myself: on various visits to Sheffield, it has often struck me that, not only by his colleagues and his students, but by the waitresses in the Senior Common Room or by barmen and barwomen in pubs, he is treated with the kind of deference accorded in Japan to the *sensei*, who is expected to be not a mere instructor or expert but a sort of sage. Like King Lear, Empson has authority in his eye; and in his remote and brusque way, he has a great deal of warmth: on my last visit to Sheffield I was very much amused and touched by a conversation between a waitress and William about a special number of a university magazine, which had included both a tribute to him by students, and a little piece by himself. The waitress was saying how deserved the tribute was; William was saying that his own contribution was rather a hasty piece of work. Neither at a surface level was quite taking in what the other was saying, they were at semantic cross-purposes, but one felt that they were at one with each other, were making the right warm noises to each other, in a way that made semantics comparatively unimportant. Restricted codes, on both sides, made possible an intimacy that elaborated codes often preclude.

It seems silly to talk about restricted codes in connection with such an acknowledgedly difficult poet. But in writing, as in life, Empson often says brief, gruff things, which you must pick up at once if at all, for expansion and elaboration would destroy them. The restricted code implies, flatteringly, that the reader or inter-locutor is, in Conrad's phrase, 'one of us'. In this sense, I go back to *The Gathering Storm* often, for what I can only call wisdom. I am by nature touchy, resentful, and liable to harbour grudges for a long time. Remembering a line and a half from a fine and patriotic poem in *The Gathering Storm*,

> As to be hurt is petty, and to be hard
> Stupidity . . .

has very often, if not often enough, helped me to check back these disagreeable tendencies in my nature. I find myself also remembering lines, apparently flippant or frivolous, for their condensed truth:

> For every style comes down to noise,

or one, about a Japanese train in Manchuria, which fascinated the young John Wain:

> For I, a twister, love what I abhor.

One would not, perhaps, call Empson a philosophical poet: simply because he would never sacrifice a genuine insight, how-ever it might seem to contradict the general directions in which his thought and life move, to a desire to appear consistent and systematic. But I would call him a wise poet. And yet wisdom is not enough. Wordsworth's *The Excursion* is a wise poem but a lot of it is flat stuff that takes a lot of plodding through. Empson's restricted poetic code, in the sense in which I have been using the phrase, leads to an off-hand elegance, a tart concision. His poems have something almost like a physical savour; 'a taste in the head', as I have described it elsewhere, very unlike other poetic tastes, as the taste of quinces is not very like the taste of any other fruit. Of course, not everybody likes quinces; and perhaps one must learn to like them (quinces, perhaps, cooked in cloves, and not every-body likes cloves either).

IV

This essay is already too long, but, though I intended to separate my impressions of a person from my impressions of a writer, I find that I have intermingled both sets, and indeed in my mind they are inextricable. I must round off, briefly. Neither of Empson's two post-Second World War critical books, *The Structure of Complex Words* and *Milton's God* (though I think the latter is a very fine book), have meant as much to my middle age as the two earlier critical books meant to my youth. I. A. Richards once said to me that *The Structure of Complex Words* was too much of a palimpsest, embodied too many layers of interest in Empson's thinking at separate times, to be wholly satisfactory. It is, of course, partly an attack on Richards's early theory of a fairly simple division between the referential and the emotive use of language. Roughly, one thing that Empson is saying is that words move us very largely *because* of what they refer to: the words 'child', 'rose', 'summer', 'kitten' will arouse pro-feelings in a large number of people and the words 'bully', 'pig', 'hyena', 'leprosy', 'cancer' will rather similarly arouse contra-feelings. The emotive charge of words is to a very large degree the charge of our habitual feelings about the things the words refer to. Yvor Winters made the same kind of point, quite independently, and it is a good point. More interesting and original was the point about how words like 'honest' or 'native', which ought to arouse pro-feelings, arouse condescending feelings, since we use them of those we think of as inferiors. Honesty is a virtue of tradesmen or servants and in Elizabethan times, in the very narrow sense of chastity, of women, thought of also as natural inferiors. Dark-skinned people, whom we rule, are natives, but we do not usually refer to ourselves as British natives. It was a good insight, but applied in rather too rough and ready a fashion. We were not getting quite pure historical textual analysis, but not getting quite pure theoretical semantics either. But there were some very sharp insights, and I never hear on the stage Othello's

> But why should honour outlive honesty?
> Let it go all,

without thinking poignantly of the difference between Iago's false trustworthiness and Desdemona's true chastity, and of the ways in which the condescension and patronage bound up with such uses of language lead us all to self-deception.

Milton's God is a work of splendid vigour, inspired by Empson's growing animus over the years against what he calls neo-Christians (many of whom may be simply cradle Christians, who have come back to their childhood faith late in life). I do not know whether he believes the God of orthodox Christianity to exist, but he seems to hate Him almost as if he did exist: he blames him for being very cruel, and Christianity for being a very cruel religion, but if you were a whole-hearted atheist you would have to say that it is because men are cruel that they invent a cruel and frightening religion (and because they are not wholly cruel that they bring in love and charity too, and that Christianity can inspire self-sacrifice and service to the poor and the sick as well as sectarian hatred, bigotry, and persecution). Men are both cruel and kind, whatever religion they have, I think, and I believe that Christian morality at its best, in Dr Johnson or Jane Austen say, is the best morality. It is about this, I suppose, that Empson and I have had our worst quarrels: the Christian hell is certainly a very horrible concept and I could not believe anybody deserves to go there, except, in black moods, myself sometimes.

But Milton's Hell in *Paradise Lost* is not particularly horrible. His devils with their long parliamentary debates and their interminable philosophical arguments are, as Empson once said at a discussion where I was taking the chair for him, 'noble creatures'. There is a hell of a lot to admire in Satan, and C. S. Lewis is very mean to treat him as ridiculous, as a comic figure, simply because his cause is lost from the start: one does not treat a General like Rommel as ridiculous because he goes on fighting bravely well after he knows that in the longer or shorter run the game is up. I suppose, though, Lewis is right in suggesting that as Satan gets more desperate he also becomes a dirtier fighter. He has *something* to resent: in the sudden promotion of the Messiah (and Milton of course is not an orthodox Christian, not even a Trinitarian; he does not believe in the eternal consubstantiality of Son and Father) there were, as Bagehot noted over a century ago, 'symptoms of a job'. One is all with Empson about Satan and about the beautiful human centrality to the story of Paradise (how right he is to say, against Eliot's theory of 'the great blind musician', that Milton paints like Claude) and of the great human love of Adam and Eve. Where I cannot go with him is in being either frightened or impressed by Milton's God. *Qui s'excuse, s'accuse*: when Milton's God says that foreseeing what people will do does not compel them to do it, he is logically right, of course, but 'God the Father turns a school divine'. Milton managed to make a very good classical epic out of rather meagre biblical raw materials. But if you compare him with two other great writers roughly contemporary with him, Bunyan and Pascal, and if you note his calm indifference to these burning topics of seventeenth-century religious discussion, reprobation, or the sense of it, conversion (the working out of one's salvation in fear and trembling), and grace, and the grace to ask for grace, you feel how untypical of the Christianity of his age Milton was. *Paradise Lost* remains, in a sense, a great Christian poem, as St Paul's cathedral remains a great Christian church: but a Shintoist Japanese walking round St Paul's might be forgiven for thinking that it is a magnificent shrine devoted to the worship of great English admirals. One of Empson's points, of course, is that Milton deserves all credit for remaining so magnificently a humanist in spite of having such a horrible religion. My point is that, in the sense of which one speaks of having a disease, Milton hardly had the religion at all. So, though *Milton's God* is a fine book, Milton is a bad stick to beat Christianity with.

Empson is a great and ferocious arguer, and, just as he was once finding neo-Christians under the bed everywhere, now he is always finding disciples of Dr Leavis. A nice girl had done a thesis on A. E. Housman for me; Empson was good enough to be external examiner, and spent a lot of time, some of it reading out Housman beautifully, much of the rest reproaching us for our slavery to Leavis's precepts and example. I cannot recall that great man ever even having mentioned Housman (whom I do not suppose him to admire much), and I did towards the end of the oral mildly murmur that over a year of rather lengthy weekly supervisions I did not remember Dr Leavis's name being mentioned. Yet Empson is very convincing and I think that both that nice girl and I were left wondering guiltily whether we were Leavisians without knowing it. And Empson's magnificent readings certainly left us both feeling that we had been shallow and condescending about Housman though, all through our lessons together, we had been thinking how much we enjoyed him.

William, in fact, is often very like one's idea of Dr Johnson. My wife, like myself, is an eager theatre-goer, and she was regaling Empson once with an account of all the plays we had crowded in, in a short London visit. 'I rarely go to the theatre, my dear,' he said gently, 'but then I am very blind and very deaf.' There was no self-pity and no demand for our sympathy: a plain statement of fact.

I never came up to Empson's early expectations of what I might do as a poet, and I think the fact that I still persist in writing poetry from time to time profoundly irritates him. I remember him once flinging a poem I had written in the 1950s (a rather good poem, I think, suggested by the mood of, but by no means a *pastiche* of, Hardy's *Satires of Circumstance*), having shaped it into a paper dart, across the floor of my Chelsea drawing room (where I also remember Kathleen Raine, who had been reading us Shakespeare sonnets, suddenly hurling the volume with extraordinary vigour and precision to hit John Davenport in the neck: John, a friend of both hers and Empson's, had been slumped half asleep in a chair, muttering that women could never read poetry aloud properly: he awoke, and shook himself in bewilderment, like a great shaggy dog that has just come out of the sea). Empson would sometimes try to be kind. I sent him some Dante versions I had been doing for the BBC. He wrote very kindly, saying that the language seemed to have a classical quality. I thanked him the next time I met him: 'I can't think what I meant when I wrote such nonsense. They are dead, dead, *dead*!' And the most generous compliments would have a sting in the tail. 'Your little book on Pound is very much better than your usual work, George . . . a good little book, in fact . . . not that it actually makes me want to *read* the old boy, again!' One comes to enjoy this gruffness (perhaps one did not *always* enjoy it in one's younger, touchier, more foolishly ambitious days) and against it one can set acts of kindness, help, hospitality, always alive in my own mind, but which it would be tedious to enumerate and describe in detail.

In one of the last of his Father Brown stories, Chesterton describes the poisoning in a pub of a cantankerous old radical who had been investigating the iniquities of the tied house system. Father Brown says that the dead man is one of the unknown great men of England, that he had been like Swift and Johnson, bitter and rough often in his speech, unmerciful to corruption or oppression, making very many enemies, but passionately beloved by his friends. I never re-read that story without thinking of Empson. Father Brown added that Swift and Johnson had this further peculiarity, that they could not abide Scotsmen. I have never seen in Empson any sign of that sort of animus against my country, except when I tried to persuade him that there was some merit in the Lallans verse of Sydney Goodsir Smith. But his general utilitarian benevolence was seen in a project, in the 1950s, for gradually replacing the red deer in the Highlands by herds of reindeer, which do much less damage to vegetation, and provide better meat: I thought this one of his agreeable fantasies and was surprised the other day to read that an enterprising Laplander has begun to put the scheme into practice. William is a very practical man: he foresaw that Dr Beeching's ruthless dismantling of the railways, besides clogging the roads with motor traffic, would create insuperable difficulties about moving soldiers in the event of another war. I think, indeed his poems show, that life has held much pain for him. But a spirit of practical benevolence and a taste for sociability have always conquered any temptation to give up life as a bad job. He is a model of courage.

NOTES

1 *Penguin Critical Anthologies: Andrew Marvell*, ed. John Carey (1969), p. 232.
2 Ibid., p. 239.
3 Ibid., p. 267.
4 'The Interpretation of the Difficult Poem', epilogue to *Interpretations*, ed. John Wain (1955); and 'Not Wrongly Moved . . .', originally a *TLS* middle article on *The Collected Poems*, reprinted in my *Vision and Rhetoric* (1959).
5 I rather doubt if Alvarez at that date was interested in Saussure: and Barthes and Lévi-Strauss were not yet visibly there to be interested in.
6 Bawdy English folk-song, widely current in sergeants' messes in the Second World War: my own slightly self-indulgent and reminiscent citation here, not Empson's in the interview referred to.
7 Unfair to Wittgenstein. Since writing this passage I have read an article in *The Human World* by Dr Leavis on Wittgenstein. Dr Leavis describes, there, how he was about to expound 'Legal Fiction' a brilliantly coherent early poem of Empson's, to Wittgenstein. Wittgenstein's instant grasp of the poem's pattern of logical analogies enabled him to sight-read it and expound it to Dr Leavis. But this was all the more impressive because Wittgenstein never spoke or wrote the English language with any nicety or correctness, and it is a tribute to the young Empson's logical coherence as well as to Wittgenstein's logical insight.

An Eighth Type of Ambiguity

Graham Hough

Long long ago when the world was young and literary criticism had just been invented we learnt from William Empson that a poem might mean more than one thing at the same time, and that far from being a defect this is likely to be a merit. This idea was not wholly new. Earlier patristic writers had employed it in the interpretation of Scripture, and it was already familiar that one literal sense and three spiritual senses could be contained in the same discourse. But Scripture being divinely inspired was a special case, and it was doubtful whether merely human authors could be credited with the same power of plurisignification. Some of them certainly claimed it—Dante, for example. Allegorical writing presented a second meaning behind the surface narrative, and in the Renaissance much heroic poetry not professedly allegorical was credited with similar concealed meanings which it was the business of commentators to unveil. But the concept of multiple meaning did not establish itself widely in the interpretation of poetry in general. It was Empson's *Seven Types of Ambiguity* that led critics and exegetes to see multiple and simultaneous meaning as part of the normal procedure of poetry; and it would be hard to exaggerate the consequences of this for later critical thinking. Neo-classic criticism had worked towards the idea of a single ascertainable meaning, presumed to be what the author had intended to put in. Romantic criticism appealed to an unbounded ocean of inspiration. Post-Empsonian criticism has been possessed by the idea of layer upon layer of implicit meanings, some of them not at all obvious, whose intentional status remains undefined. And the large body of discussion that is by now assembled in this area can be seen as directly or indirectly the consequence of Empson's work.

This has indeed become a central theme in much modern

criticism—that a literary text is a complex entity composed of different meanings, presented not as alternatives and not successively, but mutually interacting and simultaneous. It is difficult to ascribe some of these implicit meanings to the 'intention' of the author in any simple sense, and a secondary discussion has therefore grown up about the place of the author's intention in establishing the meaning of a text. Some ambiguities (Empson's second type) arise from a genuine doubt about the meaning which a particular passage can properly be said to bear. Two alternative meanings seem to be possible and instead of deciding for one or the other we accept both and resolve them in a kind of Hegelian synthesis which is the poem itself. Most ambiguities, however, take a different form. The text seems to have a plain sense about which there is no prima facie doubt, but a number of secondary suggestions can be seen to cluster round this plain sense, modifying and enriching it in various ways. The plain sense can most plausibly be described as 'what the author intended'; the status of the associated suggestions is less certain. Empson is not much interested in this question. As a follower of Richards he approaches interpretation chiefly from the point of view of the reader, and his ambiguities are generally seen as possible reactions in the reader's mind. When he does come near to stating a principle it is the traditional communicative one—that the reaction of the reader is or should be that which the author intended him to have. Yet the actual terms of his discussion allow a good deal of room for other possibilities. He admits a problem about how far the poet is conscious of his own activity. Some ambiguities are of the nature of Freudian slips, the product of unconscious forces. (I will avoid the solecism 'unconscious intention'.) There are others that Empson himself I think would describe as gifts of the language—possibilities of multiple meaning that are built into the lexicon and syntax of English, as of other natural languages. This situation evidently leaves many questions open. An ambiguity which is part of the language can be consciously exploited by the author, passively accepted, or not noticed at all. Can we, in a particular text, distinguish between these states of affairs? How would we set about doing it? If we can distinguish, what difference would it make to interpretation? What is the status for interpretation of an 'unconscious' suggestion, picked up by a reader but not intended by the author? What are we to think of a text of acknowledged literary merit which conveys to most readers a sense that the author would certainly have repudiated? An ingenious or eccentric or specially gifted reader can find a host of implied meanings in an apparently simple text. But how many of them are really there, and are those which are really there always and only those that the author intended?

In this paper I want to suggest that behind Empson's seven types of ambiguity there lurks an eighth—ambiguity between intended and achieved meaning. I shall illustrate some of its effects, and I hope to show that a recognition of its presence is an important part of the interpretation of literary texts. If I am right, it is wrong to fall into the intentional fallacy (which in its extremer forms is indeed a fallacy), but it is equally wrong to relapse into the misplaced scepticism of its opponents. It is in the interplay between intended and unintended that interpretation finds most work to be done. Since I am adding yet another item to the long series of articles on meaning and intention in literature I shall have to begin with a few remarks on the present state of play in this controversy.

The modern discussion of intention in a literary context begins with Wimsatt and Beardsley's article 'The Intentional Fallacy' (*Sewanee Review*, 1946).[1] This critical monument has by now disintegrated, as a result of its own internal contradictions, of direct assaults upon it,[2] and of more philosophical consideration of meaning and intention in a non-literary context. But the ruined site remains, haunted by the memory of an ill-defined New Critical doctrine that the intention of the author (which sometimes means his biography, sometimes his plan of work) is irrelevant (or unavailable, or both) to the interpretation (or evaluation) of a work of literature. This blunderbuss utterance could be, indeed has been, analysed into a variety of propositions, some plainly untrue, some true but on the verge of being truisms, and some doubtful. A typical literary-critical doctrine, in fact. In spite of contradictions and inconsistencies its operational purport is, however, tolerably clear—we are not to ask questions about what the author intended, but only questions about what the words mean. This injunction has been opposed in various ways. The principal philosophical reinforcements that have been brought in by the opposition are to be found in G. E. M. Anscombe's *Intention* (1963) and A. L. Austin's *How to Do Things with Words* (1962): and the most recent and direct form of rejoinder derived from these sources says that to ask questions about what the words mean *is* precisely to ask questions about the author's intentions. I will give two examples. A. J. Close (1972)[3] cites a number of 'time-honoured and still respectable axioms about literary art, according to which it is a fallacy to pursue, or feel limited by, the author's intentions: "Great works of art mean more than they literally say"; "great art transcends the original intentions of its creator and means something new to every epoch"; "we can never know, and need not concern ourselves with, what the writer intended".' He believes that these assumptions have a dubious philosophical basis, and his article is an attempt to scotch them. He concludes that 'the responses which literature seeks are securely anchored in the utterer's intentions.' Quentin Skinner, in an article (1972)[4] which sums up and adds to previous work of his own, comes to a similar conclusion—'that a knowledge of the writer's intentions in writing [in a particular sense of intention which he has isolated] is not merely relevant to, but is actually *equivalent* to, a knowledge of the meaning of what he writes'.

I do not wish at this point to question these conclusions, but to indicate the route by which they have been reached. It is by way of Austin's doctrine of illocutionary acts. This can be summarized as follows. To make any utterance is to perform a locutionary act, and to perform a locutionary act is also and *eo ipso* to perform an *illocutionary* act, i.e. to use the locution in some special way—asking or answering a question, giving information, a warning or an assurance, announcing a verdict or giving a description, etc. There are many possible illocutionary acts, and the class is not clearly defined. The essential part of both Close's and Skinner's argument is that to interpret a literary text is to identify correctly the illocutionary acts performed by the author in writing it. Illocutionary acts are intentional, so in interpreting a text we are recovering the author's intentions.

Skinner is a historian of political thought and uses non-literary examples; Close is more concerned with prose than poetry; but both in the articles cited are explicitly discussing the interpretation of literary texts. It is curious therefore that they both pass over the fact that Austin specifically *excepts* literary, fictional and poetic usage from the general course of his argument.[5]

> Surely the words must be spoken 'seriously'. . . . I must not be joking, for example, nor writing a poem.

> A performative utterance will, for example, be *in a peculiar way*

hollow or void if said by an actor on the stage, or if introduced in a poem, or spoken in soliloquy. . . . Language in such circumstances is in special ways—intelligibly—used not seriously, but in ways *parasitic* upon its normal use—ways which fall under the doctrine of *etiolations* of language.

We must bear in mind the possibility of 'etiolation' as it occurs when we use speech in acting, fiction and poetry, quotation and recitation.

Let us be quite clear that the expression 'use of language' can cover other matters even more diverse than the illocutionary and perlocutionary acts. For example, we may speak of the 'use of language' *for* something, e.g. for joking; and we may use 'in' in a way different from the illocutionary 'in', as when we say 'in saying "p" I was joking' or 'acting a part' or 'writing poetry'; or again we may speak of 'a poetical use of language' as distinct from 'the use of language in poetry'. These references to 'use of language' have nothing to do with the illocutionary act. For example, if I say 'Go and catch a falling star', it may be quite clear what both the meaning and the force of my utterance is, but still wholly unresolved which of these other kinds of things I may be doing.[6]

Perhaps Close and Skinner skip these bits out of embarrassment, for the equation of poetry with joking, and the description of literary language as an etiolation, are embarrassingly inadequate. All the same they are important; they call attention to something that is true—that utterances in poems and fictions are not on the same level as those in ordinary life; and Austin's summary relegation of literary language is not perhaps the bland Philistinism that it appears, but just a quick way of limiting his argument. However, if we are concerned with literary interpretation we cannot so limit the argument. We are bound to inquire further into the 'parasitic uses of language', the 'etiolations' which are 'not serious', not the 'full normal use'.

An obvious thing to say here (and Austin actually does say it) is that an apparently illocutionary act in poetry is not really so; it is only the mimesis of an illocutionary act. 'Go and catch a falling star' is not really a command, only the imitation of a command. Does this make any difference to interpretation? It does. If we attempt to recover the illocutionary act of the author, as Close and

Skinner tell us to, we do not find him uttering a command, we find him writing a poem. From Austin's point of view this is a special, 'etiolated' use of language; and the literary exegete has to content himself with this dusty answer.

But of course, within the fiction or the poem any illocutionary act can occur that could occur outside it; questions are asked, information is given, verdicts are pronounced, and all the rest. But these are not the acts of the author; they are imitated acts, of fictional characters, devised and combined by the author to form *his own illocutionary act*, which is the whole poem. But can anything as complex as a whole poem constitute an illocutionary act in Austin's sense? If so, it ought to be possible to say what it is doing —asking questions, warning, admonishing, describing, or what not.

The trouble with philosophical or quasi-philosophical arguments like those of Close and Skinner is that even if they are sound (I believe they are partly sound) they are so abbreviated and schematized as to be very unlike the actual process of literary interpretation. They leave out some of the real decisions that have to be made. *How much* of the text is to be taken as constituting an illocutionary act? 'Go and catch a falling star' looks like a command. In its context it is one of a series of commands to do impossible things, and at the end comes a command to find out how honesty can be advanced in the world. The implication is that this is equally impossible. We can identify the illocutionary act performed by this stanza as 'satirizing the falsity and corruption of the world'. The apparent series of commands are a rhetorical device directed towards another end, which has nothing to do with commanding.

But this is only the first stanza of the poem. The second gives a similar set of injunctions to impossible quests, and concludes that it is equally impossible to find a woman who is both true and fair. The illocutionary act here is 'satirizing women'; and this is continued, by a trope which we need not now consider, into the third and last stanza. It appears then that the illocutionary act performed by the whole poem is this one—'satirizing women'— and that the first stanza about the fate of honesty in the world is only a generalizing prologue to the specific message which is about the honesty of women.

We have now identified the illocutionary act performed by the poem, which is what Close and Skinner say we ought to be doing. It would surely be absurd to present this meagre platitude as anything like an interpretation of the poem. Perhaps we have not gone far enough. Perhaps we have relied too exclusively on the text, without inquiring from other sources what intentions could have gone or were likely to have gone into the writing of the poem. One answer to this kind of question presents itself very obviously: satire on the inconstancy of women is a vulgar and time-honoured theme in medieval and renaissance literature. Helen Gardner quotes Nashe in this connection:[7] 'Democritus accounted a fair chaste woman a miracle of miracles, a degree of immortality, a crowne of tryumph, because shee is so harde to be founde.' Professor Gardner also remarks that the listing of impossibilities is a well-known device in classical poetry, 'usually going with oaths of fidelity in the formula "sooner will . . .",', and cites Propertius, II, xv, 29–36 and Ovid, *Tristia*, I, viii, 1–10. Since Donne's impossibilities pointedly do not go with an oath of fidelity it appears that he is executing a calculated variant on a well-known theme. In the light of this information the intention behind the poem is not so much 'satirizing women' as 'writing an ingeniously novel poem on a conventional but still fashionable theme'. The two are quite different. The intention to satirize women (because you are indignant at women's frailty) is not at all the same thing as the intention to write a clever poem satirizing women (because you enjoy the literary ingenuity of the performance). Probably as in most such cases both intentions are present in some quite undeterminable proportion. But what has become of the trim outlines of the illocutionary act? They have dissolved, in a complex of fused and inseparable intentions.

I conclude therefore that to identify the illocutionary act performed by a text or part of a text is sometimes impossible, sometimes possible, desirable where possible, but always insufficient as an interpretation of the text. It is insufficient because it is schematic and generalized. To satirize women is the intention of many poems; to identify this intention cannot tell us much about this particular poem.

Let us return then to the text, or for the sake of a manageable brevity to part of it, the first stanza.

> Goe, and catche a falling star
> Get with child a mandrake roote,
> Tell me, where all past yeares are,
> Or who cleft the Divels foot,

Teach me to heare Mermaides singing,
Or to keep off envies stinging,
    And finde
    What winde
Serves to advance an honest minde.

We can indeed recover the illocutionary act performed by this utterance. We can identify the intention in writing it—to satirize the falsity and corruption of the world. But this is not to interpret the stanza. To interpret the stanza is to account as fully as possible for the unique satisfaction it brings. The satisfaction is a function of meaning—of meaning in the fullest possible sense; not only lexical and syntactical meaning, but connotative meaning, associated suggestions, rhythmical and auditory effects. These partial meanings cannot all be identified with certainty, and the way they interact must be even less certain. So there can be no final or demonstrably best reading. The individual commentator must just do the best he can. I will now do something in this direction, and if it turns out to be not very much it will at least go beyond the identification of illocutionary acts.

There is no difficulty in recovering the intended meaning in a general way—to satirize the falsity of the world. Of course we want to know this; but it is only a diagram. The achieved meaning does not contradict the intentional diagram, but it is something far more complex. The complexity here resides chiefly in the detail of the imagery from which the whole is built up. We have a catalogue of impossibilities. The first is, 'Goe, and catche a falling star'—do something impossible, catch and possess an object of haunting beauty that is by nature evanescent and unseizable. The second 'Get with child a mandrake root'—an equally impossible enterprise, but now one that is sinister and dubious. A mandrake root looks like a human being but is not; to copulate with it would be against nature. It is soporific, aphrodisiac and a fertility charm. It is also perilous, for it is supposed to shriek on being pulled from the ground, and whoever hears the shriek will die. We are in the region of perverse and dangerous sexuality. 'Tell me where all past yeares are'—i.e. find out the secrets of time, memory and survival, satisfy the insatiate metaphysical curiosity. 'Or who cleft the Divels foot'—a trivial impossibility derived from popular superstition, and casting a backward gleam of contempt on the more serious and emotionally charged impossibilities that have preceded it. Yet not all magical and mythical beliefs are contemptible—'Teach me to heare Mermaides singing'; there are no mermaids, or they don't sing, but it would be delightful if there were. It would be delightful if there were, but the world as we know it is full of vain wishes, so teach me 'to keep off envies stinging'—equally impossible, for in such a world we must long for what we have not. And then, if you can perform all these impossible feats you can perhaps perform the most impossible of all—'finde / What winde / Serves to advance an honest minde'. But you cannot do any of these things, so you cannot do that either. There is no way to advance an honest mind, just as there is no mermaids' song; and if there were it would only be a 'winde', which notoriously bloweth where it listeth, ungraspable and uncontrollable.

The common reflection on the fate of honesty in the world arrives already transfigured, because it has been realized in a picture of the world as an honest man feels it. He feels it with *Sehnsucht*, with horror and dread, with intellectual curiosity, with contempt for some of its unreal beliefs, with tenderness for others, with a dour moral realism. A mind as open, various and curious as that is not likely to get far on the narrow road of advancement.

That was a way of putting it—not very satisfactory; a periphrastic study in a worn-out critical fashion. The object of the exercise was to show how small a part of the meaning of the text is accounted for by its general intention—the intention to satirize the falsity of the world. The life is in the detail; and the cumulative effect of the detail is something different, even contrary, to the primarily identifiable intention. The achieved effect is not one of bitterness and disappointment, but of energy, curiosity, intellectual and emotional life, even if enclosed within a recognition of limits and frustrations. This is partly a matter of temperament— Donne's own diffused but ever-present energy and spirit. It is partly the ethos of a class and an age. For one of Donne's class, in his time, it was the part of a man to face the disappointments of life with wit and high spirits. But this is not an 'illocutionary act', unless a man can be said to act simply by being true to himself and the culture he belongs to.

Now I think it is quite impossible to regard the detailed imagery of this passage as 'intended' in the same sense as the general illocutionary act of satirizing or the general rhetorical organization was intended. They were intended, of course, in the minimal sense that Donne wrote them down, presumably while awake and in possession of his faculties. But if he were asked what his intention was in writing 'Go and catch a falling star' the appropriate reply would have been 'I intended to give an example of an impossible action'. And so with the mandrake, mermaids, and the rest. I do not believe that the other considerations I have advanced about these images ever reached the level of conscious intention. Such images come from we know not where—from miscellaneous reading, from a common cultural stock, from private unconscious associations. They are suggested by the exigencies of a rhyme or an accidental occurrence in the outer world. Since they are afterwards written down and put in print they are of course ratified by the conscious will: but if we are on that account to describe them as intentional I think we are stretching the concept of intention, or at any rate using it in a different sense from that employed when we said that the intention of the whole passage was to satirize. To describe the interpretation of poetry as the recovery of the author's intentions is to make the writing of poetry something like the working out of chess problems—moving a certain number of pieces that have fixed powers, with due forethought. Actually it is much more like playing tennis—reacting to unpredictable situations with unpremeditated moves, which may be abortive but may achieve an aptness and accomplishment that is absolutely unforeseeable until it happens; all done, however, within the framework of an intention—to win the game according to the rules. I see now that I am virtually paraphrasing one of the pronouncements that Close wants to scotch—'great art transcends the original intentions of its creator'.

Philosophical writers on literary theory are much afraid of ghosts. They cling to the idea of recoverable authorial intention because they fear that if they let it go they will be lost in a wilderness haunted by the whole disreputable retinue from the magician's house, and the Zeitgeist, the Dialectic, the Nine Muses, the Genius of the Language, the Mind of Europe or even the Holy Spirit itself might be upon them at any moment. I on the contrary wish to maintain that such forces as these do contribute to the composition of poetry, and I will now try to put this contention in more respectable language.

To deny the position of the extreme intentionalists does not entail adopting the old anti-intentionalist doctrine—that we must rely solely on the words on the page to reveal meaning. On the contrary, just because forces other than the intention of the author have contributed to the meaning of the poem it is important to know as much as we can about them. I applaud the two procedural rules suggested by Skinner at the end of his article: 1. 'Focus not just on the text but on the prevailing conventions governing the treatment of the issues or themes with which the text is concerned.' (Indeed I did just that, just now, in considering the prevalence of satires on women in Donne's culture, and of catalogues of impossibilities in literature accessible to him.) 2. 'Focus on the writer's mental world, the world of his empirical beliefs.' (I did that, mildly, in suggesting that Donne thought there were no mermaids.) But it must be added that with literary texts (different in this respect from the historical documents with which Skinner is mostly concerned) such considerations can give no better than probable answers, and sometimes not even that. A certain convention exists, a poet employs it; but this can tell us nothing about the intention with which he employs it—whether merely as a rhetorical device, a framework for a poem, or as an expression of conviction. As for empirical beliefs—a writer on law or government can be presumed to write consistently in accordance with his empirical beliefs. But this is just what a poet does not do. He entertains beliefs about whose empirical status he is doubtful; he makes use of ideas that he knows to be empirically false. Characteristically the poet moves in a sort of half-world where questions of empirical belief are not allowed to arise. This was particularly likely to happen with Donne (or Sir Thomas Browne), living in a culture where the new philosophy had put all in doubt, where old quasi-magical beliefs flourished side by side with new scientific ones, and old magical beliefs could still claim some sort of scientific status (see *Pseudodoxia Epidemica*, *passim*). There is no knowing what Donne really believed about mandrakes or mermaids; though as it happens it is clear enough in the text we are considering that he is using popular beliefs about them as examples of impossibilities. Better instances would be found in the passages about spheres and intelligences or the corporeal potentialities of angels, where it is quite unclear whether the ideas are used merely as metaphors or as analogies having real scientific foundations. The conclusion to be drawn is that answers to questions about what the poet empirically believed will not necessarily yield answers to questions about what he is doing in a poem.

Skinner's object in suggesting his rules is to lead us back to the author's intentions. They may do so; they are in general useful principles; but in my view they may lead somewhere else. Or of course they may simply fail. The information they provide may be irrelevant, as we have just seen. (The poet describes the moon as a crystal globe inhabited by a pure spirit; we apply rule 2 and discover that he knew very well it was made of green cheese. And nothing of interest seems to follow from this.) I wish to argue, however, that there is indeed relevant and useful information obtained by these methods, that it genuinely assists interpretation, but that what it leads back to cannot be reduced simply to the author's intention.

Yet if not the author's, whose? Or if not intentions, what? Must we believe that statements about the meaning of words and sentences are always reducible to statements about someone's intentions? It seems at first that we must. If we found what appeared to be a tomb in a lonely landscape, with the inscription *Et in Arcadia ego*, we could argue as Panofsky[8] does about whether this means 'I too was a shepherd in Arcadia', or 'Death is in Arcadia too'. We could argue about this because we suppose that someone carved the inscription, with one or the other intention. But if we were to discover that the apparent tomb was only a natural outcrop of rock, and the apparent inscription only the result of erosion, the argument would fall to the ground. There are of course natural signs, which have meaning without intention, as when we see smoke and say, 'That means fire'. But words and sentences are not natural signs and cannot be treated as such.

There is, however, a different analogy that can be applied to the behaviour of words and sentences—and applied particularly aptly to highly organized discourse like poetry. It is the analogy of involuntary symptomatic gestures. 'He said he had never been near the cash-box, but I noticed a shifty look in his eye.' 'He said "Of course I don't care for her at all any more" but as he said it his voice broke.' The shifty look and the breaking voice are certainly unintended, but equally certainly meaningful. Analogous effects can occur within language. Indeed the phenomenon of the breaking voice does occur within language, though only of course within spoken language. Something very similar, however, can happen in poetry.

Out of the day and night
A joy has taken flight;
Fresh spring, and summer, and winter hoar,
Move my faint heart with grief, but with delight
No more—O, never more.

In the third line there is both a logical and a metrical gap. There ought to be a fourth season and there ought to be a fifth foot. The manuscript is in such a mess (or so I am told, for I have not seen it) that there is no knowing whether Shelley did not finally intend to insert the missing member, and write 'Fresh spring, and summer, *autumn* and winter hoar'. The line as it stands, with autumn missing, has been praised again and again for its rhythmical and suggestive beauty. And we can see why, or partly see why. The whole poem is about loss and absence; and in a key line something that is expected is absent and lost. And the question of intention is left entirely in abeyance. We simply do not know whether Shelley intended it or not. The effect is remarkably like that of an involuntary break in the voice. Many bewildering minutes could be spent with other textual cruces—babbling of green fields, inquiring whether Hamlet's flesh was solid or Aristotle solider. In all these cases scrupulous editors labour to recover the intention of the author, and readers of poetry remain steadfastly indifferent, and simply prefer what they believe to be the best reading. But I will not pursue this line, as it brings in other considerations aside from my purpose. If Shakespeare never intended to write 'a'babbled of green fields', Theobald did. But what stands out from these textual confusions is how completely in the minds of most readers the question of authorial intention tends to disappear.

To return to involuntary symptomatic gestures. The intentionalists are right to maintain that the basic intentional act performed by the author in writing must be correctly identified. They are right too in maintaining that this frequently requires a search for evidence outside the text. Indeed it is precisely in this respect— the determining of the general intention of the poem—that such evidence is most required. Literary conventions, prevailing cultural assumptions, are not contained within the poem, but are necessary to its proper understanding. What could *Lycidas* mean to a reader who knew nothing of the long tradition of the pastoral elegy? A good deal, no doubt, but half its significance would escape him, and some of its most prominent features would remain impenetrably obscure. To that extent, and it is a very considerable extent, it is false that 'if the poet succeeded in doing it, then the poem itself shows what he was trying to do'. We need prior and external evidence about the poet's intentions. But mounted on that basic intentional structure is the whole inspectable surface of the poem in all its varied detail, much of which cannot properly be described as intentional. I am thinking of rhythmical effects, and of specific imagery, and other things besides. The example from Shelley illustrates the first, that from Donne illustrates the second. Let us look for some more. They are to be found particularly among the Empsonian ambiguities where a primary sense is obvious, its intentionality not doubted, yet other less obvious senses can be detected in the background. It was these situations that gave rise to some of the early objections to Empson's practice: 'But the writer can't possibly have meant *that*.' By now we know the answer to that kind of objection: quite likely he did not mean it, but it is there all the same.

I will take a fairly slight and simple example from Empson, as the more intricate ones would demand a discussion of his whole method, which is not my purpose now.[9]

> How loved, how honoured once, avails thee not,
> To whom related, or by whom begot;
> A heap of dust is all remains of thee;
> 'Tis all thou art, and all the proud shall be.
> (Pope, *Elegy to the Memory of an Unfortunate Lady*)

The two parts of the second line make a claim to be alternatives which is not obviously justified, and this I think implies a good deal. If the antithesis is to be serious, *or* must mean 'one of her relations was grand but her father was humble', or the other way about; thus one could take *how* to mean 'whether much or little' (it could mean 'though you were so greatly'), and the last line to contrast her with the *proud*, so as to imply that she is humble (it could unite her with the *proud*, and deduce the death of all of them from the death of one). This obscurity is part of the 'Gothic' atmosphere that Pope wanted: 'her birth was high, but there was a mysterious stain on it'; or 'her birth was high, but not higher than births to which I am accustomed'. Here, however, the false antithesis is finding another use, to convey the attitude of Pope to the subject. 'How simple, how irrelevant to the merits of the unfortunate lady, are such relationships; everybody has had both a relation and a father; how little can I admire the arrogance of great families on this point; how little, too, the snobbery of the reader, who is unlikely to belong to a great family; to how many people this subject would be extremely fruitful of antitheses; how little fruitful of antitheses it seems to an independent soul like mine.' What is important about such devices is that they leave it to the reader vaguely to invent something, and make him leave it at the back of his mind.

All that could be securely identified as intentional in these lines is the contrast between the variety of human situations in life and the uniformity in the indifferent community of death. There are three possible steps to take about Empson's commentary on them. 1. We could say that it is all a fantasy, that the implications discovered are not there. But the obscure antithesis in the second line is certainly there, to some degree disturbing to the overall intention, or additional to it. 2. We could accept Empson's explication, and say that Pope intended all these things. I do not think this at all plausible. It would be quite incompatible with any view of poetry possible to Pope to admit these multiple and partly conflicting implications in a single passage. 3. We could follow Empson and admit the co-presence of these faintly uneasy implications, but also decide that they were not part of Pope's intention in writing. If they were also incompatible with Pope's known social and personal attitudes we should perhaps be asked to believe too much in admitting them. But they are not. They expose very accurately the precarious balance of Pope's relation to the great world. More than that, they expose something that is generally true about the position of the independent man of letters in this age—something a Marxist could use in a thesis about literature as the apanage of the ruling class. Many elements that enter into the meaning of a literary text are of this kind—the result of unrecognized social forces, expressing themselves in syntax and rhetorical arrangement. Others are of a kind that a Freudian would recognize—after a reading of chapter VI of the *Interpretation of Dreams* or *Wit and its Relation to the Unconscious*. Part of the work of an interpreter of literature is to unmask these concealed meanings.

Unmasking, at any rate in popular fiction, is something that is commonly done to villains; and to do it to a work of literature is apt to suggest that something vaguely discreditable is to be revealed. Vulgar Marxists and vulgar Freudians have both often written with this purpose, and in this tone. But it is a crass error to suppose that by revealing a hidden meaning—a meaning that we have reason to suppose was unsuspected by the author—we are devaluing or impoverishing the text. Any written text is to some extent a palimpsest. The manifest layer consists of the illocutionary acts of the author—intentional by definition. We can take these to include or imply his acknowledged beliefs and assumptions. (To warn a skater that the ice is thin implies a belief that our fellow-creatures should not get accidentally drowned.) But any text also includes unrecognized assumptions and beliefs—those that the writer shares so thoroughly with his age as to be unaware of their presence, those that belong to the unexamined background of his personal life. In purely discursive writing unrecognized elements of this kind are accidents and imperfections—though doubtless inevitable imperfections. But the interpreter even of a historical document, who believes himself to be recovering the pure intended communication of the author, cannot afford to neglect them. If he takes the line that the message is what the author intended and all the rest is noise he is going to miss a good deal. The reader of Bacon or Hobbes will rightly note the overt, intentional bracketing out of established religion, by which it is left immune from the critical operations applied to other human activities. But he will also do well to note that the decorous forbearance to religion in Bacon seems really to be practised in the interests of positive science. And he can hardly help noticing that the irrepressible comic irony with which Hobbes approaches religious doctrine reveals an unacknowledged contempt for everything in religion except the institutional shell.

Now in a literary text—and it is here that the interpretation of literary texts becomes a different thing from the interpretation of pure discursive writing—the unacknowledged layers of meaning are not accidents and imperfections. They are an essential part of the totality to be examined. It was Empson's *Seven Types of Ambiguity* that brought this out into the open and made it central in critical activity. But literature and the interpretation of literature have been with us a long time, and there are not many wholly new critical discoveries. The presence of unacknowledged meanings side by side with the acknowledged ones had long been noticed in an accidental and occasional fashion, even within the sanctuary of neo-classicism. It was Dryden who first observed that Milton had made the Devil his hero. Since then *Paradise Lost* has become the classic case in English of a poem that has retained its power and celebrity unbroken, largely through a reading that contradicts the expressed intentions of the author. For Blake, Milton was of the Devil's party without knowing it. For Shelley, Milton 'alleged no superiority of moral virtue to his God over his Devil'. For Empson the poem is good because it shows how bad the God of Christian theology really is, and unwittingly sets up a lofty humanism against him. 'The root of [Milton's] power is that he could accept and express a downright horrible conception of God and yet keep somehow alive underneath it all the breadth and generosity, the welcome to every noble pleasure, which had been prominent in European history before his time.'[10]

This is not the place for a Milton controversy, or even a controversy about how Milton controversies should be conducted, especially since Empson has done it himself. My point is only to take a conspicuous instance of a poem that lives by meanings that its author must have repudiated. Dodging the theological thunderbolts, we can still advance our argument a step further by showing some of the lesser means by which this was brought about. Again and again Milton writes a glowing and magnificent passage on a classical myth, or on the exercise of some noble human faculty by the fallen angels—and then in the interests of his main design retracts it. The myth was false, the virtues exercised in vain. The architect of Pandemonium was celebrated under other names on earth—[11]

> and in Ausonian land
> Men called him Mulciber; and how he fell
> From Heav'n, they fabled, thrown by angry Jove
> Sheer o'er the crystal battlements; from morn
> To noon he fell, from noon to dewy eve,
> A summer's day; and with the setting sun
> Dropt from the zenith like a falling star,
> On Lemnos th'Aegean isle: thus they relate,
> Erring; for he with this rebellious rout
> Fell long before.

The story is false, but we are told so only after we have extracted the greatest possible imaginative pleasure from it. Similarly with the employments of the fallen angels after the departure of Satan for earth. Some practise athletic and military exercises;[12]

> Others more mild,
> Retreated in a silent valley, sing
> With notes angelical to many a harp
> Their own heroic deeds and hapless fall . . .

> In discourse more sweet
> (For eloquence the soul, song charms the sense,)
> Others apart sat on a hill retir'd,
> In thoughts more elevate, and reason'd high
> Of providence, foreknowledge, will, and fate.

It is hard to see how the devils could have been better employed had they still been angels; and the whole passage breathes a tender and elevated respect for these occupations, fit for an Athenian *kaloskagathos* or a Renaissance gentleman. Yet every item of this noble description is dutifully undercut; the military exercises end in 'wild uproar'; though it was ravishingly sweet, 'the song was partial' (i.e. partisan, unjust); the high reasonings are 'vain wisdom all and false philosophy'.

We can see something of how these contrarieties come about. The lines on Mulciber are from Homer (*Iliad*, I, 589–94); the falling all day long and dropping on Lemnos with the setting sun are quite literally translated, even, if I am not imagining it, with a modulated version of the original rhythm. They bring with them into Milton's grim theological epic the lightness, freedom, passion and generosity of Homer's Olympians. Empson remarks, 'Milton is extremely cool about the matter; one is made to sit pleasantly with him in the shade all day long, needing no further satisfaction; it is delightfully soothing to feel that the devil is all the time falling faster and faster.' But this ease and disengagement gets into Milton's text not from any concern with devils, for the Homeric passage is not about a devil at all, but about a god, who had quarrelled with the king of the gods. He is telling his own story, long afterwards, to show how dangerous it is to fall out with Zeus; and so far from having been cast into an eternity of torment he is back on Olympus, his wrongs forgotten, handing the drinks round and patching up another family quarrel. The manly exercises of the fallen angels have also a classical origin; they are derived from the funeral games in *Iliad* XXIII and *Aeneid* V.

These in their turn recall the Olympic and the Pythian games, at which poetic and rhetorical performances occurred. In discussing Satan a little earlier in the book, Milton had said that the damned spirits 'do not lose all their virtue' (II, 482). Their remaining virtues could scarcely be the theological ones, so in presenting them he goes to the great exemplars of civil and humane virtue in the ancient world; and the 'welcome to every noble pleasure' that Empson justly remarks on comes where it is least convenient to the general design.

The palimpsest again: a text written on the scarcely erased lines of an earlier text. And Milton intends what he is doing; it is part of the accepted procedure for a Renaissance syncretist epic. To identify the fallen angels with the gods of the gentiles, and to bring in with them the whole variegated tapestry of pagan mythology, is a necessary part of his plan. But willed, necessary, and intended as it is, it brings with it consequences that were certainly unintended— that the society in hell seems so much better than that in heaven.

This is the phenomenon that modern French critics call 'intertextuality'—the presence in a literary text of earlier texts, some chosen by the author, some forced upon him by his culture, but always bringing with them consequences that go beyond his intention and pass partly out of his control. This is not merely a pretentious way of saying that writers are influenced by other writers, or that literary traditions exist. It is to reveal—or open the possibility of revealing—a structure special to literature: layer upon layer of meaning, invented, inherited or deliberately acquired, held together by an authorial intention, but always retaining a partial autonomy, so that the author's intention remains only one element (the presiding element, but still only one) in a complex federal association.

In Milton's case we can see how many tensions and contrarieties were forced on him. By reason of his personal history he was in no position to be whole-hearted in condemnation of rebellion. But the psychological compulsions are less interesting than those that arise from his material and his poetic form. He is taking as his foundation extremely early mythical material (Genesis), worked up by still early secondary elaboration (scattered passages throughout the Old Testament and the New). This primitive foundation has in its turn been worked on by centuries of philosophical theology—a moral and metaphysical transformation to which it was always exceedingly recalcitrant. And he has chosen to present his myth in the form of a heroic poem—a particular kind of heroic poem (the Tassonian Christian epic) itself an adaptation of an earlier kind (the Homeric) based on still earlier mythical material derived from an entirely different religious and cultural tradition. His own theology is sophisticated and abstract; but he is obliged by his form to embody it in a story of conflict that can be presented only in quasi-personal terms. The evil and cruelty that Empson uncompromisingly exposes in Milton's epic is not, as Empson's argument requires, simply inherent in the Christian scheme. It is partly inherent in it—the doctrine of eternal punishment is a lasting disgrace to the Christian imagination—but it is partly the consequence of presenting what can only be adequately conceived in metaphysical terms as a concrete fable. A fable must have characters who act and speak; 'God the Father argues like a school divine'; and, condemned to the only terms possible to such a persona, makes a very bad case. The Christian humanism to which Milton with the better part of his mind aspired demands a more radical revision of the Christian myth than probably he was prepared to undertake; it certainly demands a more radical revision than was compatible with presenting the myth as an epic narrative. Dryden and Johnson complained that *Paradise Lost* has only two human characters; but they are only technically right, for the angels fallen and unfallen, the Father and the Son, are conceived as human characters. The epic form allows no other possibility. And in human terms—I mean human terms, not the terms of romantic satanism—most of the courage, nobility, and pathos falls to the defeated and the erring innocents, most of the cruelty, implacability, and deceit to divine omnipotence. In the background is another sort of argument altogether; but not one that could be expressed in character and action.

I seem to have been saying that it is in the unintended meanings that most of the value of *Paradise Lost* resides. This is the fault of a limited range of examples; beauty and generosity appear in Eden too, well within the intentional scheme of the whole poem. But enough has been said to show how bewilderingly the intended and the unintended are crossed and interwoven in the intricate fabric of the poem.

We can see now how natural it was for Empson, preoccupied with the actual business of interpretation, to leave the question of intention largely in abeyance. He had to leave a space round it, for it was in this ambiguous space that most of his work was to be done. Neither 'the words on the page' nor 'the intentions of the author' can alone reveal the significance of a work of literature, and no adequate interpretation of a poem has ever been made by the exclusive pursuit of either of these phantoms. We read the words on the page, but we read the gaps between the words too, and we supplement them with a complex of insight and information that come from outside the text. We identify the intention of the author, as clearly as we can; but this is only the starting-point for understanding. A poem is closer to common speech than it is to non-literary discursive writing. In responding to an utterance in face-to-face conversation we listen to the words; we listen also to the tone of voice, the silence between the words; we are aware of the non-linguistic context; we observe facial and manual gestures, the posture of a body, accompanying acts. The full meaning of the utterance is a fusion of all these factors. In reading a poem the face-to-face situation has disappeared; but it is part of the work of poetry, of the language of poetry, to create an equivalent for it. Auditory and rhythmical effects, unpremeditated images, un-solicited associations, do just this; no more willed and intended (and of course no less) than the facial expressions by which we accompany our speech. That is the situation between the poem and the reader; but there are always others present at this en-counter—a culture and a history. Looked at in another way, a poem is like an archaeological site. Beneath the baroque church is the medieval crypt, itself constructed on the ruins of a Roman basilica, and a Mithraic temple lies below. We find one text mounted upon another, layer upon layer of meaning, and we are soon led beyond the manifest text with which we started. What we discover in the end is the locus of a civilization, one of those human constructs that are neither intended nor unintended—unless they are both.

The reason why the argument about intention in literature has gone on so long and so inconclusively is that its terms have been misconceived. We have been presented with false alternatives—to explore the complexities of the inspectable text without extraneous aid, or to recover the uninspectable intentions of the author. Each method has claimed to be sufficient and to exclude the other. I hope I have shown that neither the presented surface of the text nor the inferred intention of the author is a sufficient basis for interpretation, and that so far from being mutually exclusive they are complementary. If this is so there is nothing left to argue about, and the question of literary intention can be permitted to dissolve.

As always, the matters we have been discussing seem remote from the ordinary reading of poetry. But their purpose, it should be remembered, is that what goes on in the ordinary reading of poetry, implicitly and by intuition, should be made articulate and brought fully into the light. For this we need principles and methods. These are the dogmatisms of learning. Those whose profession is learning have no call to be afraid of them; but they had better get their dogmatisms right.

NOTES

1 Reprinted in W. K. Wimsatt, *The Verbal Icon* (1953).
2 See especially F. Cioffi, 'Intention and Interpretation in Criticism', *Proceedings of the Aristotelian Society*, vol. 64 (1963–4).
3 A. J. Close, 'Don Quixote and the "Intentional Fallacy"', *British Journal of Aesthetics*, vol. 12, no. 2 (1972).
4 Quentin Skinner, 'Motives, Intentions and the Interpretation of Texts', *New Literary History*, vol. 3, no. 2 (1972).
5 Close does indeed mention this in a footnote, but does not make use of it in his argument.
6 F. L. Austin, *How to Do Things with Words* (1962), pp. 9, 22, 92, 104.
7 *Elegies and Songs and Sonnets of John Donne*, ed. Helen Gardner (1965), p. 152.
8 Erwin Panofsky, 'Et in Arcadia Ego: Poussin and the Elegiac Tradition', in *Meaning in the Visual Arts* (1955).
9 *Seven Types*, pp. 22–3.
10 William Empson, *Milton's God* (1961), p. 276.
11 *Paradise Lost*, I, 739–47.
12 Ibid., II, 546–60.

Semantic Frontiersman

I. A. Richards

There should be a special label, with analytic description (both to be supplied in ideal poetic justice by William Empson himself) for a peculiar type of comparison: that in which a point of likeness originally thought up quite consciously and with some hope that it might amuse, suddenly becomes concretely actual and starts off, like a computerized bloodhound, on the trail of its author, infallibly and relentlessly hunting him down. Long ago, when a bound copy of *Seven Types* first reached me (in Peking, it was) I used to press it on likely readers with this recommendation: 'It will make you feel you are having a lovely go of Influenza—high-fever fireworks, you know.' (Would that somebody could tell adequately what Empson did through his long years in Peking! I saw enough to know but not enough to give any account. A man who can teach *Songs & Sonnets*, reassembling a text out of his head, does more than we easily realize for passionate young students of poetry.) But to return to my whimsey. When the editor of this volume, as reasonably as eloquently, asked me to try to make my first draft of this piece be more about *Complex Words*, 'Why, of course,' I thought, 'she is quite right. It is a real work and it's absurd to have such anxieties about it!' That settled, I went to bed, and began turning its well-known pages over in what I sometimes call 'my mind'. What was this? Aches and ague-shakes: the real thing! Ten days of the London flu. Recovered, if tottery, and back home from travel, there were the remembered hopeful green covers and the scribbled margins back in my hands. What now? Down again! A full battery, weeks more of Aix les Pains and with what additions!

Maybe this alibi will be enough to get me out of dealing at once with what has been the real source all through of those anxieties. They spring from my own inability to deal fairly and properly with the definitions and notations introduced in the first two chapters. If I could understand this inability more clearly, the anxieties might fade out. But I don't; and the best thing I can do for the moment will be to jump over these first two chapters and try instead to say why Empson's minute examinations have been, are and always will be of so much value to literary semantics. To put it solidly, they raised the standards of ambition and achievement in a difficult and very hazardous art. This sort of thing often happens in sports and the sciences—great examples might be: in sport, the entire transformation of the possible that has occurred since the thirties, with the developments of aids in rock- and ice-climbing; and, in science, the consequences, shall we say, of the transistor. But in the arts of reading, arts tedious and devious as they must be, such sudden revelations of new powers are perhaps even more surprising. What I ought to point out, if I can, is some of the ways by which Empson seems to have done this.

There are of course scientific sides to all this. The very title, *The Structure of Complex Words*, shrunken down though it be from 'Theory of the functions of the complex variable', suggests a quasi-mathematic treatment that Empson disowns. (I admit I find his fondness for the word 'equation' distracting.) But lexico-graphically, he very properly discusses, in his last chapter, the use his work may be to future dictionaries. With the new compacted *NED* so handy I do not myself see 'a still bigger dictionary than the *NED*.' as either 'obviously impracticable' or 'ludicrous' (p. 391). In fact the Semantic Department of the coming Electronic Reference Source will almost certainly be soon building one up. And this is a main part of why I think his work so important. His general proposal is that the *interactions* of the senses of a word should be included and his extremely acute, detailed (and diverting) account of what the *NED* actually does offers a very powerful case to show how this could be done without making it either much bigger or any harder to use. On the contrary, rather. Indeed, it is so convincing that I am astonished his services have not, long since, been retained as advisor and consultant upon how the major dictionaries of the future should be planned. He worthily prefaces this essay by saying of the *NED*, 'Such work on individual words as I have been able to do has been almost entirely dependent on using the majestic object as it stands' (p. 391). He adds, further, 'It would be ridiculous to complain of having the work done so magnificently.'

So much for the lexicographic discernment, the expositional technique, brilliantly—even dazzlingly—displayed in this final and germinal chapter. *Where* to put *what*, so that it may be most conveniently, most safely, most economically apprehended: command of that is what I would signal here as Empson's chief contribution towards a possible scientific semantics. As a semanticist (queer though the label still seems) myself, I believe that what he has done should be taken very seriously. It is not merely a joke that we should hail The Dictionary as the true successor to Holy Writ. There, in the Dictionary, is the record, as well arranged as we can contrive, of the best (*and the worst*) that has been thought and said by prior users of the language—inspired, prophet-wise, or not, and by heavenly and infernal voices; or drearily uninspired. It is all there. The Dictionary is the custodian of all the tools of the literary man, as well as those of the most dumbfounded moron. I think as I write this of one of the most characteristic lines of Empson's poetry. Of the word Death:

It is the trigger of the literary man's biggest gun.

Anyone who can improve the *ordonnance* of future dictionaries, and Empson has done so and can do more, deserves, as Shaw declared of Ogden, 'a Peerage and a princely pension'.

Having argued this claim—as consequential as it is incontestable—I will turn now to my earlier remark, I believe fully as secure, that *Seven Types* and *Complex Words* did 'raise the standards' of the elucidative commentary on literature. This is far from being a lesser service than that I have been reporting. After all, we are by now accustomed to science advancing; but are we exactly expecting literature (and criticism, the perception of the literary endeavour—its triumphs and lapses) to tower up, endlessly, to new heights? In sad truth, we have been watching, almost all through our active days, little but dismal decline in people's power to do or say anything of significance *and* in people's ability to make out, and even less to appraise, the sorts of things being said. I invite those who question this to compare the list of poets, playwrights, and novelists available to a lecturer on contemporary English literature in 1920 with the living writers he can find to talk about today. To those who are ready to make this comparison the contrast is depressing.

In saying that Empson's best work in elucidative comment 'raised the standards' I have obviously to guard against misapprehensions. I am *not* saying that people in general, after studying him, did such work better—became more enterprising and effective. Far from it, as I have just been lamenting. And I am *not* saying that *all* of Empson's elucidative (or would-be elucidative) writing is on this new high level. I am saying only that *at his best* he is able to point out, describe, and make evident co-operations and interactions among meanings on a scale and with a subtlety and resource not to be found in previous critics. I am not claiming, either, that the new sorts of perceptions he conveys have in general the reconstitutive or seminal powers of those of Johnson or Coleridge. I *am* reporting, though, that his admiring reader often finds himself remarking: 'I never knew before that it was possible to see so much. I realize anew how much we ordinary readers may be missing.' The effect is in many ways like using a microscope. This again is a remark that can be taken amiss. As C. A. Mace wisely observed, 'A microscope is a poor instrument through which to find your way about a town.' None the less, in good hands, and on the right occasion, it can be extremely useful.

I described reading above as 'a difficult and very hazardous art' and it was not without intent that I compared Empsonic analysis with the rise of modern mountaineering. I need not labour the point that such bold attempts are much exposed to disaster. Nor need I stress that not all Empson's readers have been admiring. I can think of few writers to whom the world is much indebted who have provoked in less capable people such indignation or derision. Not every reader enjoys the feeling that something is being done that he could not possibly try to rival. That there should have been an ungenerous note in some of the reception of Empson's displays is not surprising. It is only fair, however, to add that he has not been (and indeed could not be) free from some responsibility for this.

Let me revert now to those two opening chapters of *Complex Words* which I alluded to above as occasioning for me bewilderments and anxieties. As I have said, I miss too many points and the issues grow cloudy. The 'little machine' of equations and notations causes me troubles which I am unable to diagnose helpfully. And I will not be the only one who has found these pages excessively difficult. I read on. Now and then, for a few tense sentences all seems beautifully clear, far-reaching vistas open, the taxed mind breathes deep, but alack, before long, the clouds crowd in, and one is again only *groping* through a paragraph hardly able even to see one's feet. Usually what illumines is an example. One ought, I suppose, to be able to carry it with one; but my candles—however skilfully Empson lights them—blow out. And I see moreover from the layers of marginalia that have been accumulating since the first weeks after *Complex Words* appeared and from my repeated efforts to set out Empson's symbols as a *ready vade-mecum* in table or diagram, that my uncertainties are not to be so simply set right. And yet, somehow I have to try to say what, I think, makes these two chapters such hard going—in comparison with the free felicities of so many of the specific studies that follow.

To begin with I am as certain as the case allows that Empson is right all through, well aware enough of what he is pointing out. My difficulties do not stem from faulty percipience there, but from his sentences being, as I struggle to grasp and use them, insufficient to make and maintain the relations and distinctions he employs them for. I am reminded of H. G. Wells' dread remark about trying to cut up an atom with a penknife. For me his percipiences, as I conjecture towards them, are incommensurably more refined than the clumsy terms through which he is, in these two chapters, trying to control and expound them. These terms serve him because he does not need them: he has his examples and his ways of taking them to keep his thinking in order. But his readers (at least, this one of them) has to try to follow the account without that guidance. And its terms get in his way. He is lost too often.

I recognize in writing this that I must have ways myself of recognizing Empson's percipiences apart from his terminology. I realize too that this line of speculation (which almost calls in telepathy) doubtless is much beset with delusions. I recall a morning—how long ago?—in Magdalene, when Empson suddenly ended a supervision by leaping from his chair to shout through his mirth. 'Metaphysical Poetry! Why, we've been *talking* metaphysical poetry all the morning!' No ordinary supervisee!

How frank this daring semantic frontiersman is about how little we yet know about our meanings and about the inherent difficulties of turning our language on to itself, trying to say how we say, to understand how we understand and so on. We do well here to remember Niels Bohr: 'The mental content is invariably altered when the attention is concentrated on any special feature of it. . . . An analysis of the very concept of explanation would begin and end with a renunciation as to explaining our own conscious activity.'[1]

Some time ago I ventured to observe, in *Speculative Instruments*, that 'It is not easy to let up on the pressure we are under to get (as we hope) something *said* in favour of awareness of the process of *saying*.' Which led Empson in a review to comment: 'This endeavour might seem wrong headed.' It is in fact the endeavour most of *Complex Words* is devoted to. But let me try again to say, with Niels Bohr's help, what, in part at least, is the trouble.

In the course of speculating about how widely his Complementarity Principle may apply, Bohr recorded two potentially dismaying observations. Both are germane to these bold explorations in *Seven Types* and *Complex Words*; they might indeed be pointedly discerning comments upon them:[2]

> Words like 'thoughts' and 'sentiments', equally indispensable to illustrate the diversity of psychical experience, pertain to mutually exclusive situations characterized by a different drawing of the line of separation between subject and object.

To read this lingeringly is a good way of preparing ourselves for the other:[3]

> Our task can only be to aim at communicating experiences and views to others by means of language in which the practical use of every word stands in a complementary relation to attempts at its strict definition.

It is not clear (can't be, I conjecture) how far we are to take these. They could be pretty subversive. After all, the Complementary Principle itself was once thought that: it has its saving limitary side. But how rich in outcomes it has been: enabling inquirers to combine results obtained by using formally incompatible assumptions. Get on with the inquiry and let *Ir*reconcilabilities cool their heels in the waiting room! May it continue to be so too with these semantic enterprises!

Certainly these two books have got on with the inquiry. And those who have bothered themselves for more than a brief spell about their methodological grounding have been missing an essential point as well as much wonderful fun. Conscientious scruples are out of place. However irremediably circular and reflexive our definitions and accounts are, to know that this is so is more than a little. The semantic situation that semantics itself is in, is really very entertaining. Empson has an infinity of means of making us enjoy it. At the end of his first chapter of *Complex Words*, for example:

> And by the way, in case a conscientious reader looked for another distinction, I shall make no difference at all between 'sense' and 'meaning' but try to pick the one that sounds less ugly. Indeed when talking about the word *sense* I am afraid I have sometimes thrown in the term 'interpretation' to make a third synonym, because what I have to avoid is often 'the sense, "sense" of sense', a phrase which can leave no impression on the mind except that of a sordid form of lunacy.

Sordid be it or not, the semanticist, and the meta-semanticist yet more, has, along with the poet, to accept the imputation and be ready to seem somewhat crazy.

Let us now take a closer look at Bohr's two remarks. We may find in them something that helps towards the understandings that Empson offers.

Illustrate the diversity of psychical experiences. The dictionary notes as archaic or obsolete the 'light up, enlighten, elucidate' meaning of *illustrate*, and lists as active 'explain with figures and instances' (often, alas, obfuscating) and 'provide with pictures [which too may readily perturb and distract] and examples' (which may sadly mislead). But here the older meaning 'to light, to enable to be seen' is at work. Indeed throughout semantics, what Coleridge said of reflection incessantly applies: 'Nothing is wanted but the eye, which is the light of this house, the light which is the eye of this soul. This *seeing* light, this *enlightening* eye is Reflection.'[4] We cannot, indeed, do without the great old metaphor of intellectual vision: 'I see what it means.' Perhaps here we may think that rather more *is* wanted—the things to be seen and other things to be compared (seen along) with them—but no matter. As Empson puts it in his famous common-sense way: 'People make words do what seems to be needed.'[5] Following this truly sound principle, we will make the ʳdiversityʳ[6] that the two words: *thoughts* and *sentiments* can light up to be that of two ʳequally indispensableʳ components in all ʳpsychical experienceʳ (psychical, because Bohr would be contrasting this—the sort of reflection proceeding here —with physical experience—the fixing up of an experimental arrangement, the measuring of a distance or reading of a dial). These two components have to be deeply diverse if they are to co-operate. Each needs the other, would in fact be lost without it. We have plenty of other names for the components and for their relationship—peculiarly close and intimate as it is: Cognitive (*thoughts*) and Conative (*sentiments*) are the best known of the technical terms, Referential and Affective-Volitional (or Emotive) are two more. Of literary descriptions I suppose the oldest, and one of the most striking, is in a hymn probably predating the invention of writing: [7]

> Desire in the beginning was made
> One with the first cast of thought.
> Searching their hearts with wisdom,
> The Sages found Being
> Threaded in Not-being.

This stresses the unity of the co-operation of Sense and Feeling, Intellection and Emotion . . . in the work they do together. Bohr, however, stresses rather their difference:

Pertain to mutually exclusive situations　This certainly would seem to want to separate them and to contradict the Veda. Bohr, who refers us to the Buddha and Lao Tse on Complementarity, attributes much independence to these sharply stand-offish partners. Each: 'thoughts'[8] and 'sentiments', derives its powers from its own preserves, which it should keep intact; each has its own business with which the other should not meddle; only so can they jointly and justly perform their common duty, which is nothing less than what Aristotle called 'the exercise of the highest of our faculties: intellectual speculation or contemplation' for the which, he adds, 'it is indispensable that a man be born with a gift, as it were, of sight, whereby to judge rightly and choose the good accordant to truth'. (This it was that Coleridge was echoing.) Obviously we fail, all but continually, in this, one of the chief causes being injustice in our minds: mutual meddling of thoughts and sentiments in the joint task.

Characterized by a different drawing of the line of separation between subject and object　Slippery labels, *subject* and *object*. I recall at the Moral Sciences Club in Cambridge, when Empson was in residence (he may have been there) a Welsh disputant who stumped us by asking: 'What happens when a Subject becomes an Object, and yet remains a Subject?' No one thought of quoting Hegel to him:[9]

> The individual who knows is here wrongly isolated, and then, because of that, is confronted with a mere alien Universe. And the individual, as so isolated, I agree, could do nothing, for indeed he is nothing. My real personal self which orders my world is in truth inseparably one with the Universe. Behind me the absolute reality works through and in union with myself, and the world which confronts me is at bottom one thing in substance and in power with this reality. There *is* a world of appearance and there *is* a sensuous curtain, and to seek to deny the presence of this or to identify it with reality is mistaken. But for the truth I come back always to that doctrine of Hegel, that 'there is nothing behind the curtain other than that which is in front of it'.

This would not, I think, have seemed very strange to Aristotle, whose 'exercise of the highest of our faculties' might well be described, in Bohr's words, as an endless drawing (and redrawing) of that line of separation. I admit readily, though, that Bohr's observations can be taken in surprisingly various ways. (I have given them, in verse, other and irreconcilable interpretations elsewhere. See 'Complementary Complementarities' in my *Internal Colloquies*.) It is through this versatility that these reflections can be good exercise for that highest faculty. If comments on such passages are puzzlingly yet fruitfully diverse, that is part of their merit as illustrative of the complementarity principle.

The objection to that is, of course, that such things can so easily be used as excuse for messy confusion and for careless mistakings. Any view, in whatever relations it stands to others, can be wrong in itself and not merely conflict with them.

Turn now to Bohr's second observation. Once again, Empson's sound principle is helpful with its opening words: *can only be*. Perhaps that *is* our only *worthy* task. What, however, are we to make of the rest? What is it saying of language? I take it as describing any language in which we are trying to communicate *to others*, not merely communing with ourselves. (But does it not apply even then? I think it often does.) Let us try a free paraphrase. Most of Empson's work in these two books is *experimentation in paraphrase*, and whoever writes on the theory of *that* should make himself as indebted to them as he can. A paraphrase might run:

> In *some* uses of language (better not make it *all*, or we may be only definition mongering) the more you try to give every word *one* fixed precise meaning the less will they work together in helping people to understand.

For me, the two doubtful points are: 1. about *a complementary relation*, and 2. whether it is a recommendation ('Do be careful!' 'Find a golden mean!'), or a statement of natural law, or a meta-semantic fact. ('The further from the earth you go the less you weigh.') ('Thinking about what it may mean isn't the same as seeing what it is saying.')

1. I take his *complementary* here as though it were *complementarity*. But we need not. In my paraphrase an inverse proportion is stated ('The more sugar you put in, the less puckery will it taste'). This is not at all what I understand by a complementarity relation. Possibly Bohr never meant it to be. Are there the two or more sets of mutually exclusive arrangements or assumptions—each of which yields useful results—that are needed? Not unless we shift and take the relation to be between the two *aims*: (i), the practical use, being understood, and (ii), the strict definition, having the work of every word fully ruled upon. Between these two *aims*, there would be a relation which would, I take it, be an authentic case of complementarity. We could—as with wave and quantum concepts—alternate, using results gained through one procedure with results due to the other.

2. Recommendations based on facts are hardly unknown. This could easily be advice supported by observation? The advice is good anyhow, but what about the observation? Is it just an empirical generalization, a matter of probabilities? Or could it be something deeper in semantic structuring that is being discerned: some sort of necessity in how words can do their various kinds of work?

Let us try another paraphrase; with these contraptions there is sometimes safety in numbers.

> Language is such that no word will co-operate with others unless all the partners have plenty to give and take between them.

At first sight this may look as though it might conflict with some of our reflections on Bohr's first observation. This says that words *must* meddle with one another's meanings. But no. The import there was that the referential and emotive functions can maintain their 'unity and married calm' (as Shakespeare's Ulysses has it) only by preserving their due independences. Here we are saying that the *words* (not the functions) in a sentence must be adaptive—adjust their meanings together. To bring the point out in yet another way: it is less true that the meaning of a sentence is the resultant of the separate meanings of its words than that each word's meaning *there* should further and conform with the performance of the sentence. Similarly, of course, with the sentences in a paragraph and the paragraphs in the discourse. What a model for a just society or for the good life a reasonably well-shaped composition affords!

I may fitly conclude with mention of another aspect of Empson's literary gifts: his very remarkable virtuosity as a writer of Basic English. His discussions of Swinburne and Wordsworth in Basic are truly notable achievements in a medium which can for some writers prove over-exacting. That he should have been thus interested in language control is certainly a notable aspect of his manifold venturesomeness as a writer. I see a certain appropriateness, therefore (in a volume celebrating a man of such unusually wide world-consciousness, so deeply experienced in the English language struggles of new-comers to the largest linguistic block there is, so conversant with and sensitive to the educative powers of a right entry to the language), in ending this paper with a reminder that he has been as fully concerned with the problems of a truly elementary English as with its highest and most complex poetry.

NOTES

1 Niels Bohr, *Atomic Physics and Human Knowledge*, 1958, p. 11.
2 Niels Bohr, *Dialectica*, I, p. 315.
3 Ibid., p. 318.
4 S. T. Coleridge, *Aids to Reflection*, aphorism IX.
5 Empson, *Complex Words*, p. 16.
6 ⌐————⌐: semantic marker meaning 'refer to the appropriate passage'.
7 *Rig-veda*, X, p. 129.
8 ?————?: semantic marker meaning 'with whatever meaning'.
9 F. H. Bradley, *Essays on Truth and Reality*, 1914, p. 218.

All or Nothing:
A theme in John Donne

L. C. Knights

Since William Empson has shown a life-long fascination with
John Donne—the affair began early, witness both *Seven Types* and
the first poems, and is still continuing—a note on a puzzling feature
of Donne's work will, I hope, be acceptable as a contribution to
this celebratory volume.

No one today needs to be told that Donne is a poet of paradox
and ambiguity. In the best of his poems the tensions generated by
his heterogeneous ideas have at least the appearance of being
resolved, if only by a skipping wit that dares the reader to challenge the apparent logic at the risk of appearing too solemn for
such company. There is, however, one tension that seems to have
had an especial importance for Donne, and that was too deeply
rooted in his personality to allow the kind of successful handling
that one finds in the best of the love poetry. I refer to the conflict
between his sense of the enormous importance of his own immediate experience and the sense of his own inadequacy and
unimportance, whether as John Donne or as a representative
member of the human race: the immoderate and hydroptic thirst
for 'all' (or at any rate for very widely inclusive experience) clash-
ing with the feeling of being 'nothing'.

It is a preoccupation that is not very bothersome for the reader
of most of the *Songs and Sonnets*, even though in them, as Professor
M. M. Mahood pointed out, the verbal antithesis occurs frequently
and significantly.[1] But that the preoccupation with a feeling of
nothingness in a mind so eager to reach for 'all' was in fact very
bothersome for Donne is plain from the recurrence in his letters

and verse epistles of what is almost an obsessive formula. 'The Storme', addressed to Christopher Brooke (1597), begins:

> Thou which art I, ('tis nothing to be soe).

In the impressive companion piece, 'The Calme', there is an odd extension from the vividly rendered sense of the becalmed sailors' physical incapacity ('Wee have no will, no power, no sense'—only the sense of misery) to a generalized reflection on man's littleness:[2]

> What are wee then? How little more alas
> Is man now, then before he was? he was
> Nothing; for us, wee are for nothing fit;
> Chance, or ourselves still disproportion it.

Variations of the formula used to Brooke occur in later verse letters to Sir Henry Wotton (1604)—'For mee, (if there be such a thing as I)'—and to the Countess of Bedford (1609)—'*nothings*, as I am, may/Pay all they have, and yet have all to pay'. And in a New-year's letter to the Countess (1600?):

> This twilight of two yeares, not past nor next,
> Some embleme is of mee, or I of this,
> Who Meteor-like, of stuffe and forme perplext,
> Whose *what*, and *where*, in disputation is,
> If I should call mee *any thing*, should misse . . .
>
> When all (as truth commands assent) confesse
> All truth of you, yet they will doubt how I,
> One corne of one low anthills dust, and lesse,
> Should name, know, or expresse a thing so high,
> And not an inch, measure infinity.

Characteristically Donne, in a verse letter of hyperbolical compliment (mixed with discreet advice to the Countess not to spend too much time on Court frivolities), expresses one of the central problems of human life—how can the 'inch' (man) 'measure infinity'?—but the foundation is the same acutely felt sense of personal nullity that recurs in his intimate prose letters. Sending a 'ragge of verse' to Sir Henry Goodyer, he writes: 'Sir, if I were any thing, my love to you might multiply it, and dignifie it: But infinite nothings are but one such; yet since even Chymera's have some name and titles, I am also *Yours*.' And again, to the same close friend a little later: 'Therefore I would fain do something;

but that I cannot tell what, is no wonder. For to choose is to do: but to be no part of any body, is to be nothing . . . for to this hour I am nothing, or so little, that I am scarce subject and argument good enough for one of mine own letters: yet I fear, that doth not ever proceed from a good root, that I am well content to be lesse, that is dead.'³ Such sentiments are obviously related to Donne's wretched fortunes in the years between his marriage and his ordination. But it is difficult to avoid the feeling that they are rooted in personality problems that the critic can point to, if he cannot explain: for example to what D. W. Harding has called (with the implication that it is slightly abnormal) Donne's 'sense of the transience of satisfying experience'⁴—its inability, in fact, to be 'all'.

Donne has left us in no doubt of his drive towards death. No one expends so much logic and learning as are deployed in *Biathanatos*—not at all events with that kind of intellectual verve —unless there are compelling personal reasons. And the witty and compassionate Preface⁵ is explicit: 'I have often such a sickly inclination [towards suicide] . . . whensoever any affliction as-sailes me, mee thinks I have the keyes of my prison in mine owne hand, and no remedy presents it selfe so soone to my heart, as mine owne sword.' What seems to have been a more or less permanent disposition is clearly expressed in the 'Anniversaries' written for Elizabeth Drury, where the very fact that he did not know the girl who is his ostensible subject allowed free rein for feelings to some extent necessarily curbed in more directly personal poems. Dame Helen Gardner speaks of Donne as 'a man of strong passions, in whom an appetite for life was crossed by a deep distaste for it'.⁶ But 'deep distaste' hardly does justice to the strength of Donne's revulsion from the 'fragmentary rubbidge' of the world, with its sense of protesting disappointment, that one finds in these poems, especially in the first of them, 'An Anatomy of the World': 'There is no health', 'Wee are borne ruinous'. Things might have been better once, but—with a barely disguised glance back at the lost domain of childhood—

> mankinde decayes so soone,
> We'are scarce our Fathers shadowes cast at noone . . .
>
> And as our bodies, so our mindes are crampt:
>
> 'Tis shrinking, not close weaving that hath thus,
> In minde, and body both bedwarfed us.

> Wee seem ambitious, Gods whole worke t'undoe;
> Of nothing hee made us, and we strive too,
> To bring our selves to nothing backe; and wee
> Doe what wee can, to do't so soone as hee.
>
> This man, so great, that all that is, is his,
> Oh what a trifle, and poore thing he is!
>
> Shee, shee is dead; shee's dead: when thou knowest this,
> Thou knowest how poore a trifling thing man is.

It is of course true that the second poem dwells on the joys of heaven—

> Thou shalt not peepe through lattices of eyes,
> Nor heare through Labyrinths of eares . . .

—and throughout religious belief is recommended as the only way of escaping from the miseries of a world decayed in all its parts. But most of the emotional force springs from the negative feelings; and except for three Vaughan-like lines towards the end—

> Who with Gods presence was acquainted so,
> (Hearing, and speaking to him) as to know
> His face in any naturall Stone, or Tree

—the world considered in itself has no spiritual potential; very obviously here there is no question of holding Infinity in the palm of your hand and Eternity in an hour, or of giving imaginative realization to what Coleridge called 'that other world which now is':[7]

> Turn to Luther's Table Talk, and see if the larger part be not of that other world which now is, and without the being and working of which the world to come would be either as unintelligible as *Abracadabra*, or a mere reflection and elongation of the world of sense—Jack Robinson between two looking-glasses, with a series of Jack Robinsons *in saecula saeculorum*.

In a letter Donne may appeal to traditional, and healthier, doctrine: 'You know, we say in the Schools, that Grace destroys not Nature';[8] but in the 'Anniversaries' the dichotomy seems complete.

> Be more then man, or thou'rt lesse then an Ant.

> Then, as mankinde, so is the worlds whole frame
> Quite out of joynt, almost created lame.

Rejection is the only way of escaping 'this worlds generall sick-nesse':

> thou hast but one way, not t'admit
> The worlds infection, to be none of it.

The poem may be in some respects a Renaissance version of the *de contemptu mundi* theme; but the vigour of the verse, combined with the echoes of many other of Donne's writings, prevents us from seeing it as simply that: the personal vibrations are too strong.

It is of course idle—though probably, in the twentieth century, unavoidable—to speculate on the sources of Donne's pervasive 'disconsolate melancholy', even though this cannot be explained simply by reference to his very obvious personal misfortunes. Certainly in the 'Anniversaries' there is plenty to justify Harding's comment, that 'in the fantasy he created around Elizabeth Drury Donne expressed unwittingly the familiar personal theme that for many people, of whom he was one, an unwilling and protesting separation from the fantasy perfect mother of infancy leaves the world a permanently disappointing place'. Even though Donne's mother died only two months before he did, and lived her last years with him in the Deanery, she was in a sense 'separated' from the four-year-old boy when she re-married less than a year after the death of his father. (In Chapter IV of *Young Man Luther* Erik Erikson studies the inability to mediate between 'allness' and 'nothingness' in its pathological extreme—his example is Hitler—but he also suggests the prevalence of this kind of oscillation in men of constructive genius and in very many 'ordinary' men.) But, obsessive and exaggerated as Donne's feeling of nothingness may at times have been, it is one of the permanent possibilities of our sentient life—something 'to which by reason of our weaknesse, and this worlds encumbrances, our nature is too propense and inclined', as Donne said of the death-wish in *Biathanatos* (*ed. cit.*, p. 71). We can, in short, so little take a merely clinical and detached view of his 'case', that we hope, as we read or re-read, to find the poet not repeating, but exploring, his sense of nullity, the intellectual-emotional disturbances set up when the mere inch, man, confronts immensity. Donne of course in practice found his solution in a life of austere devotion and duty, accepting fully the admirable advice that he gives in *Essays in Divinity*: 'Let no smalness retard thee: if thou beest not Amber, Bezoar, nor liquid gold, to restore Princes; yet thou art a shrub to shelter a lambe, or to feed a bird; or thou art a plantane, to ease a childs smart; or a grasse to cure a sick dog.'⁹ In the poetry, only 'A Litanie' comes to terms with the all or nothing antithesis in a sober recommendation of the middle way.

> From being anxious, or secure,
> Dead clods of sadnesse, or light squibs of mirth,
> From thinking, that great courts immure
> All, or no happinesse, or that this earth
> Is only for our prison fram'd,
> Or that thou art covetous
> To them whom thou lov'st, or that they are maim'd
> From reaching this worlds sweet, who seek thee thus,
> With all their might, Good Lord deliver us . . .
>
> That learning, thine Ambassador,
> From thine allegeance wee never tempt,
> That beauty, paradises flower
> For physicke made, from poyson be exempt,
> That wit, borne apt, high good to doe,
> By dwelling lazily
> On Natures nothing, be not nothing too,
> That our affections kill us not, nor dye,
> Heare us, weake ecchoes, O thou eare, and cry.

It is, as Helen Gardner says, 'a singularly unbitter poem, although it was written at a bitter time'.¹⁰ But although it deserves to be better known it has not the power of the Holy Sonnets or the Hymns, which deal with altogether different matters, and which, I think, do not reach across doctrinal barriers as do the no less Christian poems of George Herbert or T. S. Eliot's *Four Quartets*. Both Herbert and Eliot—like Blake in a different way—can make us feel with full imaginative power the relations between our littleness and a world of infinite possibilities, so that the 'all' is welcoming rather than frightening or oppressive. It is, however, useless to wish that a poet who has given us so much should be other than he is, especially since it is his confrontation of nothingness that results in one of his greatest poems. I refer of course to 'A Nocturnall upon S. Lucies Day'. A. Alvarez, in a fine analysis of this poem, says, 'Despite its theme, the piece has been driven continually forward by a curious restless energy. Yet that energy is entirely in the negatives.'[11] Which is true; but paradoxically the poem, by the very energy of the account of 'how it feels to reach absolute zero' and 'how it feels to *think* when you are there', becomes a kind of affirmation. After all, the poet has *made* something, alive in all its parts, which itself is a victory over chaos and the sense of nothingness that is its theme.

NOTES

1 M. M. Mahood, *Poetry and Humanism* (1950), pp. 95 ff. Professor M. C. Bradbrook reminded me of this after I had written my first draft. Professor Mahood's two chapters on Donne have an obvious bearing on the argument pursued here.

2 In a note to this passage, W. Milgate (*The Satires, Epigrams and Verse Letters of John Donne* (1967), p. 210) points out that 'the same cluster of ideas is found in *Sermons*, iii, 97, where Donne discusses the question of personal identity'. Quotations from Donne's verse letters are from this edition.

3 John Donne, *Selected Prose*, chosen by Evelyn Simpson, edited by Helen Gardner and Timothy Healy (1967), pp. 126, 129–30.

4 D. W. Harding, 'Donne's Anticipation of Experience', in *Experience into Words* (1963). Harding related this to 'an attempted insurance against some such failure of experience [as in Hardy's 'The Self-Unseeding']. In one of its forms it shows as a prolonged effort of anticipation, as though to ensure full responsiveness to the event when it did come.'

5 It is good to find Donne choosing such deeply charitable quotations from the Fathers to support his argument against 'peremptory judgements' on others.

> A devout and godly man, hath guided us well, and rectified our uncharitablenesse in such cases, by this remembrance. . . . *Thou knowest this mans fall, but thou knowest not his wrastling; which perchance was such, that almost his very fall is justified and accepted of God.* . . . An uncharitable mis-interpreter unthriftily demolishes his owne house, and repaires not another. He loseth without any gaine or profit to any. And, as *Tertullian* comparing and making equall, him which provokes another, and him who will be provoked by another, says, *There is no difference, but that the provoker offended first, And that is nothing, because in evill there is no respect of Order or Prioritie.* So wee may soone become as ill as any *offendor, if we offend in a severe increpation of the fact.* For *Climachus* in his *Ladder of Paradise*, places these two steps very neere one another, when hee sayes, *Though in the world it were possible for thee, to escape all defiling by actuall sinne, yet by judging and condemning those who are defiled, thou art defiled*, etc. (*Biathanatos* (first published 1646), pp. 18–19; *Selected Prose*, p. 27).

6 *The Divine Poems of John Donne*, ed. Helen Gardner (1952), Introduction, p. xxxv.

7 Coleridge, 'Dialogue between Demosius and Mystes', *Church and State*, ed. H. N. Coleridge (1839), p. 190.

8 *Selected Prose*, p. 153.

9 Ibid., p. 78.

10 *The Divine Poems of John Donne*, p. xxxvi. Dame Helen deals well with Donne's contribution to the ideal of 'reasonable piety' in seventeenth-century Anglicanism.

11 A. Alvarez, *The Savage God* (1971), pp. 133 ff.

12

Reflections on Johnson's *Life of Milton*

John Wain

It sometimes seems to me that the difference between academic and non-academic criticism is not that one is careful and the other slapdash, that one is learned and the other superficial, nor even that one is penny-plain and the other twopence-coloured; it is rather that the academic critic runs a fence round the subject under discussion, and keeps himself and his readers inside that fence. Any discussion of a literary text has implications that go beyond purely literary study, whatever 'literary' may mean in this context: the critic's attitude to it will depend on his general presuppositions, and the terms in which he will seek to present it to his readers will be dictated, ultimately, by his view of the world. If he is an academic critic he will try to keep all this out of sight; if he is not, he will not mind letting it appear (which is not the same thing as dragging it into long disquisitions). Speaking for myself, though I have often read academic criticism with pleasure and interest, the criticism I enjoy most, that gathers me up in the same way as imaginative literature, is the work of critics who, however learned and professional, are non-academic in the sense I have just described—those who keep a window open on the larger land-scape such as one might see in a Renaissance painting. My tutor C. S. Lewis was one such; William Empson, obviously, is another. Such men discuss literature out of a great depth of knowledge, but without allowing that knowledge to become a limiting structure. There is no barbed wire in their work. Both the two I have named, as it happens, have written studies of Milton; and from both *A Preface to Paradise Lost* and *Milton's God* it would be possible—is, indeed, unavoidable—to learn the author's personal views on religion and, by implication, largely on politics and society. The academic critic would think it tactful to keep these views as invisible as possible, and try to make himself into a lens through which the 'work itself' could be more clearly seen; these non-academic, though equally professional, critics are without that ideal of tact and so their critical work is 'literature' in its own right.

This preamble is by way of explaining why I think a note on Samuel Johnson's criticism of Milton can be relevant in a book whose intent is to pay homage to William Empson. (Apart from the more superficial consideration that Johnson and Empson are rather similar in their critical work, particularly in their blend of a studied no-nonsense manner with extreme subtlety in perception and definition, especially of verbal effects.) Milton is, in any case, a great precipitant of the views of his critics; it is extremely difficult (though some have managed it) to write about Milton without plotting one's own position; he stands so four-square as Protestant, as Puritan, as regicide and radical, and he has built up all these positions with the ferro-concrete of Renaissance human-istic pride.

Johnson, like Empson, found in Milton a particularly strong and insistent challenge to his own intellectual positions. There are, I think, signs that Johnson would have liked to avoid this challenge, if he could do so honourably. The six papers he devoted to Milton in the *Rambler* in 1751 (Nos 86, 88, 90 and 94 on *Paradise Lost*, Nos 139 and 140 on *Samson Agonistes*) come as close as Johnson ever came to a strictly delimited, technical literary study. His concern is with Milton as a verbal artist; his technique is close analysis. He studies the rhythms of Milton's verse, paying special attention to the 'pauses'; he analyses various passages to see if there is any truth in the claim put forward by Milton's admirers, that he has succeeded in that species of poetic virtuosity which makes the sound echo the sense. Is this kind of representative versification really possible, let alone desirable? Or is it a mirage? I will not pause to comment on Johnson's analysis, partly because I have done it elsewhere,[1] but mainly because what concerns us mainly here is that the younger Johnson, just coming into his power as a critic, manages to write at some length on Milton while keeping the discussion very closely literary. There are, 'to be sure', intimations of a more largely outlined suspicion; Johnson does not want Milton's example to be too widely followed, or it will undermine the foundations of neo-classic taste and then the world will no longer be safe for the kind of poetry Johnson approves of and is good at; also, he is very determined that Milton is to be admired for writing *Paradise Lost* and for virtually nothing else. Just as, in the *Life* of Milton, he refuses to see any merit in the 1645 volume, so already in 1751 he is warding off any tendency to admire *Samson Agonistes*. Its structure is undramatic; it has no progression. Johnson's view is manifestly unsatisfactory. It is interesting only as showing a mood, a settled determination to resist the pressure of Milton's huge reputation. He is frankly writing to combat the Miltonic vogue that is developing among younger poets. Even the title of his first detailed paper makes clear the intention to warn: 'A criticism on Milton's versification. Elisions dangerous in English poetry.' Already, he is aware that many people will think his attitude to Milton grudging and tetchy; at the end of the criticism of *Samson* he concludes, with a defiance that seems to mask uneasiness:

> Such are the faults and such the beauties of *Samson Agonistes*, which I have shown with no other purpose than to promote the knowledge of true criticism. The everlasting verdure of Milton's laurels has nothing to fear from the blasts of malignity; nor can my attempt produce any other effect, than to strengthen their shoot by lopping their luxuriance.

More than a quarter of a century was to go by before Johnson again sat down to a serious criticism of Milton. And now, the circumstances were such as to forbid, totally, any avoidance of the challenge. Johnson's *Lives of the Poets* are perhaps the supreme example of scholarly but non-academic criticism. Taken as a whole, which they must be, they constitute Johnson's verdict on the phase of English and European civilization he had lived through; they are the repository of his mature judgments on men, institutions, and art.

A crucial part of this judgment, naturally, concerns the transition from the conflicts of the seventeenth century to the relative stability of the eighteenth, via the events of 1688 and 1714. The formation of Johnson's attitudes in this area is very much bound up with the man's personal history and his development in general. His attitude to the Hanoverian dynasty took years to settle down; in youth he had strong Jacobite leanings, and his feelings towards the German monarchy did not become anywhere near cordial until his highly satisfactory interview with George III in February 1767. Later he settled down to an appreciation of the stability that had been a very tangible fruit of 1688—what he called 'the regularity and composure of the present time'. His complete political position—anti-imperialist, in favour of a strong central authority (e.g. *vis-à-vis* the American colonists, who were making huge fortunes while refusing to pay taxes to the home government) yet in favour of the rights of minorities such as the French Canadians—would take too long to spell out here, though it is certainly in need of spelling out, if only because his views are so often travestied. To Mr Peter Quennell, for instance, Johnson's attitude to his fellow-creatures was 'often cynical'. 'Under any guise,' Mr Quennell tells us firmly, 'the idea of human freedom excited his contempt or hatred'.[2] This, of Johnson, who was against voyages of exploration because they so often ended in dispossessing the natives: of Johnson, who raised his glass at an Oxford dinner-party with 'Here's to the next insurrection of the Negroes in the West Indies!': of Johnson, the egalitarian who wrote that 'the happiness of twenty thousand is of twenty thousand times more value than the happiness of one'![3]

It seems to me that Johnson cared very much more for 'human freedom' than Milton did. And it goes without saying that his opposition to Milton was doctrinal—as we should now say, 'ideological'. Milton had given years of his life to supporting, explicitly by his actions and implicitly in his writings, a system of government and an administration of worship that Johnson, who 'would stand before a battery of cannon to restore Convocation to its full powers', could not see as anything but dangerous and hateful. The wonder is that Johnson's report on him is not more bigoted. What saves it is Johnson's sanity and tolerance, his refusal to believe that politics can cover the whole span of experience.

When Johnson made his much-quoted remark, 'No man would give sixpence to live under one form of government rather than another', he was of course speaking in a pre-totalitarian age. Modern methods, whereby an entire population comes under surveillance all the time, were not then technically feasible. All those countless people who, in our century, have fled from their countries with nothing but what they stood up in, or been gunned down in the attempt, are obviously willing to give more than sixpence to live under one form of government rather than another. But, allowing for this change (for the worse) in the historical situation of mankind, Johnson's remark still has a ring of truth. It places him firmly on one side in a perennial difference of opinion. One of the ways in which human beings can be divided is into those who believe, and those who refuse to believe, that the introduction of a certain political system can transform a society into Paradise overnight. Many people evidently believe this with sincerity and fervour. They are in love with certain political ideas in the same way as a man can be in love with a woman. All criticism is instantly discounted and those who utter it branded as dupes or as liars inspired by jealousy and other dark motives. For many years, the people of this kind whom one encountered in England were mostly in love with the politics of Russia. They saw, with the eye of faith, that the introduction of Soviet Communism had brought heaven on earth; that there were no strikes because the workers were too happy to strike; that nobody criticized Stalin because they were gazing at him through a mist of adoration. They even kept it up during the dreadful years when there were more political prisoners in Russia than there were *people* in England. Nowadays, Russia-worship is out of fashion, but the same kind of person—in many cases, the same actual individuals— tell you with the same complete conviction that Paradise has arrived in China and/or Cuba. Those of us who are tardy in accepting these claims are not necessarily hostile to the countries about which they are made; it is just that we cannot see how any political party, however good and intelligent, could have that much influence on every department of life; it is our impression that many things escape the mesh of government and if they do not, the government is probably an evil one; and that, whoever is in power at the top, one's own struggle goes on.

Certainly Johnson lived up to this belief. His political and social convictions were strong and definite, yet he did not live his life as if people who disagreed with those convictions belonged to some alien and sinister species. Many of his friends were Whigs, including some of the closest; one thinks of his noble tribute in old age to Gilbert Walmsley, the friend and mentor of his youth.

Of Gilbert Walmsley, thus presented to my mind, let me indulge myself in the remembrance. I knew him very early: he was one of the first friends that literature procured me, and I hope that at least my gratitude made me worthy of his notice.

He was of an advanced age, and I was only not a boy; he never received my notions with contempt. He was a Whig, with all the virulence and malevolence of his party; yet difference of opinion did not keep us apart. I honoured him, and he endured me.

He had mingled with the gay world, without exemption from its vices or its follies, but had never neglected the cultivation of his mind; his belief of Revelation was unshaken; his learning preserved his principles; he grew first regular, and then pious.

His studies had been so various, that I am not able to name a man of equal knowledge. His acquaintance with books was great; and what he did not immediately know, he could at least tell where to find. Such was his amplitude of learning, and such his copiousness of communication, that it may be doubted whether a day now passes in which I have not some advantage from his friendship.

Or of Molly Aston, who 'talked all in praise of liberty' and was 'the loveliest creature I ever saw!' Nobody could accuse Johnson of failing to see the good points of a Whig. Even the celebrated remark about 'not letting the Whig dogs have the best of it' when he was composing his *Debates in the Senate of Lilliput* is not borne out by an examination of these debates, which show Johnson as remarkably impartial.

Some of Johnson's passages in praise of Milton remind us forcibly of the man's power to see good in an adversary. If Molly Aston was 'the loveliest creature I ever saw', Milton was, often, seen by Johnson as a beautiful object of contemplation. He may have been all wrong about prayer, for instance, yet, 'That he lived without prayer can hardly be affirmed; his studies and meditations were an habitual prayer.'

Within this framework, Johnson felt free to attack Milton's beliefs, and surely his freedom was justified. Pre-totalitarian that he was, Johnson had enough political vision to see very clearly the nature of totalitarianism when it should come into being. And his rejection of it, as it were in advance, is very striking.

Totalitarianism is marked by two main features. First, everything in life is party-line. One's thoughts, leisure activities, relationships, sports, clothing, hobbies, are all, in the eyes of the ruling oligarchy, correct or not correct. In the *Life of Butler*, Johnson characterizes the Commonwealth along these lines:

> We have never been witnesses of animosities excited by the use of minced pies and plumb porridge; nor seen with what abhorrence those who could eat them at all other times of the year

would shrink from them in December. An old Puritan, who was alive in my childhood, being at one of the feasts of the church invited by a neighbour to partake his cheer, told him, that, if he would treat him at an alehouse with beer, brewed for all times and seasons, he should accept his kindness, but would have none of his superstitious meats or drinks.

One of the puritanical tenets was the illegality of all games of chance; and he that reads Gataker upon *Lots*, may see how much learning and reason one of the first scholars of his age thought necessary, to prove that it was no crime to throw a die, or play at cards, or to hide a shilling for the reckoning.

The other main feature of totalitarianism is hatred of the past. Obviously the past must be forgotten, because it was an enormous tract of time during which humanity got along somehow without the benefit of whatever orthodoxy it is that governs the totalitarian society. The Rule of the Saints was an early example of totalitarian hatred of the past, as Revolutionary France in its opening stages was a slightly later one. Johnson, in that same passage of the *Life of Butler*, singles out this aspect for his attention.

The wisdom of the nation is very reasonably supposed to reside in the parliament. What can be concluded of the lower classes of the people, when in one of the parliaments summoned by Cromwell it was seriously proposed, that all the records in the Tower should be burnt, that all memory of things past should be effaced, and that the whole system of life should commence anew?

When I was young I remember being acutely embarrassed, often defensively bad-tempered, when anyone pointed out Milton's bad qualities—his rigid attitudes, his ungenerosity to political opponents as typified by the horrible sneering at Salmasius, etc. Since I was so powerfully impressed by the splendour of Milton's poetry, and felt such gratitude to him for having lived up to the demands made on him by his poetic genius, I wanted to feel this gratitude undisturbed by any side-currents. I was, in fact, very much in the position of those people whose love for the poetry of Ezra Pound caused them to adopt attitudes that were unpleasantly close to Fascism. These people—and it is the one great excuse for them—never started by being impressed with the political and social beliefs and became attracted to the poetry in consequence;

invariably, they fell in love with the poetry and decided that a man who could write like this must be obeyed in *everything*. Various poets who have held strong views about the world in general— Shelley, for instance—have had this effect on their admirers. My love of Milton's poetry did not turn me into an upholder of the Rule of the Saints, if only because I was too ignorant to understand the issues, but it had the effect of blanking off part of my mind: there was a whole area of Milton's life and personality that I could not look at. Since then, I have come to the realization that a man may be born into this world with the gifts of a great poet and may fully develop and employ those gifts, in the most honourable way and sometimes at great sacrifice to himself, without achieving balance and wisdom in every other area. Ezra Pound is the supreme example of this in our time, indeed I would like to go on record as thinking that he is the Milton of the twentieth century, with the dispraise as well as the praise that such a description implies. Another example, if we bring down the whole scale of the comparison, might be C. M. Grieve, some of whose utterances on life and politics even his *cénacle* would have rejected if they had been uttered by anyone else.

Milton was a wonderful poet who mined out his poetic vein nobly and with no thought of advantage to himself. In other respects he had, as Pound had, some of the marks of the totalitarian mind on him. He thought, or acted as if he thought, that the very complex problems of government would disappear if only people would stop being stupid and do things his way; he denied good faith to his adversaries. Johnson put his finger on these qualities and for this reason his *Life of Milton* used to give me pain; I could understand Cowper's exclaiming, 'I could thrash his old jacket till his pension jingled in his pocket!' But 'when I became a man, I put away childish things', including this kind of partisan all-or-nothing attitude, and I now think that Johnson approached the task of writing about Milton in very much the same way as I have, in recent years, approached the task of writing about Pound.[4] It is not an approach that can please the fanatic, but it ought still to be capable of engaging the attention of human beings, if there are still any such about.

NOTES

1 J. Wain (ed.), *Johnson as Critic* (1973), in Routledge & Kegan Paul's Critics Series.
2 P. Quennell, *Samuel Johnson: His Friends and Enemies* (1972), p. 260.
3 Letter to *Gentleman's Magazine*, January 1739.
4 E.g. in Dyson and Cox (eds), *The Twentieth Century Mind*, Vol. II (1972), pp. 314–26.

13

New Signatures in Retrospect

A. G. Stock

I think it was in 1918, though my memory may be out by a year either way, that the *Saturday Westminster Gazette*, then a Liberal weekly with a sedately progressive literary outlook, set as one of its weekly competitions 'A short serious poem introducing the word "hatter" '. I have forgotten the winning entry: I remember the competition because it started a group of us at school on a discussion of the poetically mentionable professions which was perhaps our first breath of criticism of those delightful Georgians. Shepherds, blacksmiths, fishermen, ploughmen, all the venerable rural crafts would pass; so would doctors, clergymen, perhaps with more circumspection teachers, but we thought university professors would not, for indefinable reasons not wholly dependent on scansion. Merchants qualified, but not stockbrokers, accountants or typists, though Tennyson could introduce a city clerk (but gently born and bred). Hatters were clearly beyond the pale. Yet any neo-Augustan poetaster could have brought one in without a blush. He might have called him something like 'the excellent artificer whose trade protects the pervious head with decent shade'—but the disguise would not have been prompted by that rustic antique poetic snobbery handed down from Wordsworth through the Romantics to our own day. A decade or so later when T. S. Eliot had made his impact on younger writers I doubt if a hatter would have been more poetically improper than a haymaker.

It is arguable that Wordsworth's sheer power damaged his successors' relation to their public for a century. Just when the kind of people who read poetry were spending more and more of their lives in towns, treating visits to the country as an intermission, he made them feel that human relationships and crises of the spirit which happened out of sight of mountains and waterfalls could only be second-class experience. Poetic reality belonged to other people, outside 'the very world that is the world Of all of us, the place where in the end We find our happiness, or not at all'. The revolt against Augustan 'poetic diction', which began as a subversive attempt to raise the dignity of common life, ended in restricting the poet's vocabulary within different but even more artificial limits. To break out needed originality and craftsmanship comparable to Wordsworth's own.

One of Eliot's achievements was to bring poetry back to town, speaking with the inflexions and wellbred reticence of the kind of people who occasionally read it outside classrooms, using the visible context of their own lives as a metaphor of their inward condition. What he said about that was uncomfortable, and naturally a generation at ease with the idiom of Wordsworth, Keats, and Tennyson reacted with the same kind of annoyance that Wordsworth had expected *Lyrical Ballads* to evoke from the Pope-nurtured public of his day: they exclaimed angrily that it was not poetry. Still, he was taking them seriously, and caught the cadence of their speech so accurately that it was difficult not to believe that it was their own inner voice speaking the truth.

One must, I think, have reservations about Eliot's or any poet's summing-up of the neuroses of a generation. Some people recognize themselves in his images, become more articulate because he gives them a language to describe themselves, and are accepted as 'the age' until a new voice expresses different attitudes which their talkativeness had thrust into the background. Something must be allowed for this confidence trick played by a convincing tone of voice; the upper classes of the 1920s may not have been so unanimously dying of spiritual thirst as Eliot depicted them. All the same, the picture he drew in *The Waste Land* with such marked distaste for almost everything in it was both recognizable and so intolerable that it was bound to evoke a reaction from those who accepted it as the truth about their own world. They might say, 'Earthly values make no sense, we must try to live by those of heaven' (which points the direction of Eliot's own later poetry), or more resiliently, 'What a rotten society! Let's scrap it and make a better one.'

The Leftist writers of the 1930s were not Eliot's disciples. Their early background was not American but firmly English, and although they belonged to much the same upper-class world they saw it from a different angle at a different stage of decay. They were perhaps indebted to him more for his existence than for what they learnt from him directly: a predecessor of that stature, by stretching the sensibilities of the reading public, had given them elbow-room to try their own experiments. By the 1930s it was less easy to shout 'That's not poetry!' at any new use of language or unexpected point of view. Also, by that time the inner void of the Waste Land had imploded into something much more like total outer collapse.

Since then change has been so much more rapid and the future so much less predictable from each successive present that it is difficult for anyone who was not grown up in the thirties to remember what the shock of the Depression felt like. In the war, the present already seemed to have obliterated the past: the war-time young had new and nerve-racking strains to undergo, but unemployment and the dread of starvation were not among them and there was little time for dreams of revolution. In the 1930s, when stacks of food were being destroyed because hungry families were penniless, capitalism was visibly breaking down as the Marxists always said it would, and you did not need to be personally a victim of the breakdown to feel that revolution made better sense, both economically and morally.

What I want to recall is the first impact of the 1930s poets on their own generation. At the beginning of that decade literature took a Leftward turn, described by George Orwell in *Inside the Whale*. *New Signatures*, which was published in 1932 and ran into three editions in two years, certainly helped it along, as the Left Book Club did later, but they did so because the trend was there, created by the Depression and asking for a voice. We recognized *New Signatures* as its new and exciting voice, but I don't think it spoke to or for working-class revolutionaries. At least, in my own experience it was never easy to explain my enthusiasm for it to the working-class students in my WEA courses. They were hetero-geneous groups, but usually about half the members were authentically working-class students, often old enough to have served in the First World War; seldom doctrinaire Marxists, but always staunch trade unionists who looked back on the General Strike as a splendid moment of class solidarity, unforgivably betrayed by the leaders. *The Silver Tassie* or *Within the Gates* always got an immediate response, and because they understood O'Casey's themes they would grow interested in his experiments in tech-nique, but *New Signatures* left them cold.

'We' who found the book exciting because it came close to our own hopes and hatreds were the Leftist intellectuals. Most of us did not like the name: according to the tone of voice it either sounded too pretentious or cast doubts on our credentials in the proletarian revolution we felt we belonged to: but there was no other way to describe us. We were on the militant workers' side more from considered conviction than from class experience, and our education had inculcated upper-class values which we now disowned. To qualify as good revolutionaries it was necessary to throw them off, and this meant a deliberate effort of self-re-education, a kind of voluntary brainwashing. So, although we recognized the same enemy, our battleground was different and more inward. It was the perennial revolt of the young against their elders, to which the conditions of our time had given a distinctively political form.

I think it was because the *New Signatures* poets, and more particularly Auden, Day Lewis, and Spender, dramatized this revolt that their effect was so powerful. This is not a reflection on the intrinsic excellence of the poems, many of which have outlived their first public and are still impressive in more general anthologies forty years later. But though excellence has staying power, it does not of itself scatter seeds unless the right winds are blowing, and their work caught the wind. Most of their contributions are essentially breakaway poems, celebrating the achievement of detachment and solitude rather than a positive commitment, but the breakaway more than the commitment was our own most pressing problem. They wrote of it more directly than the others and called up imitators, as if they had found a language for what everyone wanted to say, and later when one thought of the book it was usually their contributors that came first to mind.

In a vigorous preface, Michael Roberts presented *New Signatures* as a step towards the re-education of poetry into citizenship of the modern world. In an industrial age, he pointed out, it was time to outgrow the traditional rustic imagery and admit that machinery had entered the landscape to stay. But for the health of society it was even more important to re-learn what the nineteenth century in its obsession with science had forgotten, that 'objective' measurable facts were not necessarily the whole of truth, and to rediscover, by first believing it discoverable, a recognizable hierarchy of moral values. There were poets (he named none, but could well have had Eliot and Pound in mind) who, not finding their values reflected in the world around them, had retreated into isolation and wrote 'esoteric poetry in which it was necessary for the reader to catch each recondite allusion'—a way of writing, he implied, which amounted to an alignment with the past rather than the present, since it could be intelligible only to the classically educated elite. He was clearly not taking exception to abstruse thought, but to language that made it sound more abstruse than it was; for by way of contrast he said that Empson's own poems, however taxing intellectually, 'do something to remove the difficulties which have stood between the poet and the writing of popular poetry'.

In all this he was not claiming that a poet should 'belong to his age' by being committed to any specific political or religious creed. But he should recognize that his experience, and his effort to clarify it in words, had a bearing on that of his generation, and should look for an idiom and an imagery that connected the two—without, of course, blurring the exactitude of the thought in his mind. All the contributors to the book were there because in their various ways they were doing this, and put together they took on the collective weight of a movement. Among them he picked out, as those whose language belonged most to the living present, the 'big three' names which as the decade went on came more and more to stand in most people's minds for 'modern poetry'.

The whole discussion is of poetry as poetry, an art in which style and substance are no more separable in the completed work than they are in painting. At the same time Roberts sees style, which is something the artist deliberately cultivates, as a moral and therefore a social quality, a means through which, as a socially responsible person, the artist makes his art contribute to the common good. And towards the end of the preface Roberts remarks casually and almost parenthetically:

It is natural that the recognition of the importance of others should sometimes lead to what appears to be the essence of the communist attitude: the recognition that oneself is no more important than a flower in a field; that it may be good to sacrifice one's own welfare that others may benefit; to plough in this year's crop so that next year's may benefit; the return is certain, what matter who receives it.

Very little in *New Signatures* was recognizably communist in spirit, much less than in *New Country* which followed it a year later. There was even less that a revolutionary worker could recognize as speaking to his own condition, but that is no disparagement of the poets, who did not set out to expound experience they had not shared. There was, though, especially in the work of Auden, Day Lewis, and Spender, a vivid sense of a war to be fought and a rigorous self-re-education to be undergone in readiness for it. What exactly the war was about, whether the rigorous process was imposed by it or was itself the real value for which a war was the necessary excuse, the language of the poems mostly left uncertain. But there was in fact a class war; there were the young intellectuals I have described, whose moral conviction put them on the workers' side, their upbringing and all their inherited associations on the other, and the position the poets interpreted was theirs.

Of the three, Auden was forceful enough to have a strong effect on the other two, as both have testified in their autobiographies, but they had common ground to begin from. All three were sons of the Establishment with similar reasons for moving Leftward. Nearly thirty years later, Day Lewis wrote:

Nearly all my friends, who during this period became active in Left-Wing movements, or at least sympathetic to Left-Wing ideas, had had the same kind of upbringing. Rex Warner, MacNeice and myself were the sons of clergymen; Auden had a devout Anglo-Catholic mother: Spender came from an 'old-fashioned Liberal' family. We had all been to public schools, with their traditions both of authoritarianism and of service to the community. We had all, I think, lapsed from the Christian faith, and tended to despair of Liberalism as an instrument for dealing with the problems of our day, if not to despise it as an outworn creed. Inoculated against Roman Catholicism by the religion of my youth, I dimly felt the need for a faith which had the authority, the logic, the cut-and-driedness of the Roman church, a faith which would fill the void left by the leaking away of traditional religion, would make sense of our troubled times and make real demands on me. Marxism appeared to fill the bill. It appealed too, I imagine, to that part of me which from time to time revolted against the intolerable burden of selfhood and desired the anonymity of a unit in a crowd. (*The Buried Day* (1960), pp. 209–10)

There is a psychological difference between this kind of Leftism and that of the unemployed worker who comes to the same political position. They are allies against a common enemy, but for the worker the ruling class is, quite straightforwardly, the Enemy, the something not ourselves that makes for unrighteousness, to be attacked as soon as recognized. To the upper-class convert it is also his elders, seen with the love-hatred of the younger generation; it is the mental and emotional conditioning inseparable from growing up. For him to become a genuine revolutionary is to commit semi-suicide, cutting off the past to give the future room to take a new shape: an operation extremely difficult and emotionally painful.

A poet, at least in his poetry, has to be an integrated personality. Writing as the revolutionary he has not quite become, he must use his language with a special vigilance unnecessary to Shakespeare, who had the whole of a traditional culture to draw upon at will. Words call up the wrong echoes, evocative rhythms evoke the wrong allegiances, moments of vision in his actual experience belong to an enemy context and may have to be transplanted. On the other hand, symbols and slogans which to a worker are perhaps alive with emotional experience turn into claptrap which he cannot by any manipulation invigorate with meaning.

By alphabetical accident Auden is the first contributor, and the first of his poems neatly epitomizes the difficult poise. 'Ode (To His Pupils)' was later renamed expressively 'Which Side Am I Supposed To Be On?'—but the earlier title sets it in a tract of early Auden country. It is a campers' tract, where what appears to be a scout troop or a public school OTC is on manoeuvres: at least, the speaker sounds like a public school master in charge of operations, but the exercise is more than an exercise because the war is real and there never was and presumably never will be anything outside it. It is an inherited war, built into everyone's reflexes from birth, but in an off-duty moment the speaker allows himself to reflect on it, almost as if it were not the inescapable human condition. 'Our side' have been brought up from time immemorial on an ancestral myth

About the tall white gods who landed from their open boat,
Skilled in the working of copper, appointing our feast-days,
Before the islands were submerged . . .

Everybody knows it, nobody has a shred of evidence, nobody challenges it because you cannot question the dynamic that makes you function—and anyway, living up to the standards of the army takes all a man's energy. As for the enemy—for a brief moment he wonders why they are the enemy. Their courage is magnificent, though we always mention it in inverted commas. There are hushed-up cases of people from our side, not always despicable, who have crossed over. . . . But such talk will not do in camp. This is a time for action, which makes exacting enough demands on character.

> We entrain at once for the North: we shall see in the morning
> The headlands we are doomed to attack.

'Doomed' is a word of import. One's doom is given, not chosen, but it is part of a brave man's code to accept it.

For 'enemy' it is possible to read 'communist', but the poem is not a straight satire on ruling-class mentality. The lifelong training for an everlasting war is perhaps his vision of social reality as he saw it at the time, but his picture of it also suggests that for him, either as boy or schoolmaster, the training camp was among the best of good memories of school. He captures the atmosphere of strenuousness, of authoritarian discipline voluntarily accepted, in the name of some worthwhile purpose, vaguely understood but felt to be beyond one's mere personal interests; the implicit recognition, too, that without a war to keep in training for there is nothing to call out that comradeship in dangerous action which raises the quality of life. How much more justification does a war need? After all, public spirit, which is one of the supreme public school virtues, means suppressing what you think yourself, if the general interest seems to be endangered by it, and keenness, which is the other, means doing everything you are set to do as if it were necessary to salvation.

The spirit is handed down from an epic age, perhaps literally from Homer, the great source-book of European civilization, but not quite in its pristine glory. When fighting was accepted as a good reason for living a man could rejoice in a noble enemy to kill or be killed by: the better the foe, the more worthwhile the fight. Since then, enough Christianity has filtered in to complicate the morality without thoroughly changing it. To fight with a clear conscience we must have a war with all the right on one side, an enemy who is the enemy of God and despicable into the bargain.

The speaker sounds uneasy about it—and rightly, since extermina-
ting pests is less bracing to morale than matching courage with
courage. But under the surface the old pagan generosity survives.
Auden puts into the enemy's mouth the grand line from *The
Battle of Maldon*:

> Heart and hand shall be keener, mood the more
> As our might lessens

—and gives the speaker who quotes it the grace to acknowledge
the ring of heroism, even though he feels a slight sense of treachery
in doing so.

Auden is detached from his speaker, but not contemptuous of
him. If in this poem he was repudiating the values of his class and
upbringing, it was not without a farewell look, much more
affectionate than he gave them in poems of the next few years.

But is he doing that? The next poem, 'Doom is dark and
deeper than any sea-dingle', is one of his most haunting. It
belongs to the same country of the mind, this part of it a wild tract
of fells and potholed becks. It assumes a community somewhere
to which the speaker belongs, though nothing in it precisely
identifies the culture: only the Nordic rhythm associates it
vaguely with the Anglo-Saxon Seafarer, who also left his house in
spring. It is about an ordeal of spiritual loneliness translated into
terms of exile, not exactly sought but accepted. For it is 'Doom'
again, the inexorable, which falls on a man for some purpose not
his own. Whatever human life he encounters is too alien to break
his isolation—

> through doorway voices
> Of new men making another love.

The phrase carries no suggestion that they and their loves will
become his. Meantime his dreams are of his own kindred from
whom he is separated, and the prayer is for their safety and his
safe return. No quest is named, no monster to be found and
fought or treasure to be carried home; the ordeal appears to be the
purely private one of self-testing in solitude. It could be the
prophet's retreat to a wilderness, but that is a long way from a
change of sides.

The break with one's past, gradual or abrupt, is a normal part
of growth and not necessarily final. Auden in his twenties may
well have been too good a psychologist not to be aware that he

would go back in the end. 'We make poetry out of the quarrel with ourselves,' says W. B. Yeats, 'out of the quarrel with others we make rhetoric.' This poem, like the other, is set in a vividly imagined country of romance which is the place where inward battles are fought out, but the strongest feeling it embodies is the anguished loneliness of separation. This too is part of the break-away experience, and many of his readers must have recognized it.

Unlike Auden, who is said to have read little poetry and written none till he had found a point of view of his own, Cecil Day Lewis had practised the art from boyhood. All his earlier writing is intensely self-preoccupied, the utterance of a mind which before it could look at the world had to arrive at a standpoint to look from. His Left turn was both a commitment and a liberation, but because he was already an accomplished artist in the old tradition it meant a deliberate re-training in the use of language.

His first book, *Beechen Vigil*, was discarded later as no better than a juvenile exercise. Though there is nothing in it to set poetry on a new path, it moves on the old one with a very sure foot.

> Look not too long upon the golden hours,
> Look not too long.
> Those sirens will unstring thy powers
> That made a minstrelsy of sun and showers,
> Of every stone a song.
> Hark, how the wind's bleak trumpet stuns each hill
> To colder immobility.
> Fool!
> And canst thou quick and wakeful be
> When all thy spirit is one Philomel
> With music sweetly shrill?

The weather is too cold for Tennyson, the cadence too mellifluous for Matthew Arnold, but the music of their generation is in it: one would think those sirens had already taken him captive. By contrast, take this from *The Magnetic Mountain*:

> Nearing again that legendary isle
> Where sirens sang and mariners were skinned,
> We wonder now what was there to beguile,
> That such stout fellows left their bones behind?

It is a pointed comment on his own earlier style, as much in the scaling-down of language and the aggressively forthright metre as in the announcement of new immunity from old temptation.

The Magnetic Mountain, to which all his *New Signatures* poems belong, was not published till a year later. Taken as a whole it is weakened by diffuseness, for he had the gift of finding too many good ways of saying one thing. The result is a little like a boy's adventure story half written, with the background sketched in and the action left out. There is an Audenesque tract of unknown country, beginning where the railway ends, and a mountain somewhere beyond that, an expedition of the utmost hazard to be undertaken, a colony to be founded perhaps, with the mountain's inexhaustible mineral wealth for exploitation. All who join the expedition are muscular, tight-lipped, resolute young men in the strictest training, clear-headed about the dangers of the enterprise and the discipline and endurance needed to carry it through; all who stay behind are physical wrecks, unwholesome neurotics, sinister enemy agents, or all at once: a seductive if rather dangerously unreal picture of the Social Revolution. Massed together the *Magnetic Mountain* poems have a cumulative effect of auto-hypnosis, though for the most of us, eager to believe in regeneration by Socialist commitment, this was not an easy fault to spot at first sight. Taken separately, many of them have a buoyancy rare in our times and quite different from Auden's characteristic moods.

The *New Signatures* excerpts gave the essence of the whole book without its repetitions. The first three poems make up a kind of three-point chart for a pilgrimage. The 'Kestrel' lyric with its joyful flight-rhythms is the pure exhilaration of escape; the next ('But Two there are . . . ') makes it an escape into, not out of, hard-edged reality; in the third the Magnetic Mountain becomes the point of arrival, the triumphant moment of full self-possession. The 'Satirical Poems' (not altogether satirical) that follow are dramatic monologues by Wife, Teacher, Mother as archetypal figures who between them mark out the place they would have the man fill; they are the powers he must break away from. In 'The Observer Speaks' the poet, with an air of detachment, dismisses them all and reasserts his right to freedom.

> The tree grips soil, the bird
> Knows how to use the wind;
> But the full man must live
> Rooted yet unconfined.

(A splendid aspiration: but it only states, without solving, the everlasting problem of man and his society.)

In the whole sequence only one person, the liberated self, is of any account. The Fear and Pain of the second lyric, 'hardening the bones, keeping the spirit spare', are inescapable conditions of living, impersonal and even medicinal, but the clutching human impediments are in the wrong for thwarting him. It is poetry of revolt all right, but at least in its explicit statement, of unequivoc-ally individualist revolt. Only the language declares his alliance. In the second lyric the images are carefully chosen and mixed to express the brotherhood of trouble:

> Turning over old follies in ante-room,
> For firstborn waiting, or for late reprieve,
> Watching the safety-valve, the slackening loom,
> Abed, abroad, at every turn and tomb . . .

In the 'Kestrel' and again in the 'Mountain' lyric he borrows a note of religious ecstasy from older poets for transference from heaven to earth—as if to say, nothing imagined there is unattain-able here. His Kestrel, 'however in wind', is Hopkins' Wind-hover, made to image an achievement not Christ's, but his own. The rhythm and bits of the phrasing of the Mountain poem echo Vaughan's 'My soul there is a country Far beyond the stars', but though the feeling is ecstatic, like Vaughan's the Magnetic Mountain rivets heaven to earth.

> O there's a mine of metal
> Enough to make me rich,
> And build right over chaos
> A cantilever bridge.

It is a valiant attempt to transcendentalize industrialism, and yet here the impassioned expression on the countenance of science looks to me a little forced. It is not because the task is inherently impossible, but between this symbol and the state symbolized there is too sharp a discrepancy. The mastery of an inner chaos in an integration that holds eternity in an hour is a solitary experience and has been felt so all through the poem; when suddenly he trans-lates it into such a very collective enterprise as a cantilever bridge the jump is awkward, and the image rings a little false.

There is a question here which the intellectuals-turned-revolutionaries would have had to sort out, if war had not postponed it. At that time the hope of revolution was two things in one. Its apparent economic good sense joined us with the workers; at the same time it was that emancipation from values of the past which each one felt as his private freedom. We were disillusioned with the inherited competitive structure of life, which had neither, by the freedoms it offered, liberated our minds from the suffocating fixation on material gain, nor produced the world of peace and plenty the nineteenth century looked forward to. On the contrary, the muddle and misery were such that a normally sensitive mind could not look at them long without feeling guilty nor turn away without growing callous. If, as we believed, the collective society the USSR had proclaimed would solve all the economic problems, did it not follow that it would create a world where mental freedom was a natural and valued grace of social living? In those days, before even the Spanish War had begun to confuse us, all revolts merged in one, and the question looked merely rhetorical.

Stephen Spender came nearest to treating it seriously in 'The Funeral', of which Michael Roberts wrote in his preface:

> Poetry is here turned to propaganda, but it is propaganda for a theory of life which may release the poet's energies for the writing of pure poetry as well as provide him with standards which may make simple and direct satire possible again.

The poem describes workers, presumably in the Soviet Union, carrying the body of a comrade to the grave.

> With laughter on their lips and with winds blowing round them
> They speak simply
> Of how this one excelled all others in making driving-belts.

All the emphasis is on the work: driving-belts were the reason for his living, and what he was in his private and personal relationships is taken into no account at all. This is thrown uncompromisingly in the reader's face. It is a little unfortunate that

> This is festivity; it is the time of statistics . . .

brings in the wrong kind of smugness, by coming too close to an English school speech-day or the annual dinner of some prosperous philanthropic association.

But in the fourth verse old poetic associations are taken into the service of new values:

> They think how one life hums, revolves and toils,
> One cog in a golden and singing hive;
> Like spark from fire, its task happily achieved,
> It falls away quietly.

He has borrowed Shakespeare's 'singing masons building roofs of gold', and with a boldly mixed metaphor has mechanized the bees and transferred the song to the hive itself; and has used the spark, an age-old symbol of the individual soul, to show that total extinction at the end of one's usefulness to society is a satisfying and dignified end. Finally, he relegates the whole European tradition with its cult of the individual to 'scholars who dream of the ghosts of Greek boys'. An unfair image, but it is the nature of poetic images to be unfair; we notice it less when our emotions are already engaged on the same side.

Considered as propaganda, 'The Funeral' made its point too aggressively, to challenge rather than convert—as if the poet wanted a battle to convince himself that he felt what at the moment he ardently wished to feel. But I remember that it was an excellent catalyst, for that very reason, when it was offered to my rather stolid WEA classes for discussion. Reactions were seldom tepid or bewildered: they thought they saw at once what the poem asked them to accept, and more often than not rejected it. At least, the working-class students almost always did. They usually cherished some dream of social revolution (picturing it, no doubt, with the least possible disturbance of normal life), but if the object was to give men and women like themselves a major voice in running the country, they did not see why it should require such a reversal of all their accepted values. Giving the dignity of labour its due did not mean treating men as instruments for making driving-belts. Occasionally a young schoolteacher, fresh enough from college to have the intellectual's excitement about ideas, read the poem, more truthfully I should think, as a reflection on a certain kind of cant his soul rebelled against, seeing as the operative words—

> No more are they haunted by the individual grief
> Nor the crocodile tears of European genius.

I have dwelt on this poem, not for its durable merit but because it had this caricature-like force at the time. Some of Spender's other contributions have survived among his best-known poems, and two in particular, 'Oh Young Men' and 'I Think Continually' have the kind of quality that gave *New Signatures* its distinctive flavour. In both the phrasing is slightly precious: they sound like the work of a man who has had the best of a privileged upper-class upbringing. But they are introspective, they dig below any particular contemporary quarrel, and assert values incompatible with the received opinions of a society mentally and materially possessive. Without turning him into a pseudo-proletarian those values range him inevitably on the side of the dispossessed.

About thirty years later, when I was teaching English literature in an Indian university, 'Oh Young Men' was set for exposition in the General English paper of the All-India competitive examination for the Public Services. All the candidates were graduates, but as the paper was not an optional one only a very small proportion would have been specialists in English. Judging from the random sample that fell to me for examining, well over 90 per cent of them read the poem without hesitation as a call to Indian youth to rebel against the institution of the 'joint family', that bulwark of everything traditional and conservative in their society. It fitted their context neatly, but the Head Examiner, an outstanding scholar whose long familiarity with English poetry made the intended application self-evident to him, disallowed the interpretation. I thought the ruling unduly severe, since after all it was the candidates' grasp of the English language that was being tested, not their familiarity with English life; but it was one of those places where the two shade off into one another and make the teacher of English overseas realize the complexity of his job. It often seemed to me that these 1930s poets were the latest that most Indian students could construe into something pertinent to their own experience. The war, and the welfare state that followed it, set the younger writers against a background too remote to be easily imagined.

There were good poems in *New Signatures* which treated the modern world and its conflicts more straightforwardly: there were also William Empson's, neither negligible nor straightforward, but perplexing on a different, more detached level of thought. It was disconcerting to have to recognize a poet, unmistakably of our time, who did not appear to share that sense of the purifying

value of a sociological view of life which was what we were looking for. When one is looking for reality in sociology it is difficult
to adjust to it in metaphysics—even very tough metaphysics. But
comprehensible or not, his *New Signatures* poems had the air of
growing from actual life; the things mentioned in them existed in
their own right before they turned into symbols.

'Advance to rebuild and sleep with friend on hill', Stephen
Spender proclaims, and camping out, seen through the eyes of the
would-be volunteer who may not have tried it, becomes part of
the adventure of commitment; both friend and hill are glamorous
abstractions standing for regeneration. But 'And now she cleans
her teeth into the lake' sounds more like a real recollection of
camping for pleasure, and the abstruse reflections on physics and
metaphysics that follow are as much a part of it as the early morning
mist evaporating from the water. It is not the enactment of a
symbolic ritual but an individual mind stirred to activity by a
particular occasion.

Is the man who sleeps with friend on hill accepting reality, and
the one who goes camping for pleasure escaping from it? At that
time, when 'escapism' was a favourite fault-finding word, many
Marxists would have answered emphatically yes. The argument
rests on a doctrine of historical necessity. Things are bound to
take a certain course; whatever contributes to it is 'reality', what
does not is too trivial to deserve the name. It is useful to have a
word to distinguish what is worth taking seriously from what is
not, and historical necessity may replace the discarded idea of
revealed religion as a gauge.

'This Last Pain', however, which is a closely packed argument
about faith, is too thoroughly subversive for the average social
revolutionary, since it undermines historical necessity along with
religion, and leaves him without the assurance of inevitable
victory. On the other hand, it neither relieves man of the responsibility for discovering his own understanding of good and evil—
which both those doctrines could do—nor promises a very substantial reward for the effort.

> Imagine, then, by miracle, with me,
> (Ambiguous gifts, as what gods give must be)
> What could not possibly be there,
> And learn a style from a despair.

When he takes more direct notice of Leftist standpoints, in 'Note on Local Flora', he is hardly more reassuring. There is a tree whose cones will ripen only in a forest fire—needing its own destruction to give birth. There are mythological analogies to show that it embodies something the human imagination understands, can find attractive. (And are there seeds in man's nature that will never grow till revolution has cleared the ground of those who nourished them?) Here is the tree, transplanted from its native soil to Kew of all places, waiting hopefully for the Red Dawn of its consummation. Let the reader interpret the symbol as he pleases: it is double-edged as symbols should be.

On the whole I think we tended to bypass William Empson, respectfully, not because we were blind to the quality of the poems but because they asked for too much mental self-reliance and a different sort of response. What came home to us most at the time was the inward tension I have tried to describe, writ large in the language of social conflict; not the revolution but the mental preparation for it, the uprooting of old values in order to plant new. It was what gave to those three poets in particular their art of writing saga-fragments about a war fought in some country of the mind, soon to be transferred to earth.

In 1933 history was endorsing poetry. Dictatorships and violence in Europe, hunger-marches and derelict areas at home, made *New Signatures* a pointer to the right attitude, and its successor *New Country* took it up with more conviction. Michael Roberts in his preface said flatly that the intelligentsia had no choice but Communism—no longer because they were no more important than flowers in a field, but because short of a revolution all the cultural values they cared about were doomed—and advised them how and what to write to advance the good cause. The 'big three' all seemed to have moved on from internal debate to explicit alignment, though not quite in the docile way expected of an exemplary Marxist. The book had a substantial prose section, to which Cecil Day Lewis contributed a 'Letter to a Young Revolutionary' on the implications of joining the Party. He wrote from experience, and the sober prose assessment is strikingly unlike the poetic vision of dedicated and heroic comrades. It comes down to a resolution to drudge away, unthanked, with the wrong people in the right cause, instead of sticking to the right people in the wrong; and it slips in the ominous warning: 'You will have to keep a very constant eye on the end and a very tolerant one on some of the means.' Spender, in his closely argued essay 'Poetry and Revolution', stood up for the creative artist's vital freedom to create in his own way.

Auden's 'Prologue' ('O Love, the interest itself in thoughtless Heaven'), still one of his best poems, sets the will to revolution in a context ethical, evolutionary, historical, finally also mythological. His phrasing has that authoritative power with which a good poet, deeply concerned about his world, can sometimes put the trend of a generation's thinking into a reflection characteristically his own. The stanza,

> Some dream, say yes, long coiled in the ammonite's slumber
> Is uncurling, prepared to lay on our talk and kindness
> Its military silence, its surgeon's idea of pain

has this kind of summing-up quality, though it went through minor changes later, of the kind that show how thoroughly well-considered it was. The uncurling of the ammonite packs in the idea of revolution as a reversal of age-old order, yet a reversal within the order of nature. 'Some dream, say yes', was changed in a later version to 'Some possible dream', and afterwards restored to its original form—which gives more weight to the will to co-operate with destiny. 'Our talk and kindness' was toned down to 'our talk and reflection'. It is less brutal, but 'kindness' seems to me to be right all the same. 'Talk and kindness' epitomizes the considerate, late-Galsworthian civilization the young revolutionaries felt had become effete, and sharpens the point of the next line, which was not altered. It contains very completely the gloss upon violence in the dreams of the inexperienced. It is true that the metaphor hides an anthropomorphosis of the body politic; for the surgeon's idea, except in the vivisection of animals, is to inflict pain only for the benefit of the individual patient, not to inflict it on one for the benefit of others. Yeats, who had been closer to scenes of violence, wrote more more realistically:

> a drunken soldiery
> Can leave the mother, murdered at her door,
> To crawl in her own blood, and go scot-free

—but I doubt if anyone noticed Auden's euphemism, in a generation too young to have served in the First World War and not exposed to armed revolution except in their imagination.

Did we really in those days believe that the Revolution was

imminent? I find the question hard to answer now. It must have been clear, if we tried to think dispassionately, that the unbelievers were many and strong—the banks for instance, most of the army, the politicians in office—even in the Home Office, dutifully as they tapped telephones and sent their plainclothes men to Leftist meetings. But young Leftist intellectuals tend to be a closed group, talking a great deal to one another and seldom listening to anyone else. Perhaps the truth is that there was nothing else we could hope for with self-respect. In the next five years, however, the world was changing in ways our imagination had not foreseen, and as the hope of revolution gave place to the expectation of war, we learnt that we had been re-educating ourselves for a task we were not going to carry out. It was not an unprecedented turn of history. Euripides was fond of remarking that the gods always think of something men have not anticipated, and Auden's comment on our Victorian ancestors can be even more aptly misapplied—

Far-sighted as falcons, they looked down another future.

14

Empson's Poetry

Christopher Ricks

I

Empson might not disapprove of one's pondering a poem of his in terms of its story, since he has always stuck up for story as one of the great things about literature. Obviously so, one would have hoped, for a novel or a play. Of Virginia Woolf, Empson remarked that 'the impressionist method, the attempt to convey directly your own attitude to things, how you connect one thing with another, is in a sense fallacious; it tries to substitute for telling a story, as the main centre of interest, what is in fact one of the byproducts of telling a story' (*Scrutinies II*, 1931). Which drew him to Shakespeare: 'Even those delicate interconnections on which the impressionist method depends . . . need a story to make them intelligible, and even if Shakespeare (since I have dragged him in) could afford to abandon himself to these delicious correspondences he had first to get a strong and obvious story which would be effective on the stage.'

Some of Empson's most valuable vigilance has been in defence of story, seeing in real terms the situation out of which a person speaks. There is his salutary parenthesis about Lear which questions the status of imagery as Maynard Mack conceives it: 'he has now escaped from "the incessant conflict expressed by the images of the play" (not by the *story*, of course)' (*Essays in Criticism*, January 1967). There is yet another of the odd things about Hamlet: 'Here as elsewhere he gives a curious effect, also not unknown among his critics, of losing all interest for what has happened in the story; but it is more impressive in him than in them' (*Sewanee Review*, Winter 1953). Or there is the attack, which he has launched twice, on D. A. Traversi's incomprehension of Perdita's flower-speech: 'I think that this critical belief comes solely from being too proud to attend to the story' (*British Journal of Aesthetics*, January 1962; also *TLS*, 23 April 1964).

True, Empson's attending to the story sometimes comes to resemble a private detective dutifully making smoke without fire; his piece on *The Spanish Tragedy* (*Nimbus*, Summer 1956) hunts gamely for its unscotched quarry ('I think the point was obvious at the time, so obvious that it did not get stated in the text . . . I think, then, that the play could be produced so as to make pretty clear to the audience that Andrea had been murdered for love, but I admit that it is peculiar for the text never to say it . . . ['Correction'] I thus lose the one bit of the text which appeared to tell the secret. But Lodovico would have been unlikely to tell it anyhow, so this does not refute the theory'). Empty-handed. But never empty-hearted; witness the ebullient generosity of his reading of Joyce's *Ulysses* (*Kenyon Review*, Winter 1956), which believes in a magnanimous outcome for the story ('that Stephen *did* go to bed with Molly, very soon after the one day of the book'), and furthermore trusts that in the life of Joyce and of all concerned the outcome had been all the liberation that one could hope: 'I think it equally likely that the original Bloom couple did have a son as a result of this incident, a son by Bloom, who will now be about fifty, and that is why Joyce always felt such glee about the whole affair.'

Story, properly widened to include an apprehension of a real situation, is crucial too to Empson's criticism of poetry. *Milton's God* is in large part the reconstruction of a story which Empson glimpses in the interstices; he complains of Grant McColley's approach that 'this view lets you off attending to the story, and anything which does that ends by making you feel the poetry is bad' (p. 99). Likewise the poetry of Marvell, Empson has twice maintained, has been shrunk by critics: 'To imagine this personal situation helps you to make human sense of the paradoxes of the poem' (*Essays in Criticism*, January 1953); 'Literary critics nowadays I think lose the impact of the poem because they refuse to look at it in this real way' (*British Journal of Aesthetics*, January 1962). Empson delights in the zest of story ('*The Passionate Pilgrim* . . . starts with two genuine sonnets (138 and 144 in *Sonnets*) each of them implying plenty of story'; *Shakespeare: Narrative Poems*, 1968); and he deplores the narrow-minded squandering done by critics who throw away both a delight and a comprehension. Of 'Sailing to Byzantium', which F. A. C. Wilson misread as sailing *to* Ireland, Empson remarks: 'The effect of the mistake is that Mr Wilson ignores the "story", the actual human situation which the poet is describing with much humour and good sense' (*Review of English Literature*, July 1960). And, in a later essay, of 'Byzantium': 'One would like to have more story in the poem here' (*Essays Presented to Amy G. Stock*, 1965).

This sense of and for story is at work in Empson's criticism of the poet who means most to Empson's poems: Donne. 'The idea that the story needs explaining away is itself what needs explanation' (*Critical Quarterly*, Autumn 1966). Of 'The Expiration': 'So far they are merely lovers with feelings that drag them into conflict; but then he began inventing a larger and more Byronic story' (*Just So Much Honor*, 1972). Of 'Air and Angels': 'One needs to get the story of the poem clear'; the story in this case, it seems, is of the strong silent type: 'Between the two verses we are to assume he gets to bed with her' (*Kenyon Review*, Summer 1957).

And the story in Empson's own poems? On general grounds, I think it unlikely that poems as good as his best derive and create all their energies from those philosophical problems and pains, that siege of contrary ideas, which critics have rightly seen the poems as engaging with; certainly that siege is crucial to them, but the question for the critic—as it was for the poet—is that of the relation between such a siege and an 'actual human situation'. What is it about the two things—this contrariety and that situation —which precipitates the one thing, the poem? Riddling in so many ways, the poems are openly secretive, publicly so as poems, not privately as autobiography. And one remembers Empson's remark about Hamlet: 'he successfully kept a secret by displaying he had got one' (*Sewanee Review*, Winter 1953).

The best approach to the story in Empson's case, I think, is by first reconsidering the famous resonance of his contrarieties, his 'cymbal of clash', and then asking of the contrarieties what 'actual human situation' it is that they converge upon. Even with 'Bacchus', story is very much to the point; first, in that Empson's notes (too handily notorious) are primarily concerned to make clear the story which the poem tells; and second, in that the poem itself is concerned to progress from its initial story, a story which is allegory, to its conclusive story, a story which is an 'actual human situation'. The final twenty lines of the poem, which marry exultation and despair, give the ascendancy to the human story; in the simple words of Empson's note on the record, 'The poem then turns to an actual lady feeling what it has tried to describe.' But it is not only the poem which gains in dignity and humanity when story is respected; the same is true of a critical apprehension. Since Empson's poems are rightly known to be alive with significances (and sometimes stillborn with them, as is 'Plenum and Vacuum'), and Empson's criticism likewise, a critic is liable to be wrongly hypnotized by meaning—wrongly because exclusively, or wrongly because meaning in poetry finds itself too narrowly conceived. In 'Aubade', after the earthquake: 'Then I said The Garden? Laughing she said No.' No critical apprehension can come to anything much here which is not grounded upon the story, upon the fact that 'The Garden?' in the first place, in the actual human situation, means 'Is it safer to be out in the garden or inside the house when an earthquake has started?'

The year before he published 'Aubade', Empson made an essential point about obscurity in poetry when defending W. H. Auden against some strictures from David Daiches:

> The following line from Auden's *Orators* is quoted as 'free association', therefore demonstrably bad or rather null. It seems to me plain realism.
>
> Well?
>
> As a matter of fact the farm was in Pembrokeshire.
>
> We are told that though the separate lines of the poem have isolated prose meanings they are only connected by Auden's memory or subconsciousness, so cannot make poetry. But if you get the general context, of a man making a shameful confession, this creaking pretence of ease and nervous jerk into irrelevance is no kind of breach with 'meaning', whether with poetry or not; nor is it 'obscure'. It is a piece of horrible photography, and I remember shuddering as I first set eyes on it. But of course if a critic goes on expecting Pembrokeshire to symbolize something he is likely to get irritated. Often indeed when a poem goes on living in your mind, demanding to be re-read, you do not so much penetrate what at first seemed its obscurities as forget them; they turn out to be irrelevant. The critic therefore cannot come in and demonstrate that a poem is bad because it has no meaning—obviously, in the first place, because he may merely not know the meaning, but he can say it is too hard to know; yet there may be an answer to this too—that he is wrong to expect a meaning at the point he has chosen. (*Criterion*, April 1936)

What liberates Empson's criticism here—and Auden's line—is the respect for story. So the hope is that to ask about the story in Empson's poems will help with their meaning, not only in making clearer at some points what their meaning is, but also in making clearer at others why it is not exactly meaning that we should be expecting.

II

'Life involves maintaining oneself between contradictions that can't be solved by analysis; e.g. those of philosophy, which apply to all creatures, and the religious one about man being both animal and divine.' Empson's note to 'Bacchus' is well known, and known to widen out to take in a great many of his other poems; among them 'Arachne', which sets out life's contradictions with gruesome neatness; 'Aubade', with its antithetical refrains; and 'Let it go', where 'The contradictions cover such a range'. Empson has always been explicit about contradiction and conflict as the foundation of his poems—a true foundation for them because so for all poems and, wider yet, because of what life is. 'To take real pleasure in verse' is to feel 'so straddling a commotion and so broad a calm' (*Seven Types of Ambiguity*, p. xv). This is what we value in poems: 'That all these good qualities should be brought together is a normal part of a good poem; indeed, it is a main part of the value of a poem, because they are so hard to bring together in life' (p. 114). And what we value in myths, where 'incompatibles are joined' (*The Structure of Complex Words*, p. 242). And in goddesses: Venus in Shakespeare's poem remains somehow cool and calmly good, and 'the suggestion that the rowdy and lustful Venus keeps all these qualities makes her a goddess because she resolves the contradictions of normal life' (*Criterion*, April 1935).

Such is the *raison d'être* of ambiguity, Empson's first book of criticism; of pastoral and irony, his second; and of complex words, his third, where for instance 'the honest man in achieving normality reconciles a contradiction' (*Complex Words*, p. 196). And what is true of the arts is simply true of people: 'Indeed the way in which a person lives by these vaguely conceived opposites is the most important thing about his make-up; the way in which opposites can be stated so as to satisfy a wide variety of people, for a great number of degrees of interpretation, is the most important thing about the communication of the arts' (*Seven Types*, p. 221).

Yet there are two further dimensions of contradiction which man must accommodate to brace him. The first we glimpse in an uncharacteristic hesitancy ('it may be . . .'), when Empson remarks that 'it may be that the human mind can recognize actually incommensurable values, and that the chief human value is to stand up between them' (*Complex Words*, p. 421). One would have thought it plain that for Empson this is indeed the chief human value. Why then his hesitancy? Because he is aware of this further dimension of contradiction: that one should reject absolutes and even primacies, and should then accord an absolute status or a primacy to doing so. T. S. Eliot remarked: 'we can always accuse the pragmatist of believing his own doctrine in a sense which is not pragmatic but absolute—in other words, of eating his cake and having it too' (*New Statesman*, 29 December 1917). Similarly Empson saw that I. A. Richards was involved in some such straddling but that this was inevitable. Of Beauty in *The Foundations of Aesthetics* (by Richards, Ogden, and Wood), Empson says, reviewing the book's reissue:

> There is an inherent tug between the tentative solution of the problem, offered in the last chapter, and the theory of Multiple Definition presented before. This is inherently concerned to say that in such cases one should tabulate the sixteen or more meanings of the term in question and expect nothing further. What you have gained by your tabulation is that you can no longer be deceived—never again will an argument by an aesthetician prevent you from appreciating something unusual but good, or force you into admiring a narrow type of mysticism. But if the last chapter gives the answer, and furthermore if all the deluded aestheticians were actually fumbling after this solution, so that they would be convinced once they had been given it, then the whole position is quite different. All their sentences are simply wrong even from their own point of view, and they could be made to see it, had we but world enough and time. This fundamental ambivalence of course makes the book more interesting. But after the lapse of a generation one ought to be able to form some kind of view about which side holds the field, whether the Multiple Definition theory or the Synaesthesis theory has survived. If they both survive for ever they are only another of those tedious pairs of frustrated Kilkenny cats, like Aristotle and Plato.

The extreme brevity and caution, not to say timidity, of the final chapter puts the weight in favour of the Multiple Definition technique. But I have long been inclined to believe that the Ogden–Richards programme really did say what Beauty is, though of course only in a rough, tentative manner. If so, it is rather embarrassing for them; they are left with an Absolute Beauty on their hands, a baby which they never expected to have the trouble of bringing up. For that matter when Professor Richards wrote *The Principles of Literary Criticism*, not long after, he felt he needed to put in a chapter which in effect saddled him with an Absolute Goodness, an even more unwelcome baby. It is a familiar paradox; any serious attempt at establishing a relativity turns out to establish an absolute; in the case of Einstein the velocity of light, and I understand a good deal more by this time. (*Hudson Review*, Spring 1949)

There remains a further vista. For Empson—in poetry and in prose—insists not only that we must stand up between incommensurable values, but also that we must move, act, do something. The refusal to act or to decide, however rich its contemplation of complexity, is an act of indecision; prolonged, it can have no end but paralysis and neurosis. So among our other contradictions not the least is the tug between a reflective duty and a practical one. Empson's consciousness that 'life involves maintaining oneself between contradictions' is tensed against a further antithesis: that maintaining oneself is not enough in life. Hence his claim about the casket-scene in *The Merchant of Venice*: 'What the allegory meant to Shakespeare was probably something rather different from the Christian interpretation; I think it was that you ought to accept the actualities of life courageously even if rather unscrupulously, and not try to gloss over its contradictions and the depths that lie under your feet' (*Complex Words*, p. 124).

III

Empson has always written with poignancy and urgency about decisions. His poem 'Doctrinal Point', as he says, 'yearns to be always sure what to do' (record-notes):

> Magnolias, for instance, when in bud,
> Are right in doing anything they can think of;
> Free by predestination in the blood,

Saved by their own sap, shed for themselves,
Their texture can impose their architecture;
Their sapient matter is always already informed.

Whether they burgeon, massed wax flames, or flare
Plump spaced-out saints, in their gross prime, at prayer,
Or leave the sooted branches bare
To sag at tip from a sole blossom there
They know no act that will not make them fair.

'High Dive', his most cryptic and elaborated conception of what decision is, knows that 'One would be ashamed to walk down; the proper thing is to take a decisive action whose results are incalculable' (record-notes).

The shadowy, the complex, the inherited, the assumed, all play a part in decision. Hence Empson's view of 'the main business of a novelist':

By the very structure of the sentences, we are made to know what it felt like for the heroine to make up her mind. Of course in itself this is not new; it is the main business of a novelist to show his reader, by slow accumulations, all the elements and proportions of a decision, so that the reader knows how the character felt about it; but Mrs Woolf, so as to be much more immediately illuminating, can show how they are at the back of a decision at the moment it is taken. (*Scrutinies II*)

What sustains and invigorates *The Structure of Complex Words* is Empson's justified confidence that such verbal complexities are intimately involved in everyday decision: 'A man tends finally to make up his mind, in a practical question of human relations, much more in terms of these vague rich intimate words than in the clear words of his official language' (*Complex Words*, p. 158). And when Empson lets drop the word *decide* in writing of King Lear, it enforces respect and humanity: ' "O sides, you are too tough" implies that an explosion, even perhaps of madness, would be a relief, but as the insults sharpen he becomes wary and decides not to let them send him mad' (*Complex Words*, p. 133). A sense of Ezra Pound's personal tragedy, as well as of his misguided aesthetic, informs Empson's remark that 'the way his mind decides for him is rather too much above his own head' (*British Journal of Aesthetics*, January 1962).

There is in Empson a deep sympathy for those confronted with decision, as when he says of *Ulysses*:

All this background seems fussy and pedantic until you realize that it builds up the terrible refusal to choose, done by Stephen in the Question-and-Answer chapter . . . The chapter certainly need not be taken to mean that Stephen will never accept; surely the chief point of it is that in real life he couldn't decide, at such a peculiarly exhausting moment. (*Kenyon Review*, Winter 1956)

To remind ourselves of what, for Empson, it is that Stephen was having to decide, is a direct route to Empson's poems and to a contrariety they embody. For Stephen is deciding whether or not to sleep with Molly Bloom and (consequentially) whether to free Bloom to father a son. In Empson's poems, as in the life of any sensitive person, the fear of a commitment to love is entwined with the fear of that most daunting and exhilarating of all human commitments, the begetting of a new life. As Empson said apropos Imagery (in a sentence, incidentally, which speaks of 'the variety of life and the decisiveness of the immediate judgments upon it'), what is to be deduced from a poem is 'usually a very plain fact of life' (*British Journal of Aesthetics*, January 1962). The plainest fact of life is the facts of life. A great many of Empson's poems seem to me to comprise within their story or situation a sense of this most incalculable of high dives, the getting of children. But let me first quote one of Empson's most fervid responses to a man's decision:

Donne really does intend to boast about his marriage; you can impute bad motives to him, or lies, and you are within the field of human probability, but if you say he insinuated a 'bitter irony' into the middle of this fighting and defiant praise of the most decisive action of his life you are mistaking him for some other author. (*Just So Much Honor*)

A glory of Donne is the intensity alike of his uniqueness and of his commonalty; it is splendidly true that his marriage was specially courageous, and yet true too that for many people the most decisive action of their lives is their marriage. Unless it is their getting a child. For that act is even more awe-inspiring; of all decisions it is the most grandly simple and extensive, in being a decision to create a life which will itself then make decisions; in being so supremely irrevocable (even more so than the act of marrying); and in that its status as a decision—is it a decision, exactly?—is so insinuatingly in doubt. One could always feel that, with so much uncertainty about it, the steely responsibility of a decision need never quite make itself felt; the lap, that of the gods. And contraception has complicated and intensified all this, in that it patently heightens decision. Of Othello's jealousy, Empson has said: 'it seems to me that Othello's principles about the matter were all wrong, let alone the way he applied them. The advent of contraceptives has taken a lot of strain off the topic' (*Complex Words*, p. 245). But contraception has not simply taken strain off the decision to have children, as against the decision not to have them; on the contrary, it has in some respects intensified the strain, in that it has made choice (decision, and responsibility unignorably entered upon) more manifestly part of the act of love. Nothing ever simply reduces strain all round, and one need not be in any way unappreciative of contraception in maintaining that it does nothing to lessen, and something to heighten, certain strains inseparable from this grave decision. Most people's lives have at some point been haunted and thrilled by this gravest of responsibilities, albeit in imagination or in anticipation; not many poems recognize this but I think that Empson's poems do, sometimes being truly fearful and at other times truly robust.

IV

For anybody, begetting a child is a high and deep decision. But for those who believe certain things of life it involves maintaining oneself between contradictions. It is not rare for people to believe that the world, or the world now, is such that children should not be brought into it; it is uncommon, though by no means unheard of, for people to act upon this belief, and on principle to have no children; more usual is for people both to acknowledge the force of a grim truth and yet also to have children because of what seems a different duty and delight. I stress the ordinariness of the tug because I think that in so far as they involve such feelings Empson's poems are not a bit abstruse or idiosyncratic. But such feelings did press with further force in his case. For it is not just the conditions of modern life (rectifiable perhaps?, the would-be parent may ask faintly), but the very conditions of life which have seemed tragic to Empson. To anybody convinced of how much pain, waste, loss,

and despair there is in life, it must always be a question; believing
life to be so, why create a child to endure it?

Granted, Empson's crucially sombre word *waste* can sometimes
leave room for an accompanying delight, as when he says of
Virginia Woolf that 'her images, glittering and searching as they
are, spreading out their wealth of feeling, as if spilt, in the mind,
give one just that sense of waste that is given by life itself'
(*Scrutinies II*). But elsewhere the sad weight of Empson's words is
such as to make it a real question whether life is a gift we should
give. 'The waste remains, the waste remains and kills.'

> It is only in degree that any improvement of society could pre-
> vent wastage of human powers; the waste even in a fortunate
> life, the isolation even of a life rich in intimacy, cannot but be
> felt deeply, and is the central feeling of tragedy. (*Some Versions
> of Pastoral*, p. 5)

'Isolation' and 'intimacy' there hint at that creation, the family,
which both fosters what is good and protective in life and also
furthers life which cannot much be protected. A child, then, can
be the bleakest reminder of the loss inherent in life:

> It [a Romantic and Victorian feeling about children] depends
> on a feeling . . . that no way of building up character, no
> intellectual system, can bring out all that is inherent in the
> human spirit, and therefore that there is more in the child than
> any man has been able to keep. (*Some Versions*, pp. 260–1)

It is natural that the most resonant and yet most secure expression
of such feelings in Empson should embody one of life's contradictions: 'The feeling that life is essentially inadequate to the
human spirit, and yet that a good life must avoid saying so, is
naturally at home with most versions of pastoral' (*Some Versions*,
p. 114). Naturally at home too with Empson, the very prose makes
that clear; and yet implicated in parenthood's decision. For if life
is essentially inadequate to the human spirit, should we blithely
create new human spirits? And if we should, must it not be with
the same consciousness of an unappeasable other principle, un-
appeased but overruled, which informs our other decisions in
life?

There is no doubt about the gaiety and buoyancy that are also
strong in Empson. But the darkness is no less deep than they are.
Of *Measure for Measure* he says (and it is patently apt to his own

beliefs) that it includes 'the idea that one must not act on these absolutes prematurely. Even granting that the conditions of life are inherently repulsive, a man makes himself actually more repulsive by acting on this truth' (*Complex Words*, p. 284). The paradox, the straddling, make clear that what is at stake is close to Empson's heart, and I do not think that 'Even granting . . .' is a mere granting, a purely concessive entertaining of a supposition totally at odds with Empson's own sense of life. (Nor, of course, does it comprise the major part of his sense of life.) Empson has, after all, reprinted from his first book of poems that translation from *The Fire Sermon* which now stands as the full-page epigraph to his *Collected Poems*; it is true that he urged Allan Rodway not to make so much of it, but his way of doing so was scrupulous and therefore revelatory:

> The Fire Sermon itself is unlike most of Buddhism, and leaves Christianity far behind, in maintaining that all existence as such, even in the highest heaven, is inherently evil. Such is the great interest of it . . . But, all the same, when I mention fire in my verse I mean it to have the usual confused background of ideas, not (as Mr Rodway thinks) the specific and raging dogma of the Fire Sermon. I can be sure of this because, though I probably never thought about the Fire Sermon when writing or revising, I had already decided that I thought its doctrine wrong, though fascinating and in a way intelligible. You might say that it is present as one extreme of the range of human thought, because the poetry often tries to take the position 'what I am saying is admitted to be true, though people look at it in so many different ways'; but even so it is pretty remote, and not appealed to. (*Essays in Criticism*, October 1956)

If all existence is inherently evil, we should think twice about bringing anything into existence.

Moreover Empson has drawn attention to some such tug in two poets who particularly matter to him. Of Rochester's 'Satire on Man', he has said: 'One cannot help regarding it less as a general truth than as a source of evidence about the deep dissatisfaction or resentment with the world which drove him to his death' (*New Statesman*, 28 November 1953). And of Dylan Thomas: 'You must realise that he was a very witty man, with a very keen though not at all poisoned recognition that the world contains horror as well as delight; his chief power as a stylist is to convey a sickened loathing which somehow (within the phrase) enforces a welcome for the eternal necessities of the world' (*New Statesman*, 15 May 1954). Much of that strange loathing and welcoming is directed by Thomas to thinking about begetting, and one remembers Empson's comment on 'Before I knocked and flesh let enter': 'Jesus by choosing virginity ended an immense series of births, betraying the purpose of the creator which his mother had obeyed; but he did not end it for Dylan Thomas' (*Listener*, 28 October 1971).

Empson's recognition of the world is likewise 'not at all poisoned'. But it is styptic; I think for instance of the terms in which he ends his essay on *Hamlet*:

> The eventual question is whether you can put up with the final Hamlet, a person who frequently appears in the modern world under various disguises, whether by Shakespeare's fault or no. I would always sympathize with anyone who says, like Hugh Kingsmill, that he can't put up with Hamlet at all. But I am afraid it is within hail of the more painful question whether you can put up with yourself and the race of man. (*Sewanee Review*, Spring 1953)

A real question for Empson and not just a final flourish; a question then which must ask us why we wish to further the race of man.

And yet I can't help being aware that Empson is likely to repudiate this bit at least; I must say why I think this may be so, especially as it bears on his having given up writing poetry for the last twenty years (and very little in the ten years before that). I believe that the various tensions and contradictions involved in begetting were not only one of the important subjects but one of the important sources of energy for his poems. An enabling tension was that between the ordinary human wish to beget life and the equally ordinary sense that life is too dark and bleak a gift. But this tension has progressively slackened for Empson. In the first place, for good personal reasons—it is after all a tension more likely to precede than to follow parenthood, and Empson's giving up writing poetry dates more or less (the later poems are important but very few) from his marriage in 1941 and his becoming a father in the following years. In the second place, because of a shift of belief. Empson no longer has quite the same sense of life; or, more specifically, the main thrust of his writing for the last twenty years has been against those 'neo-Christians' who peddle a wilfully gloomy and lowminded account of this life. The necessity (quite right too) to dissociate himself from such monkishness has increasingly made Empson put his stress where he had not previously put it. His earlier semi-acknowledgment that 'life is essentially inadequate to the human spirit' could too easily be wrested to give comfort (that is, a gratifying comfortlessness) to the enemy.

In 1949 Empson could still feel that the holy enemy was 'holy optimism', as when he objected to R. B. Heilman's 'evasive pietistic technique' at work on one of 'the key sentences of the play [*King Lear*] expressing despair':

> When we are born we cry that we are come
> To this great stage of fools.

Empson rightly insisted that 'the main statement is very plain and says that life on earth is an evil. To twist it round into a bit of holy optimism seems to me to falsify the play' (*Kenyon Review*, Spring 1949). Lear's words are a key sentence in more than one way, since they seize upon the idea that the baby at the moment of its birth is uniquely able to testify to the wrong that has been done to it in having been born. As Empson said elsewhere: 'To the Freudian, indeed, it is the human infant to whose desires this life is essentially inadequate; King Lear found a mystical pathos in the fact that the human infant, alone among the young of the creatures, is subject to impotent fits of fury' (*Some Versions*, p. 249).

Still, in 1949 'holy optimism' shocked Empson; since then, it has been holy pessimism which he has set himself to challenge. 'Modern critics tend to assume both (*a*) that it isn't artistic to preach any doctrine and (*b*) that the only high-minded doctrine to preach is despair and contempt for the world' (*Kenyon Review*, Spring 1958). (What Empson's poems do with despair is not preach it—but few poems have made more, and so variously, of the word.) *Tom Jones* possesses its secret: 'Actually, the modern critic does know what kind of thing the secret is; but he has been badgered by neoclassicism and neo-Christianity and what not, whereas the secret is humanist, liberal, materialist, recommending happiness on earth.' No more than Fielding are we to concur with the Old Man of the Hill, 'who thanks God he has renounced so lunatic a world'. In the same vein, of *When We Dead Awaken*: 'there is nothing in the play to show that Ibsen isn't being "mystical", in the sense of simply praising the double suicide as a means of getting to a less nasty world' (*Kenyon Review*, Winter 1956).

It is on these grounds that Empson repudiates Maynard Mack's view of *King Lear*: 'Shakespeare's audience too would want to know what the saint will do next, after his daughter is killed; how the story will go on. It makes one realize the peculiarity of the assumptions of Professor Mack; who, as he only wants to hear a monk telling the audience to be monks, will not admit that there is any story at all' (*Essays in Criticism*, January 1967). And when Mack speaks of the play as a 'metaphor, or myth, about the human condition', Empson swoops: 'What the metaphor recommends, so far as we can gather, is becoming a monk or a yogi, on the ground that the world is inherently inadequate for us.' And yet aren't those last words, offered for our scorn, perilously close to what had once been offered for our chastened acceptance: that 'life is essentially inadequate to the human spirit'?

In 1964 Empson repudiated the slander that he had in one particular way slandered God the Father: 'I did not say he was bad because he created the world, and I think that idea a disgusting one. It is petulant snootiness to say "The world is not good enough for me"; the world is glorious beyond all telling, and far too good for any of us' (*Critical Quarterly*, Spring 1964). The energy and generosity of that are fine (and they know their enemy), but they manifest an energy of a very different kind, and of a very different direction, from that which centrally animated Empson's poems, delighted though the poems are too by the rich oddity of the world.

Let me try to stave off two misconstructions. In suggesting that Empson's poems found power and truth in the tug between a sense of life's darkness (which would sway us not to bring children into life) and a sense of the deep right wish to propagate, I am not imagining any neurosis or personal predicament in the poet; I think it ordinary to feel some such tug, and in so far as these poems feel a more than ordinary tug that is because of a public—perfectly discussable—commitment to certain beliefs, and in particular to beliefs about where we stand: between contradictions. And in stressing a shift, at least in emphasis, in Empson's sense of the world, at one with his crusade against neo-Christianity, I am not implying that he was ever much of a monk, or that he has modified his views for combative purposes, but simply pointing out that the new energies and emphases are very different—a fact which (whether as chicken or as egg) is likely to have something to do with Empson's stopping writing poetry. The holy and the monkish are certainly part of this shrubbery of ideas, for Empson as for most people. Take his words about Philip II: 'One could hardly say that he got Portugal by marriage; he got it because the more direct male heirs of that house had become too holy to produce children' (*Nimbus*, Summer 1956). Or this: 'A monk oughtn't to have a baby, but somebody else has to have babies, if only to keep up the supply of monks' (*Critical Quarterly*, Spring 1964). Or Empson's deploring the critic who finds 'The Ancient Mariner' 'a spiritual allegory in which the neophyte (the Guest) is gradually beaten down until he attains "a thorough acceptance of spiritual values", and after that, of course, he can't breed' (*Coleridge's Verse: a Selection*, 1972, p. 77).

v

The many dismaying parenthoods in the story of Oedipus have long been important to Empson; witness his poem 'Four Legs, Three Legs, Two Legs', or the play which he wrote as an undergraduate, *Three Stories*, of which *Granta* in 1927 spoke with a graceless ambiguity: 'He had achieved an almost complete mastery of his Oedipus complex, and used it for very intelligent purposes.' His criticism too has surged with it, most obviously on *Hamlet*:

> A feeling that this hero is allowed to act in a peculiar way which is yet somehow familiar, because one has been tempted to do it oneself, is surely part of the essence of the story. There is a clear contrast with Oedipus, who had no Oedipus Complex. He had not wanted to kill his father and marry his mother, even 'unconsciously'; if he came to recognize that he had wanted it, that would weaken his bleak surprise at learning he had done it. (*Sewanee Review*, Spring 1953)

But more important than the Oedipus Complex is ordinary parenthood, more simply fearful, strange, and noble. Empson's criticism has always been especially vivid, imaginative and central when it contemplates parenthood, its responsibilities and the world's. He thinks with humanity about those who are thinking about it; his rebuke to D. A. Traversi focuses upon Perdita's cool courage in using the word *breed*:

> No more than, were I painted, I would wish
> This youth to say, 'twere well, and only therefore
> Desire to breed by me.

All the talk about the flowers, which Mr Traversi finds symbolic, was unlikely to hit an audience with any shock. What did do that was the word *breed* used coolly by a young virgin. It would sound shameless if she were less fiercely virtuous; but somehow the effect of being so farmyard is to appear very aristocratic. (*TLS*, 23 April 1964; similarly, *British Journal of Aesthetics*, January 1962)

He delights in her virgin generosity and pluck, and he had manifested a comparable zest when it suddenly came to him that Tennyson was making a practical point about the high snow-pure barrenness of virginity in *The Princess*:

When I was ski-ing recently I found myself reciting that Love is of the valleys:

'nor cares to walk
With Death and Morning on the silver horns',

and suddenly realized that that grand lyric comes from *The Princess*. It means that the girls won't get husbands if they go to college, and if you start from there all the description fits in. (*Criterion*, October 1937)

There is, once more, his reading of *Ulysses*:

Bloom is described, with startling literary power so that there is no doubt about it, as having a very specific neurosis: the death of his infant son ten years before gave him a horror of the business of having a child so that he can't try to have another one. At the same time he longs to have a son, and so does Molly . . . He feels that if he could plant on her a lover he was fond of, who would even take his advice instead of jeering at him, he could even now have this son himself by his wife . . . To be sure, the novel does not ask you to believe that Bloom *did* have a son, but it does expect you to believe that on this day Bloom is getting a real opportunity to produce a son; the problem as it is shown to you is not trivial. (*Kenyon Review*, Winter 1956)

Such is the largeness of a story; it is characteristic too of Empson that he should submit himself to a detail of wording, as in his question about the first sentence of Dylan Thomas's 'A Refusal to Mourn the Death, by Fire, of a Child in London'; Empson ponders 'the distinction between *making* and *fathering*; perhaps the construction of *mankind* is a special process, as in Genesis' (*Strand Magazine*, March 1947). A special process for mankind, certainly; the difference between the birth of a child and that of a flower or a leaf is seen with cool responsible pathos in a ballad:

> She leaned her back against a thorn
> (Fine flowers in the valley)
> And there she has her young child born
> (And the green leaves they grow rarely).

'The effect of the contrast is not simple; perhaps it says "Life went on, and in a way this seems a cruel indifference to her suffering, but it lets us put the tragedy in its place, as we do when we sing about it for pleasure"' (*Complex Words*, pp. 347–8).

Parenthood, though, is more than—though never less than—giving birth. I think of Empson's insistence that when one ponders the soldier's question before the dead Cleopatra, 'Is this well done?', 'one must remember that by choosing this death she destroys her children only to avoid a hurt to her pride' (*Some Versions*, pp. 233–4). Or his response to *Paradise Lost*, where he exults in what the poetry intimates ('Nor where Abassin Kings their issue guard': 'all the references to guarding children remind us that children were the result of the fall'; *Some Versions*, p. 174); but where he excoriates Milton's God for withholding from Adam and Eve a clear warning that their posterity would suffer the results of the Fall. Or there is Empson's recent discussion of 'The Phoenix and the Turtle', which asks us to recall the story, the human situation, of Sir John Salisbury, a story of progeny: 'The subsequent poems all deal with Salisbury's domestic life, wife or child being mentioned every time, so that Shakespeare's poem acts as a watershed' (*Shakespeare: Narrative Poems*). Shakespeare's poem, moreover, is about a principled abstention from parenthood: 'Oddly enough Shakespeare manages to work the same reflection [as Jonson] into his mood of total praise; the reproduction of the Phoenix, he surmises, has only failed because of the married chastity of the couple':

> Leaving no posterity:
> 'Twas not their infirmity,
> It was married chastity.

A scarcely less mysterious abstention from parenthood is the

subject of many of Shakespeare's Sonnets, among them some
which most engaged Empson early in *Seven Types of Ambiguity*.

> Which eyes not yet created shall ore-read . . .
>   (Sonnet 81)

> These shadows of his perfection were once to have been his
> children, but Shakespeare's partly scoptophile desire to see him
> settled in love has by now been with a painful irony thwarted
> or over-satisfied, and they are now no more than those who
> read his praise. (*Seven Types*, pp. 53–4)

Empson's exploration of these Sonnets does justice to both pulls
here: first a recognition of a natural trepidation at the prospect of
parenthood, which paraphrases 'To give away your selfe, keeps
your selfe still' (Sonnet 16) as 'you are not less yourself because
you have had children' (p. 56)—indeed not, but the idea is not at
all thought to be a mad one, and has its undeniable magnetism;
but second a recognition that we too, like Shakespeare, would
have to call upon an Irish bull (with its genially mysterious self-
enfoldedness) to assert the purpose of the creator: 'You had a
Father, let your Son say so' (Sonnet 13; p. 52).

Again, there is a special urgency in Empson's challenge to L. C.
Knights (delivered twice), since it manifests the meeting of a
central plea to respect story with a most bitter childlessness:

> The great question 'How many children had Lady Macbeth?'
> had better be fitted in here. The question cannot be regarded as
> merely farcical, as one might say, 'Who wants children anyhow?'
> Macbeth is far more concerned to found a royal line than to be
> king himself; he howls on and on against the threat that his
> descendants will be supplanted by Banquo's. When Lady
> Macbeth says she would kill her child she is felt to be ridiculous
> as well as devilish, because without a child the main purpose
> would be defeated. But the murdered or the helpless child
> comes echoing back into the play all through (as Mr Cleanth
> Brooks pointed out); it is the one thing strong enough to
> defeat Macbeth and the whole philosophy he has adopted. In
> the story, however, we are left in doubt whether the Macbeths
> have any children; it would be symbolically appropriate if they
> hadn't, but Macbeth's talk would be absurd unless they have,
> as perhaps it is; and there the matter is left. It is the only crux

in the play, I think, which need be regarded as a radical dramatic ambiguity. (*Kenyon Review*, Winter 1952)

In one of his most striking speeches, Macbeth implies that he has incurred Hell for the sake of his family, sacrificing himself to found a dynasty ('To make *them* Kings? The sons of Banquo, Kings?'). He is the last person to have thought it didn't matter whether he had a son or not. (*Critical Quarterly*, Autumn 1965)

Such is childlessness as nemesis. Empson has been no less vivid about the opposite terror, parenthood as nemesis:

There are times when Lear maintains that vengeance is the due of all parenthood, however licit:

> Is it the fashion, that discarded fathers
> Should have thus little mercy on their flesh?
> Judicious punishment! 'Twas this flesh begot
> These pelican daughters.

He starts saying this as soon as he is mad; it is treated as a signal to the audience that he is now mad. (*Essays in Criticism*, January 1967)

It is Empson's sanity which rightly insists that we know Lear to be mad to consider parenthood so; but the poignancy of Lear's words, and of Empson's comment, is a matter of yet finding the hideous sentiment appallingly magnetic. As with Edgar:

> The gods are just, and of our pleasant vices
> Make instruments to plague us;
> The dark and vicious place where thee he got
> Cost him his eyes.

'And the thrill of Edgar's remark, sure enough, is to imply: "He begot a monster by it; yourself who betrayed him to torture and death."' An implication and a thrill to be resisted. The critical mind which responds so deeply and truly to such imaginings is not one which can invariably contemplate begetting with equanimity.

At the other extreme, relatedly so, is Empson's Alice. Many have thought this essay his best sustained criticism of a single work. If it is so, that may be because Empson's tart affection, sympathy, and respect for Alice are so truly matched by a deep comprehension of Lewis Carroll's bachelorhood, incorporating a dismay at most children which is by no means abolished by a delight in a special child. Empson's prose rises to a delicious hyperbole of such dismayed distaste, with the prose not shrinking at all at its imagined shrinking:

> One need not read Dodgson's satirical verses against babies to see how much he would dislike a child wallowing in its tears in real life. The fondness of small girls for doing this has to be faced early in attempting to prefer them, possibly to small boys, certainly to grown-ups; to a man idealising children as free from the falsity of a rich emotional life their displays of emotion must be particularly disconcerting. The celibate may be forced to observe them, on the floor of a railway carriage for example, after a storm of fury, dabbling in their ooze; covertly snuggling against mamma while each still pretends to ignore the other. (*Some Versions*, p. 272)

Empson is no celibate, but he is invigoratingly free from condescension towards celibates because he is not lordlily free from their dismays.

It may be objected that I am making too much of those things in Empson's criticism which respond strongly to parenthood, in that any critic who has much interest in life is likely to have something to say on so important a matter. In fact it would be very difficult to assemble worthwhile *aperçus* on parenthood and begetting from many a distinguished critic, and in any case Empson's sensibility and conscience have here been exceptionally moved. Let me quote two paragraphs from a poetry review in 1931; the humanity, lucidity, and courtesy with which the first poet is dispraised and the second praised have a lot to do with story, with what is at issue in the respective poems: two versions of parenthood and of other-worldliness.

> Mr Robinson Jeffers, like Mr Galsworthy, often seems to write from his conscience rather than his sensibility. He chooses painful subjects, one may suspect, less because he feels strongly about them than because he feels it shameful not to feel strongly about them; because one cannot be comfortable and unimaginative, with the world as it is. You may honour this feeling very much and yet say it does not produce good writing; it gives an air of poking at the reader, or trying to catch him on the raw, and it tends to falsify a dramatic issue. At the crisis of the 'Loving Shepherdess' the hero nearly remembers that her life could be

saved by a Caesarean operation; he can't quite think of it, and the word Caesar, thus suggested, becomes a vision of human and then heavenly glory, which is described very finely and apparently justifies his failure to help her. For a moment this may seem the soul of tragedy, but next moment it seems cock-eyed. He had remembered enough to tell her to go to a clinic, anyway; I speak under correction about visions, but I don't believe he would have had a vision just then if he had not been a shamefully self-centred person.

'Marina' seems to me one of Mr Eliot's very good poems; better than anything in 'Ash Wednesday'. The dramatic power of his symbolism is here in full strength, and the ideas involved have almost the range of interest, the full orchestra, of the 'Waste Land'. One main reason for this is the balance maintained between otherworldliness and humanism; the essence of the poem is the vision of an order, a spiritual state, which he can conceive and cannot enter, but it is not made clear whether he conceives an order in this world to be known by a later generation (like Moses on Pisgah) or the life in heaven which is to be obtained after death (like Dante). One might at first think the second only was meant, but Marina, after all, was a real daughter; is now at sea, like himself, rather than already in the Promised Land; and is to live 'in a world of time beyond me', which can scarcely be a description of Heaven. At any rate, the humanist meaning is used at every point as a symbol of the otherworldly one; this seems the main point to insist on in a brief notice because it is the main cause of the richness of the total effect. In either case the theme is the peril and brevity of such vision. (*Nation and Athenaeum*, 21 February 1931)

VI

It was always clear that Empson's poems were graced by Donne, and he has been explicit about it more than once:

In the twenties, when my eyes were opening, it was usual for critics to consider that Donne in his earlier poetry held broad and enlightened views on church and state, that he was influenced by the recent great scientific discoveries, and that he used the theme of freedom in love partly as a vehicle for these ideas . . . I was imitating this Donne, the poet as so conceived,

in my own verse at the time with love and wonder, and I have
never in later years come across any good reason for the
universal change of opinion about him at the start of the
thirties. (*Just So Much Honor*; similarly *Kenyon Review*, Summer
1957, and *Critical Quarterly*, Autumn 1966)

For Empson, and for his poems, Donne's love-poems embody a
defiance of church and state, an adventurous freedom brought
home by 'making the idea of the inhabited planet a symbol of the
lovers' independence from the world' (*Sewanee Review*, Summer
1955). Hence Empson's title 'Donne the Space Man'. Or, twenty
years earlier:

> The idea that you can get right away to America, that human
> affairs are not organised round one centrally right authority
> (*e.g.* the Pope) is directly compared to the new idea that there
> are other worlds like this one, so that the inhabitants of each
> can live in their own way. (*Some Versions*, p. 75)

My argument about Empson's poems does not entail a consideration of just how much truth there is in this view of Donne; but it
entails some other questions. If Donne's poems celebrate freedom
and independence, do they limit that to independence from
church and state? Or do they in some way recognize those other
threats or limitations upon the freedom and independence of
young lovers, those involved in parenthood, both in our being
children and in our perhaps begetting them? After all, 'one
centrally right authority' may be that of the family from which we
depend (often at one with church and state but not to be escaped
by escaping those); an inherent obstacle to young lovers' simply
being able to 'live in their own way' is the family, both that
to which we belong and that which may come to belong to
us.

Praising Donne, Empson spoke of 'that secret largeness of
outlook which is his fascination' (*Some Versions*, p. 84). Some of
that secret largeness is to be divined, I think, in the particular way
in which the poems celebrate young love's freedom from parenthood, young love seen at a moment when it has the right, for now,
to be free from responsibilities which it inherits, and the right
to be free, as yet, from responsibilities to its heirs. Donne's best
poems are rich in the way Empson suggests, rich with a buoyancy
of freedom; yet they feel quite without sentimentality, whereas

there would be sentimentality in a presentation of young love as naturally, always, everywhere, for ever independent of all which family brings as dependence. ('All my perfumes, I give most willingly/To embalm thy father's corse; What? will he die?')

In Donne's poems there is a marked absence of such dependences; absence, in that they seldom directly figure; marked, in that they persistently surface as metaphors or ways of speaking. Young love is presented as possessing a season; or its deserved weightlessness is made real to us (and made a recognition of the realities of life) by the fact that as it floats so little clogged by gravity we see it accoutred with what would ordinarily be weight. Accoutred with metaphors. Donne's poems do not feel irresponsible, they feel non-responsible—but responsibly so, honouring a season when anything else would be too glum a gravity. In short, I think that Donne's poems repeatedly move us to a recognition of responsibilities inseparable from love, those of parenthood; responsibilities, though, which young love should not as yet confront but which no one should imagine not to exist.

J. B. Broadbent has said of Donne that 'he has to wriggle, joke, argue himself out of the dead end, the shut bedroom, whence, like Mellors' cottage, history and children, as well as wives and busybodies, are excluded' (*Poetic Love*, p. 224). But a consciousness of exclusion, the sense that a door is shut which cannot, should not, always stay so: this is very different from an ignorance or an ignoring. Children, wives: can they not continually be heard in Donne outside that shut door? They make their presence felt—as metaphors or figures, yes, but not forbidden to call up the real and the literal.

As a man Donne was to have ample reason to be exceptionally aware of his family, his in both directions: the greatness of his mother's family behind her, her three marriages, his five siblings; and in due course his intrepid marriage, his nine children and two others stillborn (in Empson's words, 'gradually killing his wife by giving her a child every year'; *Kenyon Review*, Summer 1957); eventually the death of his mother in her eighties, two months before his own death.

The curious weight of the early poems, though, at one with their weightlessness, is partly a matter of their intimation that 'the right true end of love' is not, as young lovers should be forgiven (liked, even) for supposing, making love but making life. An intimation recurrently to be glimpsed in metaphors, asides, or details of the story.

> But since my soul, whose child love is,
> Takes limbs of flesh, and else could nothing do,
> More subtle than the parent is
> Love must not be, but take a body too.
>
> ('Air and Angels')

At one extreme there are the bitterly unreal realities of 'The Curse', with its 'if he had not / Himself incestuously an heir begot', and 'His sons, which none of his may be', and its 'stepdames'. At the other extreme there are the children, agog, who appear in 'Farewell to Love' as part of a metaphor which tells how lovers sadly tire of their treat; the children hot for gingerbread grow into those riddling lines, so variously punctuated, which tell how

> that other curse of being short,
> And only for a minute made to be
> Eager, desires to raise posterity.

The desire to raise posterity is there—in bidding farewell to love —made explicit; elsewhere some sense of it animates poems as different as 'The Good Morrow' ('were we not weaned till then, / But sucked on country pleasures, childishly?'), and 'The Indifferent' ('Will it not serve your turn to do, as did your mothers?'). True, the getting with child in 'Song' is 'Get with child a mandrake root'; true, the midwife in 'Elegy 19' is an audacity of metaphor:

> Then since I may know,
> As liberally, as to a midwife, show
> Thyself:

What is 'begot' in 'The Will' is love, and in 'A Nocturnal upon S. Lucy's Day' it is the poet ('I am re-begot'); what the lovers 'produce' in 'A Lecture upon the Shadow' is two shadows, and the infants that grow are 'our infant loves'; what is 'pregnant' in 'Love's Alchemy' is the alchemist's pot, and in 'A Valediction: of Weeping' his loved one's tears:

> For thy face coins them, and thy stamp they bear,
> And by this mintage they are something worth,
> For thus they be
> Pregnant of thee.

Yet is it not the case that these last lines, and the others too, depend for their liberating force upon invoking, even while resisting, the idea of that more usual pregnancy, that usual way in which a woman coins those miniatures which bear her stamp?

It is this tacit sense, so richly humane, of what begetting truly is that seems to me to hold Donne's poetry together, ranging as it does from, say, 'The Flea' to 'The Ecstasy'. For what gives 'The Flea' a bounding lightness and not just a levity is the notion that the flea is like a child of their love:

> Me it sucked first, and now sucks thee,
> And in this flea, our two bloods mingled be . . .
>
> And pampered swells with one blood made of two . . .
>
> Oh stay, three lives in one flea spare,
> Where wee almost, nay more than married are.
> This flea is you and I, and this
> Our marriage bed, and marriage temple is;
> Though parents grudge, and you, w'are met,
> And cloistered in these living walls of jet.

That the flea is in a way their baby informs even the diminutive horror when it is murdered in its miniature innocence of blood. And, vaster but related, 'The Ecstasy' insinuates through its metaphors a world not metaphorical:

> Where, like a pillow on a bed,
>   A pregnant bank swelled up, . . .
>
> And pictures in our eyes to get
>   Was all our propagation . . .
>
> When love, with one another so
>   Interinanimates two souls,
> That abler soul, which thence doth flow,
>   Defects of loneliness controls . . .
>
> As our blood labours to beget
>   Spirits, as like souls as it can,
> Because such fingers need to knit
>   That subtle knot, which makes us man . . .

My point is not that such metaphors give away what the poem is *really* up to; rather, that the poem's meaning is the relation between the metaphorical sense and the literal world from which they are drawn. It speaks beautifully, not slightly, of the soul; but 'that abler soul' which flows from interinanimation, and which controls 'defects of loneliness', is estimated truly by being seen against the ordinary child of love, a child who controls the defects of loneliness in another manner. It is the literal meaning which, never belittling soul, yet protects the poem (in Donne's great words elsewhere) 'From thinking us all soul'.

The rich love-poems of Donne, then, to which the young Empson richly responded, seem to me alive with thought and feeling about begetting and posterity and about the relation between a true worldliness and a true unworldliness; alive in a way which was to create such a life in Empson's own poems. Empson's recent criticism of Donne has spoken of the ordinarily biographical things about Donne: his need to 'feed his wife and children'; 'if she is dead, there is nothing to keep him out of the Church any longer, and (though the thought is not fit for verse) money will have to be got hold of for all those children' (*Critical Quarterly*, Autumn 1966). But for my purposes the emphasis is different; and when Empson remarks gruffly that 'Donne says nothing in verse about his children because he found them merely a nuisance, but this didn't keep him from being devoted to his wife; I expect Blake and D. H. Lawrence would have felt the same, if they had not been spared', I need to urge the claims of a different angle: not why Donne says nothing in verse about his children, but whether he says anything about the thought of childing—a thought superbly fit for verse.

'The separate planet stood for freedom' (*Kenyon Review*, Autumn 1949). But Empson and his poems are aware that freedom is an equivocal matter; his note on *free* in 'Sonnet' says he 'was trying to give the word the impact of a contradiction; as in "Letter IV", where it probably doesn't come off either'. In 'Letter IV' it is used of the stars and the music of the spheres, and one of the most important implications of the space-travel metaphor concerns a responsibility inseparable from the freedom it attests. Freed from the claims of church and state (and of one's parents too), the lovers must enter upon a special responsibility; to be upon a new planet is to take all the responsibility for posterity there. It therefore seems to me of great importance that Empson should have said of Adam and Eve before the Fall that 'they indeed are the type case of lovers on a separate planet' (*Kenyon Review*, Summer 1957)—they, the father and mother of mankind. It is the grandeur of this responsibility (any lover ought to feel some such grandeur and awe, as if henceforth a new series of births will begin) which leads Empson to use a word like *colonise* ('When he colonises such a planet with a pair of lovers'; *Critical Quarterly*, Autumn 1966). It is this too which lends depth to Empson's feeling for the line in 'The Good Morrow', 'Let us possess one world, each hath one, and is one':

> The sound requires it to be said slowly, with religious awe, as each party sinks into the eye of the other; it is a space-landing. Then there is a pause for realization, and the next verse begins in a hushed voice but with a curiously practical tone: 'You know, there's a lot of evidence; we really are on a separate planet'. (*Kenyon Review*, Summer 1957)

For the curious practicalities of life on a separate planet have much to do with creating a posterity and a society from scratch. One kind of loneliness is epitomized in the lovers' each being a planet; of the 'Valediction: of Weeping', Empson says that 'now he sees another aspect of space-travel—if they become separated, the gulfs between them are absolute. He sees her with a terrible clarity falling away from him on her tiny planet' (*Critical Quarterly*, Autumn 1966); 'Once the lovers are separated they are absolutely separated, so great is the isolation of these starry habitations' (*Kenyon Review*, Summer 1957). But there is also the possibility of a different isolation, alone together the two of them upon what is insufficiently a habitation. It is such a loneliness which Empson glimpses when he brings Donne back to earth:

> It is from this background that he was keenly, even if sardonically, interested in the theology of the separate planet—from fairly early, though he did not come to feel he was actually planted on one till he realized the full effects of his runaway marriage. By the time he took Anglican Orders I imagine he was thankful to get back from the interplanetary spaces, which are inherently lonely and ill-provided.

An odd and compelling angle, then, upon the responsibilities of and for parenthood is implicit in this metaphor of newly inhabited planets which Empson drew from Donne. That Empson sensed this is clear, I think, not only from that remark about Adam and Eve but also from the beginning and the end of 'Donne the Space Man'. It ends with a discussion of 'A Nocturnal upon S. Lucy's Day' which twines together childbirth, the separate planet, and Empson's own poems:

> He [J. B. Leishman] deduces that 'The Nocturnal' was written in Paris on the night of the 13th December 1611; Donne was there with the Drury family, and anxious about his wife's coming child-birth (Izaac Walton says he knew by telepathy that not the wife but the child was dead, and so it was, but one can well believe there was a certain amount of confusion). As a young man I snatched at any chance to hear wisdom drop from Mr T. S. Eliot, and he once remarked that the test of a true poet is that he writes about experiences before they have happened to him;[1] I felt I had once passed this test, though I forget now in which poem. The doctrine makes one very doubtful of any dating of poems by internal evidence, and I should think it might be true of Donne . . . But still, the only definite reason for supposing that Donne refers to a separate planet in 'The Nocturnal' is that he does it so often in other poems, sometimes obviously, but often so vaguely that we are only sure of it because the poem becomes better if we recognize it.

As for the start of 'Donne the Space Man', it is so clear in the connections it weaves, and so weird in the apt double-duty which it asks—on the one page—the word *kids* to do, that it seems to me incontrovertible evidence that, in responding to Donne, Empson responded to a special responsibility and *élan* about begetting that were implicit in the loved metaphor:

> Donne, then, from a fairly early age, was interested in getting to another planet much as the kids are nowadays; he brought the idea into practically all his best love-poems, with the sentiment which it still carries of adventurous freedom . . . No reasonable man, I readily agree, would want space travel as such; because he wants to know, in any proposal for travel, whether he would go farther and fare worse. A son of my own at about the age of twelve, keen on space travel like the rest of them, saw the goat having kids and was enough impressed to say 'It's better than space travel'. It is indeed absolutely or metaphysically better, because it is coming out of the nowhere

into here; and I was so pleased to see the human mind beginning its work that I felt as much impressed as he had done at
seeing the birth of the kids. One does not particularly want,
then, to have Donne keen on space travel unless he had a
serious reason for it.

VII

I think, then, that the complex of thinking and feeling involved in
begetting—man's desire to raise posterity—is 'the right handle to
take hold of the bundle', or at any rate a right handle, in considering Empson's poems. Sometimes explicit; sometimes like
Donne's planets, an implicit part of that 'secret largeness of outlook' which Empson shares with Donne, and so part of the
poem's richness—richness having been defined in a powerful
parenthesis by Empson (*Some Versions*, p. 145): 'the sense of richness (readiness for argument not pursued)'. As to the tacit, there
is some reassurance in Empson's fine exploration of the fact that
'Every one of [Hamlet's] soliloquies . . . contains a shock for the
audience, apart from what it says, in what it doesn't say' (*Sewanee
Review*, Winter 1953).

Ian Hamilton has complained that the inaugurating perception
in an Empson poem is seldom chosen 'because it can discover
something of an important experience that the poet has already
had' (*the Review*, June 1963). Indeed no; the usual thing is for an
Empson poem to be about an experience not yet had (one half-
feared and half not); in so far as the poem embodies an experience,
it is usually the experience of not yet having had such-and-such an
experience. Empson has said that in the last thirty years or so 'the
motives which made me want to write had I suppose largely
disappeared. I didn't feel I had to do it anyway. I think many
people actually feel they've got to go on, because it's the only
way they can support their wife and children or something' (*the
Review*, June 1963). I hope it will not seem impertinently intrusive
if I suggest that Empson's marriage and parenthood have effected
a shift of motives, partly because much in his poems had obscurely
to do with parenthood. (And on such happy yet disconcerting
losses, see his poem 'Success'.) Nor am I suggesting that he re-
makes other poets in his own image if I say that one of the en-
deavours he is at present engaged on—proving that Marvell did
marry—matters in part because the marriage, in Empson's view,

is involved in Marvell's giving up poetry and becoming a different kind of writer. And that this further matters because it has at least some relation to Empson's own career.

Love and war make up much of Marvell, as of Empson. His *Poems* were published in 1935, and *The Gathering Storm* in 1940. He has pungently repudiated one particular accusation:

> The idea that Empson lost his nerve with the second volume has always seemed to me very unreasonable. The first book, you see, is about the young man feeling frightened, frightened of women, frightened of jobs, frightened of everything, not knowing what he could possibly do. The second book is all about politics, saying we're going to have this second world war and we mustn't get too frightened about it. Well, dear me, if you call the first brave and the second cowardly it seems to me that you haven't the faintest idea of what the poems are about. (*the Review*, June 1963)

Both volumes are brave in their way; and one remembers 'Courage means Running', with its laconic confidence: 'Usual for a man / Of Bunyan's courage to respect fear'. But what yokes the two volumes is the fact that the approach of a world war lends a further gravity to the decision whether or not to beget children. (Incidentally, I think it touching and noble of Empson to have given to his two sons—among their middle names—the names of the two Allied victories which coincided with their birth.)

'Just a Smack at Auden' makes the yoking clear; true, it mocks the funk of those who are apocalyptically, with ripe relish, 'waiting for the end', but its mockery is not at all directed at the idea that the fears are farcical. A richly ironical poem, yes, but 'an irony has no point unless it is true, in some degree, in both senses' (*Some Versions*, p. 56).

> Shall I send a wire, boys? What is there to send?
> All are under fire, boys, waiting for the end.
> Shall I turn a sire, boys? Shall I choose a friend?
> The fat is in the pyre, boys, waiting for the end.

'Shall I turn a sire, boys?': it is a scorching question, and of the three *Shall I*'s here, the only one which needed to be clad in the asbestos of whimsical wording. To speak of fatherhood as to 'turn a sire', is of course, to intimate a distaste for those who let such a question be mainly a matter of ministering to their finicking self-importance, but that does not deny that the question is indeed important, too important to be left to fluttering apocalypticists. 'The fat is in the pyre': any life is already in the funeral flames. The impulses are contradictory even in this hosing-down poem, but then Empson's attitude to the approaching war was rightly compacted of contradictory impulses: people needed to be made truly, and not falsely, afraid. There is such a thing as false insecurity as well as false security. Usual for a man of Empson's courage to respect fear. Think of his superb laying-bare of Dryden's 'Charge, charge, 'tis too late to retreat' ('Song for St Cecilia's Day'):

> It is curious on the face of it that one should represent, in a mood of such heroic simplicity, a reckless excitement, a feverish and exalted eagerness for battle, by saying (in the most prominent part of the stanza from the point of view of final effect) that we can't get out of the battle now and must go through with it as best we can . . . Evidently the thought that it is no good running away is an important ingredient of military enthusiasm . . . Horses, in a way very like this, display mettle by a continual expression of timidity. (*Seven Types*, p. 198)

But it is Auden that Empson's poem (good-humouredly enough, in his case) is just a smack at, and one should recall Empson's first exploration of Auden. His 'Note on "Paid on Both Sides"' (*Experiment*, Spring 1931) deals, after all, with a work which imagines love within a feud tantamount to civil war. John Nower, whose father has been killed in the feud, is in love with Anne from the enemy family; John has to decide whether to plunge upon marriage, and whether to escape (emigrate) with or without her. He tries to straddle it all—but he has Anne's brother shot as a spy. His decision to do so precipitated from Empson the most elaborate analysis that he has ever made of a decision:

> He has the spy shot partly to tie his own hands, since he will evade the decision if he can make peace impossible, partly (the other way round) because it will make peace difficult, so that the attempt, if he chooses to make it, will expose him to more risk (for this seems to make it more generous), partly from a self-contempt which, in search of relief, turns outwards, and lights on the man who seems likest to himself, for he too is half a spy in his own camp; partly because he must kill part of himself in

coming to either decision about the marriage, so that it seems a
first step, or a revenge, to kill by an irrelevant decision the man
likest him (for whom he must at the moment, from the point
of view which still excites horror in him, feel most sympathy),
partly because only by making a decision on some associated
matter can he string himself up to know his own mind on the
matter in question, partly because what is in his own mind
makes him feel ashamed and guilty among his supporters, so
that he mistakenly thinks it necessary for his own safety to prove
to them he is wholeheartedly on their side.

What matters to my argument is the way in which the decision
which here so fascinates Empson is entwined with marriage,
family, and parenthood within what is in effect war. Given war's
world it seems impossible either to create marriage here or to flee
and create it elsewhere. Moreover Empson saw that Auden was
implying a further relation: 'John, the hero of the play, is born
prematurely from shock, after the death by ambush of his father';
'And yet it is precisely the painfulness and dangerousness of these
expulsive forces that make it possible for him to give birth to a
decision.'

That was 1931, but Empson has never lost interest in this
cluster of feelings and moral concerns. It is not a coincidence that
the three examples in 'Argufying in Poetry' (*Listener*, 22 August
1963) should run from 'Byzantium', described as 'a fascinating bit
of science fiction', via a love-complaint by Wyatt, to 'Letter to
Anne Ridler', in which 'the young G. S. Fraser, on the troopship
taking him to Africa, considered why men allow themselves to be
conscripted':

> Or freedom, say, from family love and strife
> And all the female mystery of a room
> That half supports and half imprisons us
> May drive a man from father, mother, wife
> And every soft reminder of the womb.

The reasons why Empson finds this 'magnificent' are among the
reasons why his own poems are magnificent.

'And every soft reminder of the womb': a world of war gives
special pain and pathos to the question 'Shall I turn a sire?' Which
recalls that the first Shakespeare play to be discussed by Empson
in terms of its plot was *Troilus and Cressida* (1932 and 1935).

'Certainly the play is not interested in marriage so much as in the prior idea of loyalty, but it was to the interest of these lovers to marry so as to have a claim against being separated' (*Some Versions*, p. 35). And yet it is the father's claim not to be separated from his daughter that determines the tragedy. (It is apt, incidentally, that in speaking of *Troilus and Cressida* Empson should have provided the best summary of what one feels about those of his poems which do not come off: 'Much of the language of *Troilus*, I think, is a failure; it makes puzzles which even if they can be unravelled cannot be felt as poetry'; *Some Versions*, p. 41.)

'To marry so as to have a claim against being separated': this cannot but call up Empson's best and contemporaneous poem, 'Aubade'. The best because it has plenty of story; because it fuses, as no other poem does so richly, the two principle preoccupations (of bold commitment and of shrewd good sense); because it marries the love-poems and the war-poems; and because it deserves the praise which Empson gave to Swinburne's best poem, 'The Leper': 'a story where both characters are humane, and indeed behave better than they think; Swinburne nowhere else (that I have read him) succeeds in imagining two people' (*Complex Words*, p. 78).

> 'Aubade' is about the sexual situation. When I was in Japan, from 1931 to 1934, it was usual for the old hand in the English colony to warn the young man: don't you go and marry a Japanese because we're going to be at war with Japan within ten years; you'll have awful trouble if you marry a Japanese, and this is what the poem is about . . . It just says 'All right, we can't marry, we must expect to separate'. (*the Review*, June 1963)

> > A bedshift flight to a Far Eastern sky.
> > Only the same war on a stronger toe.
> > The heart of standing is you cannot fly.
> >
> > Tell me more quickly what I lost by this,
> > Or tell me with less drama what they miss
> > Who call no die a god for a good throw,
> > Who say after two aliens had one kiss
> > It seemed the best thing to be up and go.

The piercing pathos of that penultimate line is achieved by its being so parenthetical; the sentence sweeps pitilessly on past the

words 'after two aliens had one kiss' and simply swallows them
up. But the force of the understatement springs from those largest
and most ordinary things that should follow a kiss: marriage,
children. The two people will never become that three or more
which is a new world, an inhabited planet; the bleak stoical
arithmetic of 'two aliens . . . one kiss' divides, not multiplies.
What is so expansive in the poem is not only its largeness of
moral feeling (the decent expediency of 'up and go' never either
demeaning or truckling to the tragic dignity of 'the heart of
standing'), but its strange power of heartening: 'Up was the
heartening and the strong reply.' It celebrates an experience, and
a mutuality, yet a great part of that experience was a sense of
future experiences not to be had here. In its way a 'Valediction:
Forbidding Mourning', its personal fervour and generosity are
at one with its sense that in times of war such a loss is simply to be
expected.

VIII

'To an Old Lady' is rightly revered. The dignity with which it
conceives of another's dignity; its calm refusal either to melo-
dramatize or to sentimentalize the great gulf it contemplates; its
ability to withhold and yet not to grudge: these make the most
serious use of the spacemanship which Empson learnt from Donne.

> Ripeness is all; her in her cooling planet
> Revere; do not presume to think her wasted.
> Project her no projectile, plan nor man it;
> Gods cool in turn, by the sun long outlasted.
>
> Our earth alone given no name of god
> Gives, too, no hold for such a leap to aid her;
> Landing, you break some palace and seem odd;
> Bees sting their need, the keeper's queen invader.
>
> No, to your telescope; spy out the land;
> Watch while her ritual is still to see,
> Still stand her temples emptying in the sand
> Whose waves o'erthrew their crumbled tracery;
>
> Still stand uncalled-on her soul's appanage;
> Much social detail whose successor fades,
> Wit used to run a house and to play Bridge,
> And tragic fervour, to dismiss her maids.

Years her precession do not throw from gear.
She reads a compass certain of her pole;
Confident, finds no confines on her sphere,
Whose failing crops are in her sole control.

Stars how much further from me fill my night.
Strange that she too should be inaccessible,
Who shares my sun. He curtains her from sight,
And but in darkness is she visible.

The last stanza soars; the second stanza does something more
disconcerting, it leaps. We should be sufficiently surprised by the
line 'Bees sting their need, the keeper's queen invader' to ask with
some urgency what it is up to. For one thing, it is the only moment
in the poem when the planetary metaphor is replaced by quite
different figure of speech; elsewhere the planet fades (for instance
the fourth stanza), but nowhere else is it abruptly and totally
replaced by an altogether alien metaphor. Why the brusqueness
Moreover the train of thought is odd. The first two lines of the
stanza follow on naturally enough, making their crucial point
about systems of belief. You cannot get to her planet; (and there
with something of a shrug, a diverting concession) and even if you
could, you would only do damage as well as make a fool of your
self.[2] But then there is this odd leap into a very extreme further *and
even*: and even an invader of the highest authority, the grandest of
ladies, and absolutely essential to the place, the queen-bee, finds
herself stung for her pains. The line is a bizarre moment of
uncalled-for aggression, not only in being about aggression but in
the way it behaves in the poem; it is itself an invader, and we have
to ask what sting, what need, makes it suddenly insist upon making
its presence felt. Simply, what are we to make of this reminder that
there is a way of life (the bees whom we are so often asked to
admire; see Empson's large response to 'The singing mason
building roofs of gold', *Seven Types*, pp. 112–13), a way of life so
suspicious of any invasion that it will kill the only means it has of
reproduction? What, in short, has the threat to reproduction to
do with the poem?

   For a start, the poem beautifully uses a question which is bound
to be felt in any poem 'to an old lady' that insists 'do not presume
to think her wasted'. We are not to think of her as an old maid
but we are positively not to think of her so—that is, the matter is
to arise. Such, after all, is the most immediately presumptuous

way in which people are prone to presume that an old lady's life is wasted; a presumption from which Empson is always challengingly free, as in the implied rebuke in *Seven Types* (p. 247): 'The object of life, after all, is not to understand things, but to maintain one's defences and equilibrium and live as well as one can; it is not only maiden aunts who are placed like this.' (The poem's use of *maids* very totally to mean servants plays its part as a negative implication, 'what you imply but to exclude', in the words of 'Letter V'.) Certainly it is part of the point of the metaphor 'appanage' that it should call up its literal sense too: provision made for younger children. Likewise of 'successor', again a metaphor but again not to be narrowly conceived as to the way in which it works upon us (quietly strengthened as it is by Empson's putting *whose* instead of 'of which the'). And what is not metaphor at all, but story—'Wit used to run a house'—invokes a family and a household rather than a solitary life. Empson's subject is not the solitariness of solitary life, but of the unsolitary one, 'the isolation even of a life rich in intimacy'. And that the bees and their propagation have something really to do with the poem seems to me confirmed by the happiness which Empson felt at the reception of the poem by the old lady herself: 'My mother, but when she came across it in print she luckily thought it meant her own mother, thus showing that it tells a general truth' (record-notes). The right thing to be delighted about, but the general truth then includes a sense of a vista, of parents' parents and of children's children. The general truth is about parenthood, not about a friend's or an acquaintance's distance from us. Empson in the record-notes has paraphrased ' . . . Who shares my sun' as 'though isolated we shared a system closer than the great minds in books', and the system in question is a family. It is after all natural to think of the solar system as a family. So that when Empson says without qualification ' "Sun" not "son" is meant', I wish his comment to be resisted or amplified. Of course the literal sense of son would ruckle the line; but I don't think that all suggestion of son can be or should be eliminated, even if the proper way to put it is to say that the phrase means *sun-not-son* rather than means *sun*, not *son*. The effect of the word 'share' is to make it even harder altogether to preclude an intimation of the family; and in any case I think it inherently improbable that a man who so honours Donne and whose own poems can speak of Lucifer as 'Sun's Son' could imagine that all trace of *son* could so easily be vetoed.

The point matters because the succession (appanage, successor) of grandmother, mother, son is part of what creates as well as of what created the poem. The poem is warm with family feeling (strangely, given its recognition of cooling and of inevitable distance), and family there has to include not only progenitors but also the absent descendants. One aspect of the proper (and public) self-consciousness of the poem is its sense that no life can simply be thought of as wasted which has brought a new life into the world, and that this bears upon those who have not, or not yet, done so. At which point we should ask about that calmly surprising opening, which so ripens in the poem, and which seems so utterly to earn the right to its audacious appropriation of great Shakespeare: 'Ripeness is all'. The first words of this poem to an old lady are those in which a son offers comfort to a parent. It is an odd comfort, not only in that Gloucester could never in certain respects be comforted by it; what he can say is what the old lady might say of her poem, 'And that's true too', a dignified austerity of comfort. But we need to remember just how Edgar thought it best to comfort his father: by recalling the birth which we were given as well as the death approaching us. The ripeness is that of gestation as much as of moribundity:

> Men must endure
> Their going hence, even as their coming hither;
> Ripeness is all.

The range of Empson's poem is a matter of its taking within itself a sense of the coming hither as well as of the going hence. It sees the paradox of any family, that the very light it shares makes for a daily invisibility. 'And but in darkness is she visible': the darkness is that of a night-time realization, of sadness or despair or memory, and also of the shadow of death. The poem has its cool light, and its source is revealed when for a moment it flashes into fieriness, stung by need.

The infinite spaces precipitate a multiplicity of feelings.

> You were amused to find you too could fear
> 'The eternal silence of the infinite spaces' . . .
>   ('Letter I')

Amusement and fear meet in the love-poems.

Although, as a matter of fact, most of them turned out to be love poems about boy being too afraid of girl to tell her anything, the simple desire to think of something rather like Donne was the basic impulse. But I think my few good ones are all on the basis of expressing an unresolved conflict. (*the Review*, June 1963)

Of 'The Ants', the first poem in the *Collected Poems*, Empson has said: 'It is a love-poem with the author afraid of the woman' (record-notes). But we need to distinguish fears; it will not do just to assume that every boy is afraid of a girl, because anybody fears rebuff and any other body can be dangerous—both true, but only part of what seems to haunt Empson's poems. What we should (women included) fear in women is their power to bring forth life, a power which is both mysteriously generous and unperturbed by scruple. In 'The Ants' the woman is thought of as a tree of life, teeming not just with leaves but with the parasitical greenfly and with the ants parasitical upon the greenfly. The ants, with sinister care, protect the greenfly so as to live, via them, upon the tree's life.

> We tunnel through your noonday out to you.
> We carry our tube's narrow darkness there
> Where, nostrum-plastered, with prepared air,
> With old men running and trains whining through
>
> We ants may tap your aphids for your dew.
> You may not wish their sucking or our care;
> Our all-but freedom, too, your branch must bear,
> High as roots' depth in earth, all earth to view.
>
> No, by too much this station the air nears.
> How small a chink lets in how dire a foe.
> What though the garden in one glance appears?
>
> Winter will come and all her leaves will go.
> We do not know what skeleton endures.
> Carry at least her parasites below.

I don't want to linger over this poem, mainly because I am still unhelpfully perplexed by it, though moved; it is enough for now for me to suggest that there is special force in Empson's note: 'The ants build mud galleries into trees to protect the greenfly they get sugar from, and keep them warm in the nest during winter'. A travesty of a warm nest; and of the strange activity of the womb. There is a sense of what the grandest parasites are; there is the aphids' 'sucking', and in the association of 'branch' with 'bear' a feeling that any woman is a family tree. This is indeed what women must bear, and it is very different from man's 'all-but freedom'. And in the admonition 'How small a chink lets in how dire a foe' there is the sharpest sense of begetting—rightly thought of as an intimidating prospect, and with the fear braced against unmanliness or panic by that humour and coolness of archaism with which the poems outfrown indignity, as in 'Shall I turn a sire?'

'Invitation to Juno' thinks of the centaur bred by Ixion from the delusive cloud substituted for Juno (an act of begetting for which he was as punished as if he had had the real goddess); of the 'gennets for germans' which 'sprang not from Othello'. It asks: are all attempts at 'inheriting two life-periods' doomed?

> Courage. Weren't strips of heart culture seen
> Of late mating two periodicities?
> Could not Professor Charles Darwin
> Graft annual upon perennial trees?

The name Darwin is called upon because it so stands for a great family—a family can in its way inherit two life-periods. But being about a transcendent act of breeding doesn't here make for a good poem. It admonishes: 'Courage.' But there is not enough fear for it to mean more than cheer up. And that is because no woman —no sense of woman—is allowed into it; Juno, or rather the cloud that simulated her, lurks only in the title, and the poem grants all its room to males: Lucretius, Dr Johnson, Othello, Ixion, and Charles Darwin. Like a club; Invitation to Athenaeum. The point is not the presence of ideas but the absence of that human situation which makes a poem convince our nerves. Another poem of 1928 shows the difference.

Value is in Activity

Celestial sphere, an acid green canvas hollow,
His circus that exhibits him, the juggler
Tosses, an apple that four others follow,
Nor heeds, not eating it, the central smuggler.

Nor heeds if the core be brown with maggots' raven,
Dwarf seeds unnavelled a last frost has scolded,
Mites that their high narrow echoing cavern
Invites forward, or with close brown pips, green folded.

Some beetles (the tupped females can worm out)
Massed in their halls of knowingly chewed splinter
Eat faster than the treasured fungi sprout
And stave off suffocation until winter.

The maggot, the seed, the mite, the pip; out to the apple, and then to the juggler, to the circus-tent, and to the world; and then swoop in again, back down to the beetles within the world. The metaphysics of the poem have been well scrutinized by Martin Dodsworth (*the Review*, June 1963); the metaphors tense the metaphysics. And as in 'To an Old Lady' there is a sudden, and similar, fierceness: 'Some beetles (the tupped females can worm out) . . .' The very parentheticalness is a jolt, an eruptive energy which might splinter the poem if the brackets did not pinion its arms; and 'tupped' is like no other word in the poem. For among the 'Inhabitants' who at first gave the poem its title, there with 'the central smuggler', the maggots, the dwarf seeds, the mites, and the 'close brown pips', are the future beetles with which the tupped females teem—and which make it a good thing for male beetles that the females 'worm out'. Many feelings play over such a notion; it is with affection as well as perturbation that we may think of an embryo as a 'central smuggler'. How sharply and oddly 'dwarf seeds unnavelled' invites us forward to think of birth, and then 'scolded' sees them as children. How quiescent the 'close brown pips, green folded', with future apples folded within those folded pips. Pips and seeds are reproduction as much as 'tupped', a word which certainly must not be allowed to domineer, and yet which must be allowed to be—as was 'Bees sting their need . . .'—the jolt which shakes the kaleidoscopic poem so that we see its pattern.

The title, 'Value is in Activity', would suggest (as well as Aristotle on happiness) that value and activity can especially be seen in the value and activity of perpetuating life.

> We gain
> Truth, to put it sanely, by gift of pleasure
> And courage . . .
> ('Courage means Running')

Truth, and life too; the act of begetting is the gift which marries pleasure and courage. The act of begetting is a type case of activity, not just because it makes possible great vistas of others'

activity ('Cradle within cradle', in the words of Yeats which appear
in Empson's epigraph to 'Autumn on Nan-Yueh'), but also
because in its irrevocable decisiveness it most violates that other
deep wish of ours, to foresee. 'High Dive' is Empson's elaboration
of the necessity to act. The idea of the poem is 'that one must go
from the godlike state of contemplation even when attained either
into action which cannot wholly foresee its consequences or into
a fixed condition, due to fear, which does not give real knowledge
and leads to neurosis' (Notes). I believe that the poem, exceptionally hard to construe, sees the type case of an 'action which cannot
wholly foresee its consequences' as the act of begetting; and if so,
I think it simply and importantly right. I realize that action is not
here limited to such an act, and moreover that any attempt to
write about activity would inevitably find itself using words which
invoke begetting. Yet the poem seems to me to go further than
a poem would be obliged to, or advised to, unless it wished to
invoke begetting. I think it characteristic too of Empson, as of
Donne, that his metaphors are not reduced to blank obedience
but are allowed to ask for themselves a richer presence. So that
when the attained contemplation, from the diving-board, is given
as

> I Sanctus brood thereover,
> Inform *in posse* the tank's triple infinite,

we should see this brooding as indeed like that of the Holy Ghost,
intent upon the creation of life (rather than intent upon some
action or other). Likewise when, within this same sentence, the
ripples are seen as 'maggots', and when in the next sentence they
'rut or retract', we should not ignore the teeming life of maggots,
and the sexual suggestions of 'rut or retract' (though the main
sense is 'form ruts or draw back'). We are told that their ripples
are 'Thicker than water'—a phrase which insists upon the human
family, and which Empson emphasizes by enclosing it (needlessly,
otherwise) in quotation marks, alone in the poem. (It is an
important phrase in 'Bacchus', too:

> Making a brew thicker than blood, being brine,
> Being the mother water which was first made blood,
> All living blood, and whatever blood makes wine.

Empson's note says: ' "Blood is thicker than water", but blood
connects us with near relations, as the phrase is used, and this with

all life'.) The water will 'clot . . . unless . . .'; will clot into the
inactivity of neurosis, here invoked in the line 'These doves
undriven that coo, Ark neuroses'. It is a baffling phrase; the only
sense that I can make of it is to think that the animals that went in
two by two are likely to have suffered from the neuroses con-
sequent upon the whole survival of their kind being now dependent upon their power to propagate; and one of the poor doves
saw its only mate sent forth three times, not even to return the
last time (Genesis viii 12). The responsibility would make
propagation a weighty enough matter to foster any number of
'Ark neuroses' ('Sitting two and two, boys, waiting for the end').

Now the two stanzas that particularly matter. The water will
clot unless one

> Unchart the second, the obstetric, chooses,
> Leaves isle equation by not frozen ford,
> And, to break scent, under foamed new phusis
> Dives to receive in memory reward.
>
> Fall to them, Lucifer, Sun's Son. Splash high
> Jezebel. Throw her down. They feast, I flee
> Her poised tired head and eye
> Whose skull pike-high mirrors and waits for me.

Unless one chooses the second alternative, an 'unchart' because it
leads to the uncharted but is a way out; and it is 'obstetric', it
brings to birth. And in bringing to birth, one 'leaves isle equation
by not frozen ford'; the isle equation is that of believing that man
is an island ('Each of us enisled, boys, waiting for the end'; and
Empson has observed that 'most of the later sayings of Donne
still famous are also a renunciation of separateness; as in "no man
is an island; he is a piece of the Continent, a part of the Main" ';
Kenyon Review, Summer 1957). The 'not frozen ford' by which one
leaves the paralysing equation is in human terms love, and the
act of love, and the woman's obstetric act. Any act can be disastrous; Lucifer's fall was (yet he is 'Sun's Son', not man's son), and
so was Jezebel's. The dive into life can be the dive into death.
Lucifer falls; Jezebel is thrown down. That we are to recollect
the very words of II Kings ix 30 is clear from *tired*, which mostly
means 'attired' (and is pronounced by Empson on the record as a
disyllable, as is 'poised'): 'And she painted her face, and tired her
head, and looked out at a window'. Then since 'Throw her down'

gives the exact words of Jehu's order, we should remember just
who they were who received the command: 'And there looked out
to him two or three eunuchs. And he said, Throw her down. So
they threw her down'.

'High Dive' is too secret, too racked, a poem, but critics have
been right to think that its preoccupations are crucial to Empson.
In the same way, we should not leave as solely metaphors the
terms in which 'Dissatisfaction with Metaphysics' chooses to
speak:

> Whose hearth is cold, and all his wives undone . . .

> Adam and Eve breed still their dotted line,
> Repeated incest, a plain series.

The same with 'Earth has Shrunk in the Wash', which Empson has
summed up as 'Civilized refinement cutting one off from other
people' (Notes): 'Space-travel compared to neurotic isolation and
the dangers of the increase of power' (record-notes). It ends:

> One daily tortures the poor Christ anew
> (On every planet moderately true)
> But has much more to do,
> And can so much entail here,
> Daily brings rabbits to a new Australia,
> New unforeseen, new cataclysmic failure,

> And cannot tell. He who all answers brings
> May (ever in the great taskmaster's eye)
> Dowser be of his candle as of springs,
> And pump the valley with the tunnel dry.

The rabbits brought to a new Australia are an unwished-for
colonization and a teeming mischief; 'entail' is free to revert to its
oldest sense, to settle an estate in succession; and the 'unforeseen'
becomes particularly a matter of the unforeseeable effects of
procreation. 'Dowser' is, as Empson says in the Notes, 'a pun on
putting out a light and smelling out water'; that the same word can
bring forth the waters of life and can put out the candle of life is
the centre of the poem's puzzlement. 'And cannot tell'.

Again, the best stanza of another flawed heterogeneous poem,
'Letter IV' (Empson is dissatisfied with it), is its opening, which
imagines a grotesque birth and then a grotesque kind of parturi-
tion; at once heroic and mock-heroic—the child cicada a tiny

Childe Roland—like many of the begettings, love-tunnellings and brave acts of building which most move Empson:

> Hatched in a rasping darkness of dry sand
> The child cicada some brave root discovers:
> Sucks with dumb mouth while his long climb is planned
> That high must tunnel through the dust that smothers:
> Parturient with urine from this lover
> Coheres from chaos, only to evade,
> An ordered Nature his own waste has made,
> And builds his mortared Babel from the incumbent shade.

No one else's love-poem would set itself such a long climb; the triumph of life is seen as a triumph over the inevitable waste, using waste instead of denying it. 'Bacchus' too celebrates birth: 'The laughing god born of a startling answer'; 'Incestuous Chaos will breed permanent', and so too must Order, or it will leave the world to Chaos. Chaos or nothingness—'Four Legs, Three Legs, Two Legs' is disturbed by 'The delta zero': Oedipus 'short-circuited life by keeping it all in the family' (Notes).

I believe that almost all of Empson's poems have to do with the way in which we do or do not short-circuit life. Even 'This Last Pain', perhaps the poem in which Empson devoted the most of his energies to drawing abstractions taut, needed to begin with a grim repudiation implicit in the application of the word *fathers*:

> This last pain for the damned the Fathers found:
> 'They knew the bliss with which they were not crowned.'

The poem needed too at its centre the deep pun on 'conceivable':

> 'What is conceivable can happen too',
> Said Wittgenstein, who had not dreamt of you;

You there being as wide as the world; any *you*, including those not yet conceived, or you, gentle reader ('Which eyes not yet created shall ore-read'), as undreamt of by me the poet as by Wittgenstein. Any individual human being is conceived and yet inconceivable. The poem needs this pun not only because of its tension between an intangible idea and a tangible person, but also because the pun is then itself in tension with the end of the poem:

> Feign then what's by a decent tact believed
> And act that state is only so conceived,
> And build an edifice of form
> For house where phantoms may keep warm.

> Imagine then, by miracle, with me,
> (Ambiguous gifts, as what gods give must be)
>   What could not possibly be there,
>   And learn a style from a despair.

What keeps warm the poem's ending, what fleshes its phantoms
and abstractions, is the robust return in 'so conceived'; the act of
imagining, of so conceiving, is as odd, as trusting, as precarious
and as implicated in hope, as the act of conceiving life. 'Ambiguous
gifts, as what gods give must be': of such gifts, the most 'by
miracle' is the gift of life.

   Last of the more covert instances is the end of 'Your Teeth are
Ivory Towers'. Like many of Empson's endings, it soars and
broods:

>   He who tries
> Talk must always plot and then sustain,
> Talk to himself until the star replies,
>
> Or in despair that it could speak again
> Assume what answers any wits have found
> In evening dress on rafts upon the main,
> Not therefore uneventful or soon drowned.

The delicate stoical wit of this gains from our being alive to a
great many aspects of the brave doomed life on the raft, but I
think we need particularly to sense that the raft cannot but short-
circuit life; what it most epitomizes is not only certain death but
the impossibility of furthering life. 'Not therefore uneventful or
soon drowned'—but the greatest eventfulness of all is out of the
question. Many readers of Empson's poems have, I think, found
the feeling of this ending to be quite different from any other in
Empson, and the shape of the ending is indeed unique in his work.
In all of his other poems in *terza rima*, the end of the poem returns
to its beginning; a cycle is completed. Indeed they usually invoke
some such circularity or return. 'Arachne', with its bubbles, sends
back its last rhyme to its first pair; 'The Scales', with its tunnels,
likewise; 'Reflection from Rochester', with its search for a pattern,
is doubly concluded, sending back its last pair to its first pair; and
'Courage means Running', its last rhyme to its first pair. Alone of
the *terza rima* poems, 'Your Teeth are Ivory Towers' short-
circuits the life of its verse-form; it leaves its final rhyming not

fully consummated, no third rhyme ever forthcoming to grace the
conjunction of 'found' and 'drowned'.

IX

For the rest, I want to end by doing the lavish thing, and quote in
sequence ten of Empson's poems which are among his best,
remarking briefly why I think they too are animated by these
concerns.

Camping Out

And now she cleans her teeth into the lake:
Gives it (God's grace) for her own bounty's sake
What morning's pale and the crisp mist debars:
Its glass of the divine (that Will could break)
Restores, beyond Nature: or lets Heaven take
(Itself being dimmed) her pattern, who half awake
Milks between rocks a straddled sky of stars.

Soap tension the star pattern magnifies.
Smoothly Madonna through-assumes the skies
Whose vaults are opened to achieve the Lord.
No, it is we soaring explore galaxies,
Our bullet boat light's speed by thousands flies.
Who moves so among stars their frame unties;
See where they blur, and die, and are outsoared.

The ordinary dawn turns out to have its feat of creation; for our
own bounty's sake we are to share the lavish relaxation of 'her own
bounty's sake' and its power of vivifying. The stars have faded
from the lake, but her toothpaste re-creates them, and as they fly
apart it is as if we were flying towards them. The poem is Empson's
most exuberant evocation of a delight in creative multiplicity;
the creation of those mimic stars (and the evening and the morning
were the fourth day) is at one with a full sense of a tenderly
human erotic generosity: 'who half awake / Milks between rocks
a straddled sky of stars'. And just as Empson has always been
fascinated by the idea that any man can become a Christ (the idea
occurs throughout his criticism), so here my lady can become
Madonna. The vaults of the skies which 'are opened to achieve the
Lord' are open to the achievement of a fecundating glory (reminiscent of Tennyson's 'St Agnes' Eve' in its erotic fervour but

triumphantly secular). The Madonna's body went to heaven without bodily decay; 'through-assumes' incorporates the way in which any woman's body can in love assume as much, both because an ecstasy makes physical decay at once unthinkable and insignificant, and because the creation of any new life, whether by a Madonna or not, confutes decay. The jet-like boost which 'Madonna' gives is powered by the delighted implication that for a virgin to conceive is nowhere near as grand and jubilant a thing as for a woman to do so. The 'bullet boat light's speed' ('The toothpaste specks as they go apart on the water look like approaching a constellation at more than the speed of light'; record-notes) includes an evocation of the moment of conception. And then in the last two lines, which Empson has summarized as 'a great enough ecstasy makes the common world unreal' (Notes), there is an extraordinary combination of triumph with chastening gravity, since 'are outsoared' suggests both a diminution and a something else's victory. 'Who moves so among stars their frame unties': the impulse of the line is thrilled yet sober, responsible, and admonitory. Nothing here smoothly 'makes the common world unreal' in any airy way because the claims of the common world are supremely there in the wish to create a pattern of stars that will not blur and die and be outsoared. The feeling of vigilance in the closing lines creates what Empson found in 'The Good Morrow': religious awe, a hushed voice wonderfully implicated in the curiously practical. I realize that these impulses are not presented as the self-evident subject of 'Camping Out', but then one of the strengths and challenges of all Empson's poems (one of the ways by which they move you to make human sense of them) is that they are proudly unostentatious about their subjects. Welcoming but wary, they are open secrets. 'Camping Out' is not a poem about camping out, or about toothpaste specks; but camping out and space-travel are both modes of lovers' freedom. The poem makes richly courteous use of its toothpaste specks rather as Marvell's 'The Mower to the Glowworms' is courteous to its friendly helpful glowworms. It is only by seeing that the adventure and pathos of begetting are in the poem's air that we can grasp how it earns its buoyancy and grave calm; or grasp how Empson is here moved to a love-poem which so exhilaratingly casts out fear; casts it out, not denies its existence; a fear that would be natural to a bullet boat at the speed of light as to the creation of a new inhabitant of the starry habitations.

It is fecundity in 'Camping Out'; in 'Letter II', it is destructive barrenness. 'The young couple are merely curious about each other, therefore they lose interest in whatever they think they have found out; a nagging process' (record-notes).

> Searching the cave gallery of your face
> My torch meets fresco after fresco ravishes
> Rebegets me; it crumbles each; no trace
> Stays to remind me what each heaven lavishes.
>
> How judge their triumph, these primeval stocks,
> When to the sketchbook nought but this remains,
> A gleam where jellyfish have died on rocks,
> Bare canvas that the golden frame disdains?
>
> Glancing, walk on; there are portraits yet, untried,
> Unbleached; the process, do not hope to change.
> Let us mark in general terms their wealth, how wide
> Their sense of character, their styles, their range.
>
> Only walk on; the greater part have gone;
> Whom lust, nor cash, nor habit join, are cold;
> The sands are shifting as you walk; walk on,
> The new is an emptier darkness than the old.
>
> Crossing and doubling, many-fingered, hounded,
> Those desperate stars, those worms dying in flower
> Ashed paper holds, nose-sailing, search their bounded
> Darkness for a last acre to devour.

The barrenness is brought alive to us precisely as *not* creating new portraits, merely using the old ones up; and the central metaphor of the portrait deserves, once more, not to be dwindled into being simply metaphor, slackly exchangeable with many another way of putting it. The effect within the poem is to intimate that there have been ancestors. Ancestors first appear in the poem as available to condescension, the disconcerting lordliness of 'these primeval stocks' ('the early race that made the pictures'; Notes). But then, after 'the golden frame', they change, as by evolution and history, and what was a cave gallery becomes an ancestral gallery of family 'portraits' ('how wide / Their sense of character, their styles'). True, as in Marvell's 'The Gallery' each such picture is in the first place conceived of as a facet of the lover's character; but the effect of the metaphor is to suggest a short-circuiting, a line of ancestors coming to an end. Such is the taunting sadness of 'fresco after fresco' (Italian, *fresh*) as each fresh apprehension crumbles. The sight of each fresco 'ravishes / Rebegets me', but the ravishing only re-begets him and is no begetting. The Notes by Empson say: 'They have a ground in common only so long as there is something new to find out about each other.' Indeed, the whole poem is a penetrating and shaming evocation of this particular form of *egoisme à deux*; it is important to see that two is the number, two only, no created other to create the newly unforeseeably interesting. The drastic shift of manner and tone in 'Whom lust, nor cash, nor habit join, are cold' (there is nothing else that is hortatory, let alone so lavishly and Gallicly sententious, in the poem) should challenge us to ponder what it really is that joins and warms lovers; lust, cash, and habit are a determinedly low-minded trio, especially as we would have expected a high-minded admonition, and to find it so is to be aware of other possibilities for the list. 'What each heaven lavishes' is only some facet of her; not a lavishness beyond the one or the two of them. The two are contrasted with the many portraits, and with the stars, the flickering flames, and the tendrils of smoke (like the smoke from sophistication's cigarettes) that spill many-fingered from the fearful torch. The immense series of births is curtailed; their inability to create anything newly of interest to each other is implicit in their condescension towards the past and their blankness towards the future. What gleams is not life, since it is killingly out of its element: 'A gleam where jellyfish have died on rocks'. 'No trace / Stays to remind me'. It is this short-circuiting of life which furnishes one of the senses in which 'The new is an emptier darkness than the old'. And the force of the final stanza, which with effortless surprise moves up and out, 'nose-sailing', into a rich surrealism of style quite new to the poem, is in its travesty of fecundity; neither its 'crossing' nor its 'doubling' can urge the creative sense of those words; and its many fingers, its 'desperate stars, those worms dying in flower', have the bizarre vitality of death. Of Milton's Death, indeed, to whom 'nose-sailing' is a grim guide; Death scenting his victims even before they become such:

> So saying, with delight he snuffed the smell
> Of mortal change on earth. As when a flock
> Of ravenous fowl, through many a league remote,

Against a day of battle to a field
Where armies lie encamped, come flying, lured
With scent of living carcasses designed
For death, the following day, in bloody fight:
So scented the grim Feature, and upturned
His nostril wide into the murky air . . .

'Camping Out' experiences a delighted creating; 'Letter II', a sterility which is a travesty of vitality (a vitality associated with art-work and with worms). 'Arachne' fears the pride which thinks it can create on its own, the one of it, not even the two of them.

Twixt devil and deep sea, man hacks his caves;
Birth, death; one, many; what is true, and seems;
Earth's vast hot iron, cold space's empty waves:

King spider, walks the velvet roof of streams:
Must bird and fish, must god and beast avoid:
Dance, like nine angels, on pin-point extremes.

His gleaming bubble between void and void,
Tribe-membrane, that by mutual tension stands,
Earth's surface film, is at a breath destroyed.

Bubbles gleam brightest with least depth of lands
But two is least can with full tension strain,
Two molecules; one, and the film disbands.

We two suffice. But oh beware, whose vain
Hydroptic soap my meagre water saves.
Male spiders must not be too early slain.

It is the pounce within the final pounce which so unpredictably wrests the poem, and which we need to tremble at if we are 'to make human sense of the paradoxes of the poem'. It is disconcerting enough when in the last stanza the poem is suddenly seen to be a love-poem. 'We two suffice.' The peremptory chill of that sentence is not only that a 'we' suddenly asserts itself where there has as yet been no I or you, but also that this three-word sentence (the barest of sufficiencies) follows upon sentences which have been fifty, twenty-one, and twenty-four words long. The poem had seemed to be serenely braced, a dazzling act of abstraction-acrobatics, itself walking the velvet roof and dancing on pin-point extremes. And then the last stanza converts all those extremes into the high strategy of a silky, thoughtful counter-threat,

designed to meet a thoughtless threat. At first, in simply insisting
that we two need each other, since neither soap nor water can
alone create the bubble; and then with the altogether unexpected
leap which takes the earlier 'Birth, death' with nothing like the
earlier calm: 'Male spiders must not be too early slain.' For all
its cold courtesy (akin to the counter-threats in Shakespeare's
Sonnets), it is a weird and violent end. We had not been much
thinking about the title 'Arachne'; had come gradually I think to
forget it squatting over the poem; and then she is what the poem
finally, superbly uncalled-for, drives at. The 'King spider' who is
'man' (and there is, one now realizes, a trick with 'man', as in
'Invitation to Juno', that man's world of a poem) is the counter-
part and rival to Arachne, 'a queen spider and disastrously proud'
(Notes). For the last line enters upon a different dimension of
threat and fear: that a woman can be so predatorily proud as not
just to destroy life but to preclude it. The female spider who jumps
that gun and the proud Arachne who challenged the goddess,
hanged herself in despair, and was changed into a spider: these
coalesce. The sudden pounce of the last line cannot but call up
the eruption into 'To an Old Lady' of 'Bees sting their need . . .',
with its same wilful perilous precluding of a life-series. And is it
only the accident of their having become famous as the epigraph
to Robert Lowell's 'To Speak of Woe that is in Marriage' that
makes one remember those words of Schopenhauer? 'It is
the future generation that presses into being by means of
these exuberant feelings and supersensible soap bubbles of
ours.'

Empson does not read 'Arachne' on the record:

> I left it out because I'd come to think that it was in rather bad
> taste. It's boy being afraid of girl, as usual, but it's boy being
> too rude to girl. I thought it had rather a nasty feeling, that's
> why I left it out. (*the Review*, June 1963)

One sees what he means, and 'Arachne' will always be a poem
that one changes one's mind about. But its fierceness is true and
deep, and I think that the end—just because it is a meticulous
slow-paced warning—includes its own plea for something other
than pride all round. I am reminded of another poem in which a
man might be considered too rude to a woman, one which has,
on and off, a rather nasty feeling, and one about which Empson

has written with passion: Donne's 'The Apparition', with its chillingly torrid conclusion:

> and since my love is spent,
> I had rather thou shouldst painfully repent,
> Than by my threatenings rest still innocent.

Just as Donne's ending with *innocent* (and not with *repent*) holds open, imperiously but magnanimously, the door to something else, so Empson's threatenings, 'Male spiders must not be too early slain', incorporate some intimation that it is even now not too late. Even so, a central source of energy in 'Arachne' is the full tension of feelings about begetting, and it is worth remembering where 'hydroptic' comes from. In Donne, it evokes the death-bed in a poem which Empson is not alone in thinking of as enshrining Donne's fears for his wife's child-bed:

> The general balm th' hydroptic earth hath drunk,
> Whither, as to the bed's-feet, life is shrunk,
> Dead and interred.
> ('A Nocturnal upon S. Lucy's Day')

It sums up, too, the fierce father in 'Elegy 4: The Perfume': 'By thy hydroptic father catechized'.

'The Scales' is a catechism by a figure not only fatherly but also avuncular. This girl, should she be patted (small, child-like, a miniature landscape like that of a sand-castle), or is she a grander adventurous landscape? 'The Scales'—'in the sense of the first estimate of size which decides what kind of tool to use; an excuse to a woman for not showing enough love' (record-notes).

> The proper scale would pat you on the head
> But Alice showed her pup Ulysses' bough
> Well from behind a thistle, wise with dread;
>
> And though your gulf-sprung mountains I allow
> (Snow-puppy curves, rose-solemn dado band)
> Charming for nurse, I am not nurse just now.
>
> Why pat or stride them, when the train will land
> Me high, through climbing tunnels, at your side,
> And careful fingers meet through castle sand.

Claim slyly rather that the tunnels hide
Solomon's gems, white vistas, preserved kings,
By jackal sandhole to your air flung wide.

Say (she suspects) to sea Nile only brings
Delta and indecision, who instead
Far back up country does enormous things.

The right and usual commentary on this poem which speaks of
Alice is Empson's essay on Lewis Carroll:

> A desire to include all sexuality in the girl child, the least
> obviously sexed of human creatures, the one that keeps its sex
> in the safest place, was an important part of their fascination
> for him. He is partly imagining himself as the girl-child (with
> these comforting characteristics) partly as its father (these
> together make *it* a father) partly as its lover—so it might be a
> mother—but then of course it is clever and detached enough
> to do everything for itself. (*Some Versions*, p. 273)

'So it might be a mother': this is what vibrates the delicious
perplexity of scale, the gravity and tremor, in those lines about
'nurse', and this is what animates the ample triumph of the poem's
concluding lines, which are at once the most casual of gestures
(vaguely across a continent) and the most princely of admonitions.
Still, 'an excuse to a woman for not showing enough love'? The
lurking presence of an excuse is to be sensed in a most marked
absence from those last lines; delta and indecision at the mouth of
the Nile, yes, and enormous things far back up country. But is
there nothing between? What of the great fecundating power of
the Nile, neither indecision nor those vaguely enormous things
but the one superbly decisive (decisive for Egypt) enormous thing
which is the life of Egypt and which epitomizes the mysteries of
the genial powers of life. From 'castle sand' to 'jackal sandhole'
to the Nile: the shift is not just into grandeur but into the life-
giving. I think of 'the fructuant marsh' in that poem by Empson
which begins 'Egyptian banks . . . ', and of the line about the
Sphinx in 'Four Legs, Three Legs, Two Legs': 'Behind, Sahara,
before Nile and man', on which Empson comments: 'I have never
seen anything in print about how dramatically she is placed between
the desert and the sown' (Notes). 'The Scales' does not speak of
the Nile's most real power, its most enormous thing, but far back
up country the poem knows of it, and is itself fecundated by its

richness of implication, in suggesting a richness of possible
motherhood in the girl ('so it might be a mother') from which for
now the speaker, preferring an excuse, averts his perplexed eyes.
Not showing enough love, perhaps, but with the tenderest of
affection and indeed a great sense of why love is the grandest of
the enormous things.

'Homage to the British Museum' may seem altogether remote
from any such concerns. Its subject, clearly enough (it is Empson's
most gruffly lucid and humorous poem), is modern man's all-
but-paralysing consciousness of the range and variety of beliefs
alive in the world; it is aware of the paradox that would grant an
absolute status, a supremacy, to its own large relativism. (Empson
says of Fielding: 'he does not find relativism alarming, because
he feels that to understand codes other than your own is likely
to make your judgments better'; *Kenyon Review*, Spring 1958.)
Aware, too, that the only way out of this paradox is through
good-humour, a repeated willingness to admit (admission as
paradoxically the way out), and a quizzical freedom from fluster.

> There is a Supreme God in the ethnological section;
> A hollow toad shape, faced with a blank shield.
> He needs his belly to include the Pantheon,
> Which is inserted through a hole behind.
> At the navel, at the points formally stressed, at the organs of
>   sense,
> Lice glue themselves, dolls, local deities,
> His smooth wood creeps with all the creeds of the world.
>
> Attending there let us absorb the cultures of nations
> And dissolve into our judgment all their codes.
> Then, being clogged with a natural hesitation
> (People are continually asking one the way out),
> Let us stand here and admit that we have no road.
> Being everything, let us admit that is to be something,
> Or give ourselves the benefit of the doubt;
> Let us offer our pinch of dust all to this God,
> And grant his reign over the entire building.

Yet even here what has moved Empson to speak with such largeness of mind is the largeness of begetting. It is not only that this
'Supreme God' is Tangaroa, the sea god, in the act of creating the
other gods and man; he is seen as wonderfully able to do all the

creating all by himself, and so to absorb the powers of woman-
hood within his manhood. He shows that we can imagine, though,
we cannot enter, a world in which it is not any longer true that

> two is least can with full tension strain,
> Two molecules; one, and the film disbands.

He alone has the right to think that he can create it all alone; he
possesses the true pride of which Empson's Arachne was the
travesty. 'A desire to include all sexuality . . .', 'clever and
detached enough to do everything for itself': Alice too belongs to
this odd family of Arachne, the supreme god, and the phoenix-
like tree of 'Note on Local Flora'.

The supreme god's face is a blank shield, still to receive lineage
and arms. His belly is a comical womb, a bit like an unaggressive
Wooden Horse—'He needs his belly to include the Pantheon', not
as we need ours. His 'navel' is even more delightful a supereroga-
tion than those of Adam and Eve. We are from the first line in the
world of mock-heroic (often, incidentally, as in Dryden and Pope,
a world of primal acts of creation), but there is no demeaning.
And that this should be so is a consequence of the shrewd calm
with which the poem contemplates the greatest-ever act of
begetting; one is one and yet not all alone.

The world of 'Note on Local Flora' is mock-heroic too, and it
again celebrates an extraordinary begetting, not in the backward
vista but in the forward.

> There is a tree native in Turkestan,
> Or further east towards the Tree of Heaven,
> Whose hard cold cones, not being wards to time,
> Will leave their mother only for good cause;
> Will ripen only in a forest fire;
> Wait, to be fathered as was Bacchus once,
> Through men's long lives, that image of time's end.
> I knew the Phoenix was a vegetable.
> So Semele desired her deity
> As this in Kew thirsts for the Red Dawn.

The poem is itself a hard cold cone which then miraculously
ripens. The buoyant snap of the eighth line—'I knew the Phoenix
was a vegetable'—is that of a ripened conclusion (though it
importantly does not conclude the poem); the poem's first
sentence had ripened through seven lines to bring this triumphant

jauntiness to birth. I appreciate that, among other things, the poem is a political *aperçu*; but that does not alter the fact that what animates it, what makes it ripen in the mind (ripeness is all), is its relief as it contemplates this apocalyptic begetting. Miraculous, in that the cones are already gestating ('Will leave their mother only for good cause') but somehow have not yet been fathered ('Wait, to be fathered as was Bacchus once'); and in that what Donne called 'the phoenix riddle' is solved, newly solved and yet one had always dimly known that must be it. The tree is not to feel any pain; yet the last two lines of the poem are chastening (as so often in an Empson poem), for they expand from the previous line's single succinctness into a graver tone and a larger movement, and they bring before us not just the fathering of Bacchus but the woman who was destroyed in bringing into the world 'The laughing god born of a startling answer' (Empson's 'Bacchus'). Semele, burnt to destruction by the god she loved, reminds the poem of the pangs of birth and of the terribly unforeseen; Kew is securely and therefore insecurely within the real world; 'thirsts' stands in an oddly challenging relation to Bacchus; and the Red Dawn is something from which only this extraordinary tree (not native here, remember, though 'local flora') can have no impulse whatsoever to flinch. I am not out to darken this invigorating poem, but I think that the crisp weight of its joking is a matter of its knowing the usual gravity of birth; indeed it is invigorating just because it speaks from Kew and not from Turkestan. The gaiety of 'Note on Local Flora' and of 'Homage to the British Museum', like the joy of 'Camping Out', derives its pungent force from appropriating to itself these lavish grotesqueries of begetting (the phoenix tree, the all-creating god, the Madonna); the gaiety banishes the usual anxieties and trepidation that are rightly involved in begetting—banishes them, which is not the same as ignoring them; they must put in a spectral experience so that they can be exorcised. 'Note on Local Flora'—the mother as a mysterious tree—is in its way an exorcism of the darker mysteries involved in the woman as tree in 'The Ants'. I think too of 'The World's End', and of Empson's feeling for 'the gulf that lies so snugly curled', possibilities of independence and freedom, conceivabilities which lie like embryos never to be given birth, there 'Where nameless Somethings in their causes sleep'.

For the tree, fire is a thirsted-for begetting. In 'Missing Dates', 'The complete fire is death.' It is a poem about life as a long day's

dying and about inevitable waste; what reinforces the feeling that
it is the grimmest of Empson's three villanelles is the way in
which the two refrains—'Slowly the poison the whole blood
stream fills', and 'The waste remains, the waste remains and kills'
—manifest the same impulse, oppressively at one, whereas they
stand at something of an angle to each other in 'Villanelle' ('It is
the pain, it is the pain, endures', and 'Poise of my hands reminded
me of yours'), as in 'Reflection from Anita Loos' ('No man is sure
he does not need to climb', and ' "A girl can't go on laughing all
the time" ').

> Slowly the poison the whole blood stream fills.
> It is not the effort nor the failure tires.
> The waste remains, the waste remains and kills.
>
> It is not your system or clear sight that mills
> Down small to the consequence a life requires;
> Slowly the poison the whole blood stream fills.
>
> They bled an old dog dry yet the exchange rills
> Of young dog blood gave but a month's desires.
> The waste remains, the waste remains and kills.
>
> It is the Chinese tombs and the slag hills
> Usurp the soil, and not the soil retires.
> Slowly the poison the whole blood stream fills.
>
> Not to have fire is to be a skin that shrills.
> The complete fire is death. From partial fires
> The waste remains, the waste remains and kills.
>
> It is the poems you have lost, the ills
> From missing dates, at which the heart expires.
> Slowly the poison the whole blood stream fills.
> The waste remains, the waste remains and kills.

When he reads this poem and speaks of it, Empson usually denies
that 'missing dates' had for him any real connection with the
true, the frustratedly amatory, meaning of the phrase; he was
using it only to mean appointments that fell through, opportunities missed. And yet it is impossible to feel that when 'the poems'
suddenly surface at the end they can really be thought of as
carrying much of the gravity of the poem. I like the oddity of

their sudden intervention, but I think it important that they should seem so desolatingly much smaller than the dark intimations of this poem itself. For the pull towards death, towards a sense of waste and death in life, is very much a matter of feeling so many possibilities of life unbegotten. 'The consequence a life requires' has, I think, to include some sense of the many things consequence can be (the act of most consequence which a life requires is to perpetuate the sequence of life). The old dog who gets the young dog's blood gets a cruel parody of begetting (the generations the wrong way round, moreover), as 'a month's desires' suggests—and how long is a month to a dog? The waste-tombs of ancient death and the waste-mounds of modern life between them leave no room for that soil which should be the ground of present life, new life. Yet I don't think that 'Missing Dates' is clear to itself about the consequence this poem requires. Perhaps because it is the poem which most raises to a glare the two focuses (upon life as dark and upon life as the creation of light); perhaps because it so completely lacks a sense of anybody or anything else addressed, whether a tree, a general audience or a person —it self-communes as no other poem of Empson's does, its *you* a desolating vacancy; perhaps because it allows so little room to Empson's humour, whether sardonic or affectionate; perhaps because its refrains concur as hammer-blows rather than converging as pincers: at any rate I find that it presents a mind troubled like a fountain stirred, and the poem itself sees not the bottom of it. 'Or tell me with less drama . . . '

Of 'The Teasers' one is fearful of saying anything at all because of the high scorn which Empson let play upon G. S. Fraser:

> When dear old George Fraser says it was all against being horrified by women when they're menstruating, and offering my person to all the women in the world and so forth, I was much shocked. I don't entertain these shocking sentiments at all, do you see? Absolutely nothing to do with what is in my mind; I wouldn't even have thought it was in George's mind. (*the Review*, June 1963)

> Not but they die, the teasers and the dreams,
> Not but they die,
>   and tell the careful flood
> To give them what they clamour for and why.

You could not fancy where they rip to blood,
You could not fancy
    nor that mud
I have heard speak that will not cake or dry.

Our claims to act appear so small to these,
Our claims to act
    colder lunacies
That cheat the love, the moment, the small fact.

Make no escape because they flash and die,
Make no escape
    build up your love,
Leave what you die for and be safe to die.

Empson has insisted that the four stanzas which make up 'The Teasers' were salvaged from a long poem and that they cannot really be made sense of. I shall say only that it is clearly an erotic poem; that 'the careful flood' (at once cautious, full of unforeseen cares, and both destructive and creative—the Nile's flood as well as Noah's) creates life, 'what they clamour for' ('the clamour of life' is a prominent phrase in Empson's 'Ignorance of Death'); that the fantasies of life are no more evanescent than our love-hopes and our acts of love, and yet that this should not move us to escape but to build. I believe that the last stanza sees begetting as the true recourse which is not falsely an escape; sees it as the way 'to build up your love', and as the paradox: 'Leave what you die for and be safe to die.' *Leave* both as quit and as leave behind you when you go; what we all die for—whether in terms of ideals or of the hungry generations—is our progeny, and it is only in doing so that we can 'be safe to die'. 'To give away your selfe, keeps your selfe still': that was the line from Shakespeare's Sonnet 16 which Empson paraphrased as 'you are not less yourself because you have had children'.

'Safe': the word is at home in 'Thanks for a Wedding Present', one of the very few poems in the *Collected Poems* that are later than the 1940 volume.

Thanks for a Wedding Present

[It was a compass on a necklace with the poem:

> *Magnetic Powers cannot harm your House*
> *Since Beauty, Wit and Love its walls de-Gauss.*

And if, when nights are dark, your feet should stray
By chance or instinct to the Load of Hay
With me drink deep and on th' uncharted track
Let my Magnetic Power guide you back.]

She bears your gift as one safe to return
    From longer journeys asking braver fuel
        Than a poor needle losing itself an hour

Within a *Load of Hay* needs heart to learn.
    She wears the birth of physics as a jewel
        And of the maritime empires as a flower.

I think this a lovely poem and am surprised that it never seems to get mentioned. What is especially fine in it is that it carries out its delicate double-duty so unassumingly: it needs to incorporate gratitude to the giver within a larger gratitude to the woman who has given so much larger a gift, herself; and this without slighting the wedding present and its friendly love. Likewise it needs to praise the wedding present and more vastly to praise the woman (and moreover without self-congratulation); and this it does by letting us feel that it is not only the compass, but the wearer, who is delighted in as a jewel and as a flower. The serenity and safety of the poem derive, I think, from the tact and secret largeness with which it includes a sense of what the right true end of love in marriage is. The poem has two sentences only, one beginning 'She bears your gift', and the other 'She wears the birth'; the parallelism, the internal rhyme, and the words 'bear' and 'birth' all seem to me to ask us to feel something of a rich future such as we are usually guided to glimpse in an epithalamium. The dignity of the poem is achieved by its compacting so much of what had always been the preoccupations of Empson's poems: the compass; safety and yet adventurous 'longer journeys asking braver fuel'; physics; the maritime empires. But just as the giver's verses had spoken of 'your House' (and in so doing could not but suggest, as it were, a royal house), so the birth of physics and of the maritime empires, those past discoveries of richness, should be felt as indeed births. The poem's climax, they expand to a full sense of the human situation, and of future births as rich.

    The last four poems in the *Collected Poems* are 'Let it go' (which is 'about stopping writing poetry'; record-notes); 'Thanks for a Wedding Present'; 'Sonnet' (published 1942, on 'the cultures of

man'); and—translated in 1951 and published in 1952—'Chinese
Ballad'. I think it sheer grace that 'Thanks for a Wedding Present'
and 'Chinese Ballad' should form the points that they do in the arc
of Empson's poetry. 'The bit of a *Chinese Ballad*, about resistance
to the Japanese, is direct translation; I felt that it achieved without
effort the metaphysical poetry which we struggled to write when
I was young' (record-notes).

> Now he has seen the girl Hsiang-Hsiang,
>   Now back to the guerrilla band;
> And she goes with him down the vale
>   And pauses at the strand.
>
> The mud is yellow, deep, and thick,
>   And their feet stick, where the stream turns.
> 'Make me two models out of this,
>   That clutches as it yearns.
>
> 'Make one of me and one of you,
>   And both shall be alive.
> Were there no magic in the dolls
>   The children could not thrive.
>
> 'When you have made them smash them back:
>   They yet shall live again.
> Again make dolls of you and me
>   But mix them grain by grain.
>
> 'So your flesh shall be part of mine
>   And part of mine be yours.
> Brother and sister we shall be
>   Whose unity endures.
>
> 'Always the sister doll will cry,
>   Made in these careful ways,
> Cry on and on, Come back to me,
>   Come back, in a few days.'

Love in time of war, with the poignancy of what war does to
parenthood; the intrepid journey; the respect for courage and for
decision; the fording of the river (which had once been 'Leaves
isle equation by not frozen ford') and its unobtrusive paradox
about the right choice ('He crosses the stream where it turns
because it is wider therefore shallower there', Notes); the pathos

of the utterly disparate time-scales ('Cry on and on, Come back to me, | Come back, in a few days'); and at its heart symbolic be-getting of dolls (how different from those 'dolls' on the 'Supreme God'), of two people, an act of self-begetting, offering a magical reassurance and an unmagical epitome of faithfulness, and which recalls the children begotten by the ordinary magic of birth: all this, the fullness of the poem's respect for what it contemplates, is achieved because the subject so fully reconciles so much in Empson's thinking and feeling. He took no liberties, and it is altogether right that the only point on which he needs to say any-thing should be this: 'I added the bit about children, but I under-stand that is only like working a footnote into the text, because the term specifically means dolls for children' (Notes). What is created is what is honoured: an assurance that though life may be essentially inadequate to the human spirit, the human spirit is essentially adequate to life.

Empson has said that when he finished *The Structure of Complex Words* he felt *Nunc dimittis* (*Mandrake*, Autumn–Winter 1955–6). Fortunately he was not so possessed by the feeling as to write no further criticism. But given the particular kind of conclusive triumph which 'Chinese Ballad' is, there is a simple dignity, clear-sighted and touching, in its having been Empson's *Nunc dimittis* as a poet.

NOTES

1 Compare *Some Versions*, p. 100: '. . . as often happens to poets, who tend to make in their lives a situation they have already written about'.

2 A magnificent bit of Empson's Englishness, 'and seem odd'. As in his remarks on Donne's marriage: 'He couldn't have been certain when he did this that it would break his career, because it wouldn't have done if the father hadn't behaved foolishly; the father first insisted on having Donne sacked and then found he had better try to have him reinstated, which Egerton refused on the very English ground that the fuss about the matter had been sufficiently ridiculous already' (*Kenyon Review*, Summer 1957).

15

William Empson

Francis Berry

I

AN EARLIER POET'S HELL

Often too sane, Cowper was at times mad
Outright, his 'Castaway'. On whose conscience should
Lie that? the Father's? the Son's? the Ghost's? Not ours!
Or the churches', inspired by love but teaching terrors?
'You'll be castaway for ever if you're not good.
Avoid:
Don't spell God backwards.'
                                        Dare it:

Dog.

Then hell. Despair.
On whose conscience lies this insanity?
His timid own? or that of christianity?

Nowadays we are inclined to blame the Reverend Something
    Newton.
But was not all the mollycoddling he had of dear old Mrs Unwin
God?

Fear.
Like his own weak wild pet hare.

II

THE LATER POET, TO WHOM GOOD WISHES, AND HIS INTOLERABLE HELL

When the object of homage is Empson, why recall an earlier
    William?
The later William's *Milton's God*, 'considered as a contribution
To the advancement of critical studies', may not indeed rate—
However consistent in its wit, characteristic in its hate—
Equal to the wiry speed of *Seven Types*, the splash of the *Pastoral*
(Brilliant on *Alice*, expert on the 'Elegy'), yet it is undeniable
(Not excepting the exercised precisions of the *Complex Words*) that,
In its No to the Christian hell, this *God* is the most compassionate
And the most compulsive Empson that this William has yet
    written.
May he write more, as indignantly brave, fantastically right

Or wrong—will live long characteristically brave and joyfully
    write
The books that he needs to, books glorious in a freedom from spite
But exquisitely naughty in wit, and may he rise—early or late—
To deliver no 'style of despair' but in his own cheerful spirit;
May he analyse the analysable, and of the indefinable
May he be less contemptuous than of the bad detective novel.
Then, cunning mathematician, *Times* crossword solver, may the
    surge or spate,
In his old age, of making verses, sparkle again, so that a *Complete*
Poems will double their present number, and may this contribution
By Empson be a crowning delight for this extraordinary William.

Fear.
But no timidity here.

III

THE SHEFFIELD PROFESSOR

(*a*)

In the teaching of a variety of text,
His policy was 'variety of opinion'.
Remember the mixture that he mixed:

Atheist, catholic, quaker, scrutineer;
Oxford, marxist, la-dee-la and fiddle-de-dee;
Post-christian roamer, the sweet-girl pagan.

Let us praise the jovial man,
His splitting jokes at various bars,
Quick chinese walk, the ruddy tan.

And let us praise the lucky man,
Chestnuts pulled for him from many fires,
Endearing helplessness, as endear it can.

And let us praise the plucky man,
His wit the stronger as the pain grew worse.
He'll end with pride as he began.

And let us praise the courtly man,
Concern for invalids, the touching airs
Of Wykehamist blent with Old Japan.

And let us praise the Yorkshire man
Emerging from his 'burrow' to stalk the moors;
In pork-pie hat, his county to scan—

Strong in the line of East Riding squires.

(*b*)

Witty and lucky and plucky this man.
He came as a legend, he left as a myth
At the bars, by our fires, with his verse, with his prose,
His extraordinary dares, his amazingly wise—
Or his occasionally wild, quite lunatick—flairs

He left with even more lustre than he began.

(*c*)

To finish this section—and with a grand slam:
Let us now praise the Sheffield burrow!
For eighteen sessions the Empson home.

Often from here, when disaster did loom,
Would he answer the Dean, or other such bother,
With an eye-weeping frolic, dispersing the gloom.

The joke a good way, confronting a horror.
A purgatory now, no hell hereafter.

IV

THE GENIAL SAGE

Hating cruelty, he hated hell,
All the christian implements of pain,
In gaols the rope, in schools the cane.
'More christian than a christian',
Say some. He'd deny it to the full,
Preferring Buddha,
   Loathing an idea of sacrifice.
   It was obscene.

At crossword, chess problem, textual crux,
Pet Algebra, wiser than Confucius;
Choosy at cooking—Yorkshire or Chinese,
Detective novel for his evening ease;
At puzzling out this game of intellects
No-one shrewder.
   And then he rests, his face averse
   To mask of Benin.

Emeritus, you'll be active. Marvell next?
Nervous as Cowper, you did re-act
More bravely from the start of Yokefleet story
To bestow at last on Sheffield your own glory.
And for all heretics, traitors, or others racked,
Did properly shudder;
   Naturally more generous
   Than Origen even.

V

WHAT THE ANGELS SAID

'He jauntily attacked while others despaired
Of our Chief's unfortunate public image, and everyone
Forgave, except One.

                         Look
What he said about Him in his *Milton.*'
And while they're busying the pages of that book,
Wing-fanning them over,
'We're lucky to have had him', conclude.
'For, about that unfortunate image of God,
This one *cared.*'

16

An Empson Bibliography

Moira Megaw

This bibliography aims to cover all the published work to the end of 1973, but it does not include the reprinting of poems in later anthologies or of passages or chapters from Empson's books, and includes only a selection of letters. Reprints of criticism which has not been printed by Empson in book form are noted where known and in the case of these reprints additions by the author are noted and revisions also, where known. The titles of poems which have been altered in revision are entered as they are given in *Collected Poems* 1955 (abbreviated as *CP* 1955) together with the original titles. Poems uncollected in *CP* 1955 are denoted by an asterisk.

Acknowledgments are due to Peter Lowbridge for his excellent bibliography on which this one is based (*the Review*, nos 6 and 7, June 1963) and to the editor of *the Review*, Ian Hamilton, for permission to use it; also to Professor Empson, Professor Ricks, Professor Rintaro Fukuhara, Martin Dodsworth, and John Scattergood for their help.

1927

POETRY

'Poem about a Ball in the Nineteenth Century', *Magdalene College Magazine* VIII (June), p. 111. Reprinted in *Experiment*, no. 7 (Spring 1931), p. 59.

REVIEWS

Book reviews

Time and Western Man, by Wyndham Lewis; *Right Off the Map*, by

C. E. Montague: *Granta* (21 Oct.), p. 47.

Aspects of the Novel, by E. M. Forster; *Mood Without Measure*, by Richard Church; *A Chinaman's Opinion of Us*, by Hway-Uny: *Granta* (28 Oct.), pp. 61–2.

The Life of the White Ant, by M. Maeterlinck; *Others Abide*, by H. Wolfe; *Poems from the Greek*; *Poems from the Chinese*, by Arthur Waley; *Poems from the Persian*, by E. Browne; *Latin Anthology*; *Poems from the Irish*: *Granta* (4 Nov.), p. 89.

The Monthly Criterion, vol. VI, nos 1–5, ed. T. S. Eliot; *The Secret of Father Brown*, by G. K. Chesterton: *Granta* (11 Nov.), pp. 104–5.

Proper Studies, by Aldous Huxley; *A Subaltern on the Somme*, by Mark VII: *Granta* (18 Nov.), p. 123.

The Prospects of Literature, by Logan Pearsall Smith; *Oxford Poetry 1927*: *Granta* (25 Nov.), p. 154.

All At Sea, by O. and S. Sitwell; *The Wild Body*, by Wyndham Lewis; *Reluctantly Told*, by J. Hillyer; *Mind*, ed. R. J. S. Mc'Dowall; *Lions led by Donkeys*, by P. A. Thompson; *Cressage*, by A. C. Benson; *George Leigh Mallory, a Memoir*, by D. Pye: *Granta* (2 Dec.), pp. 192–4.

Film reviews

Granta: 6 May, p. 410; 13 May, p. 430; 20 May, p. 438; 27 May, p. 463; 10 June, p. 522; 14 Oct., p. 18; 4 Nov., pp. 84–5.

MISCELLANEOUS

Humorous verse and prose sketches (with J. H. E. P. Marks), *Granta* (18 Nov.), p. 116.

1928

POETRY

'To an Old Lady', *Cambridge Review*, vol. 49 (20 April), p. 347. Reprinted in *Cambridge Poetry 1929*, p. 35.

'Sonnet' (title in *CP* 1955: 'The Ants'), *Cambridge Review*, vol. 49 (27 April), p. 369.

'Invitation to Juno', *Cambridge Review*, vol. 49 (4 May), p. 387. Reprinted in *New Signatures*, ed. M. Roberts (1932), p. 72.

'Rolling the Lawn', *Cambridge Review*, vol. 49 (4 May), p. 388.

'Une Brioche pour Cerbère',* *Cambridge Review*, vol. 49 (4 May), p. 388.

'Relativity' (title in *CP* 1955: 'The World's End'), *Cambridge Review*, vol. 49 (11 May), p. 406.

'Letter' (title in *CP* 1955: 'Letter Two'), *Cambridge Review*, vol. 49 (6 June), p. 485. Reprinted in *Cambridge Poetry 1929*, p. 38.

'Arachne', *Cambridge Review*, vol. 49 (6 June), p. 490. Reprinted in *Cambridge Poetry 1929*, p. 40; and in *Recent Poetry 1923–1933*, ed. Alida Monro (1933), p. 50.

'New World Bistres',* *Cambridge Review*, vol. 49 (6 June), p. 492.

'Inhabitants' (title in *CP* 1955: 'Value is in Activity'), *Cambridge Review*, vol. 49 (6 June), p. 506.

'Villanelle', *Cambridge Review*, vol. 50 (26 Oct.), p. 52. Reprinted in *Cambridge Poetry 1929*, p. 37; and in *Recent Poetry 1923–1933*, p. 51.

'Sea Voyage', *Cambridge Review*, vol. 50 (16 Nov.), p. 131.

'Legal Fiction', *Cambridge Review*, vol. 50 (30 Nov.), p. 171. Reprinted in *Cambridge Poetry 1929*, p. 39.

'Letter' (title in *CP* 1955: 'Letter One'), *Experiment*, no. 1 (Nov.), p. 4. Reprinted in *New Signatures* (1932), p. 66; and, under the title 'Letter One', in *The Year's Poetry 1935*, ed. D. K. Roberts, G. Gould and J. Lehmann, pp. 92–3.

'Part of Mandevil's Travels', *Experiment*, no. 1 (Nov.), pp. 38–9. Reprinted in *Cambridge Poetry 1929*, p. 33.

'Disillusion with Metaphysics' (title in *CP* 1955: 'Dissatisfaction with Metaphysics'), *Experiment*, no. 1 (Nov.), p. 48.

'Flighting for Duck', *Magdalene College Magazine*, vol. 9 (Dec.), pp. 19–20.

REVIEWS

Book reviews

Possible Worlds, by J. B. S. Haldane; *Archimedes or the Future of Physics*, by C. L. Whyte; *Hunting Under the Microscope*, by Sir A. Shipley: *Granta* (27 Jan.), p. 229.

The Feet of the Young Men, by 'The Janitor'; *Mr. Teedles, the Gland Old Man*, by T. Le Breton; *Condemnations of the Action Française*, by L. Ward: *Granta* (3 Feb.), p. 250.

King Arthur: A Dramatic Opera, by John Dryden; *Hermes or the Future of Chemistry*, by T. W. Jones; *British Farmers in Denmark*, by J. R. Bond *et al.*; *The Book of Opportunities*, by R. H. Platt: *Granta* (17 Feb.), pp. 285–6.

The Sleeping Sword, by B. Goolden; *The Monthly Criterion*, vol. VII, nos 1–2: *Granta* (24 Feb.), p. 304.

The Bridge of San Luis Rey, by Thornton Wilder; *Hollywood Love*, by C. N. Williamson; *Potiphar's Wife*, by E. C. Middleton; *Cornelian: A Fable*, by H. Acton; *They Return at Evening*, by H. R. Wakefield; *A Lecture on Lectures*, by Sir A. Quiller-Couch; *Opposite Things*, by M. C. Sturge: *Granta* (9 Mar.), pp. 339–40.

Flights into Antiquity, by A. Weigall; *Wanderings in Medieval London*, by C. Pendrill; *War Among Ladies*, by E. Scott; *Fraudern Bear*, by B. Mowshay; *The Way the World is Going*, by H. G. Wells; *The Pre-War Mind in Britain*, by C. E. Playne; *Sweeney Todd, the Demon Barber of Fleet Street*, by D. Pitt; *Jazz and Jasper*, by W. Gerhardi; *Gemel in London*, by J. Agate: *Granta* (27 April), pp. 375–6.

The Eugenics Review: *Granta* (4 May), p. 396.

Blue Trousers, by Lady Murasaki, trans. by Arthur Waley; *Words and Poetry*, by G. Rylands; *Power and Pillars*, by R. Kircher; *Sex Relations without Marriage*, by A. H. Gray; *Another Country*, by H. du Coudray: *Granta* (11 May), pp. 419–20.

An Experiment with Time, by J. W. Dunne: *Cambridge Review* (25 May), pp. 446–7.

How a Play is Produced, by K. Capek; *The Boy Prophet*, by E. Fleg: *Granta* (25 May), pp. 457–8.

Why Mr. Bertrand Russell is not a Christian, by H. G. Wood; *The Beast with Five Fingers*, by W. F. Harvey: *Granta* (1 June), pp. 481–2.

ABC of Adler's Psychology, by P. Mairet; *Keeping Up Appearances*, by R. Macaulay; *Four Boon Fellows*, by A. J. Brown: *Granta* (8 June), pp. 519–22.

Triforium, by Sherard Vines: *Cambridge Review* (23 Nov.), p. 161.

Film and theatre reviews

Cambridge Review: 27 April, p. 375; 4 May, p. 396; 25 May, p. 452; 6 June, p. 513; 19 Oct., pp. 33–4.

Granta: 19 Oct., p. 42; 26 Oct., p. 63; 9 Nov., p. 111; 16 Nov., p. 120; 23 Nov., p. 154; 30 Nov., p. 197.

LETTER

Reply to Desmond Flower concerning Empson's review of *Berlin*, *Cambridge Review*, vol. 49 (11 May), pp. 412–13.

MISCELLANEOUS

Humorous verse and prose sketches, *Granta* (3 Feb.), p. 243; (2 Nov.), pp. 74, 85; (16 Nov.), p. 123; (30 Nov.), p. 180. With J. H. E. P. Marks (12 Oct.), p. 8.

1929

POETRY

'Camping Out', *Experiment*, no. 2 (Feb.), p. 15. Reprinted in *New Signatures* (1932), p. 71.

'Earth has Shrunk in the Wash', *Experiment*, no. 2 (Feb.), p. 45.

'Sleeping Out in a College Cloister', *Magdalene College Magazine*, vol. 9 (Mar.), p. 46. Reprinted in *The Venture*, no. 6 (June 1930), p. 265.

'Insomnia',* *Cambridge Review*, vol. 50 (19 April), p. 373.

'Letter Three', *Experiment*, no. 3 (May), p. 7.

'Essay',* *Magdalene College Magazine*, vol. 9 (June), p. 79.

'UFA Nightmare',* *Experiment*, no. 4 (Nov.), p. 28.

'Letter Four', *Songs for Sixpence*, ed. J. Bronowski and J. Reeves.

Cambridge Poetry 1929 (reprints of: 'Part of Mandevil's Travels', p. 33; 'To An Old Lady', p. 35; 'Villanelle', 'Letter Two', p. 37; 'Legal Fiction', p. 38; 'Arachne', p. 39).

CRITICISM

'Ambiguity in Shakespeare's Sonnet XVI', *Experiment*, no. 2 (Feb.), pp. 33–5.

'An Early Romantic' (critical essay on Vaughan), *Cambridge Review* (31 May), pp. 495–6.

'The Sacrifice' (on Herbert's poem), *Experiment*, no. 3 (May), pp. 41–4.

'Some Notes on Mr Eliot', *Experiment*, no. 4 (Nov.), pp. 6–8.

Book review

Diversion (a play), by J. Van Druten: *Cambridge Review* (8 Mar.),
p. 355.

Film reviews

Granta: 1 Feb., p. 262; 3 May, p. 420.

MISCELLANEOUS

Humorous prose sketch (with J. H. E. P. Marks), *Granta* (8
Mar.), p. 352.

1930

POETRY

'Note on Local Flora', *Experiment*, no. 5 (Feb.), p. 26. Reprinted
in *New Signatures* (1932), p. 70.
The Venture, no. 6 (June), p. 265 (reprint of 'Sleeping Out in a
College Cloister').
'Poem' (title in *CP* 1955: 'The Scales'), *Experiment*, no. 6 (Oct.),
p. 12. Reprinted in *New Signatures* (1932), p. 67.
'Description of a View', *Experiment*, no. 6 (Oct.), p. 13.

CRITICISM

'O Miselle Passer!' (reply to John Sparrow's criticism of I. A.
Richards), *Oxford Outlook*, vol. 10 (May), pp. 470–8. (See
'Letters' 1931.)
Seven Types of Ambiguity, Chatto & Windus.

REVIEWS

The Elizabethan Underworld; Harman, Greene, Dekker and Others, ed.
A. V. Judges: *Nation and Athenaeum* (5 July), p. 444.
Studies in Elizabethan Imagery, by Elizabeth Holmes: *Criterion*, vol.
9, no. 37 (July), pp. 767–74.

The Metaphysical Foundations of Modern Science, by E. A. Burtt: *Criterion*, vol. 10, no. 38 (Oct.), pp. 167–71.

LETTER

'Shelley' (reply to Edmund Blunden's review of *Seven Types of Ambiguity*), *Nation and Athenaeum* (29 Nov.), p. 291.

1931

POETRY

Experiment, no. 7 (Spring), p. 59 (reprint of 'Poem about a Ball in the Nineteenth Century').

CRITICISM

'A Note on W. H. Auden's *Paid on Both Sides*', *Experiment*, no. 7 (Spring), p. 60.
Seven Types of Ambiguity (American edition), Harcourt Brace.
'Virginia Woolf', *Scrutinies*, vol. 2, pp. 204–16.

REVIEWS

Recent Poetry: 'The Pursuit', by P. P. Graves; 'The Grave of Arthur', by G. K. Chesterton; 'Dear Judas', by Robinson Jeffers; 'The Glance Backward', by Richard Church; 'The Gum Trees', by Roy Campbell; 'Marina', by T. S. Eliot: *Nation and Athenaeum* (21 Feb.), p. 672.
'Sound and Meaning in English Poetry', by Katherine M. Wilson, *The Criterion*, vol. 10, no. 40 (April), pp. 529–34.

LETTER

'Practical Criticism' (continuation of debate with John Sparrow), *Oxford Outlook*, vol. 11 (Mar.), pp. 54–7.

MISCELLANEOUS

'Learning of English', *Japan Chronicle* (25 Nov.).

1932

POETRY

'This Last Pain', *New Signatures*, p. 68. (Reprints of: 'Letter One', p. 66; 'The Scales', p. 67; 'Note on Local Flora', p. 70; 'Camping Out', p. 71; 'Invitation to Juno', p. 72.)
'Homage to the British Museum' and a reprint of 'Note on Local Flora', *Poetica* (Japan), (Jan.).

CRITICISM

'Marvell's Garden', *Studies in English Literature*, published by the English Literary Society of Japan (Aug.).
'Marvell's Garden', *Scrutiny*, vol. 1, no. 3 (Dec.), pp. 236–40.
'The Double-Plot in *Troilus and Cressida*', *The Rising Generation* (Japan), 67, pp. 366–7, 402–3.
'Harold Monro', *The Rising Generation*, 67, p. 151.
'*Mrs Dalloway*', *The Rising Generation*, 68, pp. 182–3.

MISCELLANEOUS

'A Comparative Experiment in Text Simplification' (Pandora and the Box put into Basic), *The Bulletin of the Institute for Research in English* (Japan), no. 88 (Oct.–Nov.), pp. 6–8.
'Basic English', *Japan Chronicle* (17 Aug.).

1933

POETRY

'Bacchus', *New Verse*, no. 2 (Mar.), p. 8. Reprinted in *The Fox and Daffodil*, a poetry magazine (ed. in Japan by T. Sone and T. Kitamura), no. 5 (1934).
Recent Poetry 1923–1933 (reprints of: 'Arachne', p. 50; 'Villanelle', p. 51).

CRITICISM

'La Double Intrigue et L'Ironie dans le Drame', *Le Théâtre Elizabéthain. Cahiers du Sud*, 10, Numéro Spécial (Juin), pp. 36–9.

'They that have power. . . .' (on Shakespeare's sonnets) *Studies in English Literature* published by the English Literary Society of Japan, vol. 13, pp. 451–69.

'T. E. Hulme's *Speculations*', *The Rising Generation*, 69, pp. 2–3.

'Introduction to *Selected Essays*' by T. S. Eliot, trans. into Japanese by T. Kitamura, published by Kinseido, Tokyo.

'Proletarian Literature', *New English and American Literature* (Japan), (Aug.).

LETTERS

'An Experiment in Text Simplification', *Bulletin of the Institute for Research in English Teaching*, no. 90 (Jan.), pp. 3–4.

'Concerning "Basic English"', *Bulletin of the Institute for Research in English Teaching*, no. 91 (Feb.), p. 3; no. 92 (Mar. p. 7; no. 96 (July), p. 7; no. 98 (Oct.–Nov.), p. 10.

MISCELLANEOUS

'Words with Meaning', *Japan Chronicle* (23 Feb.).

1934

POETRY

'Letter Five', *The Year's Poetry 1934*, ed. D. K. Roberts, G. Gould and J. Lehmann, p. 94.

The Fox and Daffodil, no. 5 (reprint of 'Bacchus').

Poems by William Empson containing fourteen poems to be included in *Poems* (Chatto and Windus, 1935). Printed for private circulation. The Fox and Daffodil Press (Japan).

CRITICISM

'*The Beggars' Opera*', *The Rising Generation*, 70.

Notes on 'Arachne', *The Rising Generation*, 71.

MISCELLANEOUS

'On the Teaching of Literature', trans. S. Narita, *Literary Art* (Japan).

1935

POETRY

'Bacchus Two', *Criterion*, vol. 14, no. 57 (July), p. 572.
'Travel Note' (title in *CP* 1955: 'Four Legs, Three Legs, Two Legs'), *New Verse*, no. 16 (Aug.–Sept.), p. 9.
'Doctrinal Point', *The Year's Poetry 1935*, p. 90. (Reprint of 'Letter One', pp. 92–3.)
Poems (Chatto & Windus). Including first publication of: 'Plenum and Vacuum' and 'High Dive'.

CRITICISM

'Proletarian Literature', *Scrutiny*, vol. 3, no. 4 (Mar.), pp. 332–8.
Some Versions of Pastoral, Chatto & Windus.

REVIEWS

The Indus Civilisation, by Ernest Mackay: *New Statesman* (27 April), p. 592.
Coleridge on Imagination, by I. A. Richards: *Criterion*, vol. 14, no. 56 (April), pp. 482–5.
Poems, by George Barker: *New Statesman* (18 May), pp. 720–2.
Basic Rules of Reason, by I. A. Richards: *Spectator* (14 June), pp. 1024–6.
Basic in Teaching, by I. A. Richards: *Spectator* (14 June), pp. 1024–6.
An Enquiry into Moral Notions, by John Laird: *Spectator* (29 Nov.), p. 912.

LETTERS

Concerning 'Basic English', *Spectator* (2 Aug.), p. 191.
Concerning a review of *Some Versions of Pastoral* in the previous issue, *Times Literary Supplement* (7 Dec.), p. 838.

MISCELLANEOUS

The Outlook of Science by J. B. S. Haldane, put into 'Basic' by W. Empson, Psyche Miniatures.

Science and Well-Being by J. B. S. Haldane, put into 'Basic' by W. Empson, Psyche Miniatures.

'The Need for Translation Theory in Linguistics', *Psyche*, vol. 15, pp. 188–97. (Reprinted in *Structure of Complex Words* as Appendix III, minus one footnote.)

1936

POETRY

'Courage means Running', *Contemporary Poetry and Prose*, no. 1 (May), p. 6. Reprinted in *The Year's Poetry 1936*, ed. D. K. Roberts and J. Lehmann, pp. 62–3.

'The Small Bird to the Big' (a poem by C. Hatakeyama, trans. W.E.), *Listener* (5 Aug.), p. 252.

'Echo' (a poem by C. Hatakeyama, trans. W.E.; title in *CP* 1955: 'The Shadow'), *Contemporary Poetry and Prose*, no. 7 (Nov.), p. 130.

'Reflection from Rochester', *Poetry* (Chicago), vol. 49 (Nov.), p. 68. Reprinted in *The Year's Poetry 1936*, pp. 64–5.

The Year's Poetry 1936 (reprints of: 'Courage means Running', pp. 62–3; 'Reflection from Rochester', pp. 64–5).

CRITICISM

'Feelings in Words', *Criterion*, vol. 15, no. 59 (January), pp. 183–99.

'The Best Policy', *Life and Letters*, vol. 14, no. 4 (Summer), pp. 37–45.

'Timon's Dog', *Life and Letters*, vol. 15, no. 6 (Winter), pp. 108–15.

'Sense and Sensibility', *Psyche*, vol. 16, pp. 150–64.

REVIEWS

The Dream in Primitive Cultures, by J. Steward Lincoln: *Spectator* (10 Jan.), pp. 64–6.

Human Ecology, by J. W. Bews: *Spectator* (17 Jan.), p. 103.

The Psycho-Biology of Language, by G. K. Zipf: *Spectator* (14 Feb.), p. 270.

Confessions of a Ghost Hunter, by Harry Price: *Spectator* (10 April), p. 675.

The Wilderness of Zin, by Sir Leonard Woolley and T. E. Lawrence; *Abraham*, by Sir Leonard Woolley: *Spectator* (17 April), p. 714.

The Place of Meaning in Poetry, by David Daiches; *The Appreciation of Poetry*, by P. Gurrey: *Criterion*, vol. 15, no. 16 (April), pp. 518–21.

Bali and Angkor, by Geoffrey Gorer: *Spectator* (8 May), p. 844.

The Unlimited Community, by J. W. Friend and J. Fiebleman: *Spectator* (7 Aug.), p. 246.

The Allegory of Love, by C. S. Lewis: *Spectator* (4 Sept.), p. 389.

Apes and Monkeys, by E. G. Boulenger; *Jubilee and her Mother*, by Lorna Lewis; *Interviewing Animals*, by Dr Bastian Schmid; *Animal Life of Yesterday and Today*, by J. Morewood Dowsett: *Spectator* (30 Oct.), pp. 766–8.

The Onlie Begetter, by U. Nisbet; *Principles of Shakespearean Production*, by G. Wilson Knight; *A Study of 'Love's Labour's Lost'*, by F. A. Yates: *Life and Letters*, vol. 15, no. 5 (Autumn), pp. 201–4.

The Problem of 'Hamlet', by A. S. Cairncross: *Life and Letters*, vol. 15, no. 6 (Winter), pp. 210–11.

MISCELLANEOUS

'The Faces of Buddha' (on Buddha faces in art), *Listener* (5 Feb.), pp. 238–40.

1937

POETRY

'Bacchus Four', *Poetry* (Chicago), vol. 49 (Jan.), pp. 188–9. Reprinted in *Poetry* (Chicago), vol. 59 (Feb. 1942), p. 266.

'Missing Dates', *Criterion*, vol. 16, no. 65 (July), p. 618.

'Aubade', *Life and Letters*, vol. 17, no. 10 (Winter), pp. 68–9.

CRITICISM

'About Grigson', *Poetry* (Chicago), vol. 49, no. 4 (Jan.), p. 237.

'Statements in Words', *Criterion*, vol. 16, no. 64 (April), pp. 452–67.

'The Phases of the English Dog' (Part I), *Life and Letters*, vol. 17, no. 10 (Winter), pp. 29–36.

Shakespeare Survey by William Empson and George Garrett, Brendin Publishing Co. ('The Best Policy', pp. 5–21, and 'Timon's Dog', pp. 22–36, by W.E.).

REVIEWS

More Poems, by A. E. Housman: *Poetry* (Chicago), vol. 49, no. 4 (Jan.), p. 228.

The Hero, by Lord Raglan: *Life and Letters*, vol. 16, no. 7 (Spring), pp. 155–6.

Scepticism and Poetry, by D. G. James; *New Literary Values*, by David Daiches; *The Future of Poetry*, by Dallas Kenmare; *Introduction to Modern Poetry*, by Martin Gilkes; *Modern English Poetry* by Bhawani Shankar: *Criterion*, vol. 16, no. 65 (July), pp. 705–7.

Psychology: The Changing Outlook, by F. Aveling; *In the Realm of the Mind*, by C. S. Myers: *Spectator* (20 Aug.), pp. 324–5.

The Philosophy of Rhetoric, by I. A. Richards: *Criterion*, vol. 17, no. 67 (Oct.), pp. 125–9.

LETTER

'Reply to Grigson', *Poetry* (Chicago), vol. 50, no. 2 (May), p. 116.

MISCELLANEOUS

'London Letter', *Poetry* (Chicago), vol. 49 (Jan.), pp. 218–22.
'Ballet of the Far East', *Listener* (7 July), pp. 16–18.

1938

POETRY

'Just a Smack at Auden', *The Year's Poetry 1938*, ed. D. K. Roberts and Geoffrey Grigson, pp. 48–50.

CRITICISM

'The Phases of the English Dog' (concluded), *Life and Letters*, vol. 18, no. 11 (Spring), pp. 36–42.
'Sense in *Measure for Measure*', *Southern Review* (Louisiana), vol. 4, no. 2 (Autumn), pp. 340–50.
English Pastoral Poetry (American edition of *Some Versions of Pastoral*), W. W. Norton.

1939

REVIEW

Modern Poetry and the Tradition, by Cleanth Brooks: *Poetry* (Chicago), vol. 55, no. 3, p. 154.

1940

POETRY

'Bacchus Three', *Poetry* (Chicago), vol. 56 (April), p. 18.
'Poem' (title in *CP* 1955: 'Success'), *Horizon*, vol. 1, no. 5 (May), p. 315.
'The Teasers', *Furioso*, vol. 1, no. 2, p. 13.
The Gathering Storm, Faber & Faber (with a preface to the explanatory notes not included in *CP* 1955). Including first publication of: 'Your Teeth are Ivory Towers', 'The Fool', 'Ignorance of Death', 'The Beautiful Train', 'Manchouli', 'Reflection from Anita Loos', 'Advice', 'Anecdote from Talk', 'China', 'Autumn on Nan-Yueh'.

CRITICISM

'Honest Man', *Southern Review* (Louisiana), vol. 5, no. 4 (Spring), pp. 711–29.
'Basic English and Wordsworth' (a radio talk), *Kenyon Review*, vol. 2, no. 4 (Autumn), pp. 449–57.

REVIEWS

China and Peace and War, by Madam Chiang Kai-Shek: *Spectator* (15 Mar.), p. 386.

Christopher Marlowe, by F. S. Boas: *Life and Letters*, vol. 26, no. 36 (Aug.), pp. 173–5.

Selected Poems of Thomas Hardy, ed. G. M. Young: *New Statesman* (14 Sept.), pp. 263–4.

The Mongol Empire, by M. Prawdin: *Life and Letters*, vol. 27, no. 38 (Oct.), pp. 51–3.

D. H. Lawrence and Susan his Cow, by William York Tindall: *Horizon*, vol. 2, no. 12 (Dec.), pp. 344–6.

MISCELLANEOUS

'Passing Through USA', *Horizon*, vol. 1, no. 6 (June), pp. 425–30.

'A Chinese University', *Life and Letters*, vol. 25, no. 34 (June), pp. 239–45.

1941

REVIEW

The Foundations of Empirical Knowledge, by A. J. Ayer: *Horizon*, vol. 3, no. 15 (Mar.), pp. 222–3.

1942

POETRY

'Sonnet' ('Not wrongly moved . . .'), (also reprint of 'Bacchus Four'), *Poetry* (Chicago), vol. 59 (Jan.), p. 266.

MISCELLANEOUS

'Did You Hear That?' (on Japanese students), *Listener* (1 Jan.), p. 9.

'These Japanese', *Listener* (5 Mar.), pp. 293–4, 309.

1945

POETRY

'Sonnet' ('Not wrongly moved . . .'), *The War Poets*, ed. Oscar Williams.

1946

REVIEW

A Daughter of Han, by Ida Pruitt; *A Japanese Village*, by John F. Embree: *New Statesman* (29 June), p. 477.

1947

CRITICISM

'To Understand a Modern Poem' (on Dylan Thomas' 'A Refusal to Mourn'), *Strand Magazine* (Mar.), pp. 60–4.

'Thy Darling in an Urn' (on *The Well-Wrought Urn* by Cleanth Brooks), *Sewanee Review*, vol. 55 (Oct.), pp. 691–7.

Seven Types of Ambiguity (second edition, revised), Chatto & Windus.

1948

CRITICISM

'The Structure of Complex Words', *Sewanee Review*, vol. 56 (April), pp. 230–50.

'Emotions in Words Again', *Kenyon Review*, vol. 10, no. 4 (Autumn), pp. 579–601.

'The Style of the Master', Empson's contribution to *T. S. Eliot, A Symposium*, compiled by Richard Marsh and Tambimuttu, pp. 35–7.

1949

POETRY

Collected Poems (revised text with a new prefatory note, American edition), Harcourt Brace and Co. Including first publication of: 'Let it Go', 'Thanks for a Wedding Present'.

CRITICISM

'Fool in *Lear*', *Sewanee Review*, vol. 57 (April), pp. 177–214.
'Donne and the Rhetorical Tradition', *Kenyon Review*, vol. 11, no. 4 (Autumn), pp. 571–87.

REVIEWS

The Foundations of Aesthetics, by I. A. Richards, C. K. Ogden, and James Wood: *Hudson Review*, vol. 2 (Spring), pp. 94–7.
This Great Stage, by Robert B. Heilman: *Kenyon Review*, vol. 11 (Spring), pp. 342–54.

1950

CRITICISM

'Wit in the "Essay on Criticism"', *Hudson Review*, vol. 2, no. 4 (Winter), pp. 559–77.
Some Versions of Pastoral (second impression, with errata), Chatto & Windus.
'My Credo: Verbal Analysis', *Kenyon Review*, vol. 12, no. 4 (Autumn), pp. 594–601.
'George Herbert and Miss Tuve' (on an article by Rosemond Tuve: 'On Herbert's "Sacrifice"', *Kenyon Review*, vol. 12, no. 1, pp. 51–75), *Kenyon Review*, vol. 12, no. 4 (Autumn), pp. 735–8.
Some Versions of Pastoral (American edition), New Directions.

1951

CRITICISM

'Sense in *The Prelude*', *Kenyon Review*, vol. 13, no. 2 (Spring), pp. 285–302.

'Emotions in Poems', *The Kenyon Critics*, Cleveland.
The Structure of Complex Words, Chatto & Windus.
The Structure of Complex Words (American edition), New Directions.

LETTER

'The Staging of *Hamlet*', *Times Literary Supplement* (23 Nov.),
p. 749.

1952

POETRY

'Chinese Peasant Song' (title in *CP* 1955: 'Chinese Ballad'), *Nine*,
no. 9 (Summer–Autumn), p. 316. Reprinted under the title
'Chinese Ballad' in *New Statesman* (6 Dec. 1952), p. 683.
New Statesman (6 Dec.), p. 683 (reprint of 'Chinese Ballad').

CRITICISM

'Dover Wilson on *Macbeth*', *Kenyon Review*, vol. 14, no. 1 (Winter),
pp. 84–102.

REVIEWS

The Year One, by Kathleen Raine: *New Statesman* (1 Nov.), p. 518.
Purity of Diction in English Verse, by Donald Davie: *New Statesman*
(13 Dec.), p. 724.

LETTER

'This a good block' (textual point in Lear), *Times Literary
Supplement* (19 Dec.), p. 837.

1953

CRITICISM

'Answers to Comments' (contribution to 'The Critical Forum', on
Marvell's poetry), *Essays in Criticism*, vol. 3, no. 1 (Jan.),
pp. 114–20.

'Hamlet When New' (Part I), *Sewanee Review*, vol. 61 (Winter), pp. 15–42.

'Hamlet When New' (Part II), *Sewanee Review*, vol. 61 (Spring), pp. 185–205.

'Falstaff and Mr Dover Wilson', *Kenyon Review*, vol. 15, no. 2 (Spring), pp. 213–62.

'Bare Ruined Choirs' (contribution to 'The Critical Forum' on Shakespeare's sonnets, with a further note answering criticism by F. W. Bateson), *Essays in Criticism*, vol. 3, no. 3 (July), pp. 357–8, 362–3.

Seven Types of Ambiguity (third edition, revised), Chatto & Windus.

'The Loss of Paradise', *The Northern Miscellany of Literary Criticism*, no. 1, pp. 17–18.

REVIEWS

Science and Aesthetic Judgement, by S. J. Kahn; *The True Voice of Feeling*, by Herbert Read: *New Statesman* (21 Mar.), pp. 343–4.

Selected Poems, by Wallace Stevens: *Listener* (26 Mar.), p. 521.

Daybreak in China, by Basil Davidson: *New Statesman* (20 June), p. 750.

Conscience and the King, by Bertram Joseph; *Hamlet ou Les Personnages du Fils*, by Jean Paris: *New Statesman* (3 Oct.), p. 380.

Report on Mao's China, by Frank Moraes; *Window on China*, by Raja Hutheesing: *Listener* (8 Oct.), pp. 595–6.

Poetic Process, by George Whalley; *Aspects of Language*, by W. J. Entwistle: *New Statesman* (31 Oct.), p. 530.

Poems by John Wilmot, Earl of Rochester ed. V. de S. Pinto: *New Statesman* (28 Nov.), pp. 691–2.

1954

REVIEWS

Flaming Minister, by G. R. Elliott: *Kenyon Review*, vol. 16 (Winter), pp. 163–6.

Collected Poems, by Dylan Thomas; *Under Milk Wood*, by Dylan Thomas: *New Statesman* (15 May), pp. 635–6.

LETTERS

'Empson, Adams, and Milton' (reply to R. M. Adams' article 'Empson and Bentley'), *Partisan Review* (Nov.–Dec.), pp. 699–700.

On Hopkins' 'Windhover', *Times Literary Supplement* (1 Oct.), p. 625.

On 'The Elizabethan stage', *Times Literary Supplement* (10 Dec.), p. 801.

1955

POETRY

Collected Poems (with a revised prefatory note), Chatto & Windus. Including first publication of 'The Birth of Steel'.

CRITICISM

'Yes and No' (contribution to 'The Critical Forum', on the previous number of *Essays in Criticism*), *Essays in Criticism*, vol. 5, no. 1 (Jan.), pp. 88–90.

Seven Types of Ambiguity (American edition), Noonday Press.

REVIEWS

Mandarin Red, by James Cameron: *Listener* (9 June), p. 1039.

The Shores of Light, by Edmund Wilson; *The Language of Criticism and the Structure of Poetry*, by R. S. Crane; *The Verbal Icon*, by W. K. Wimsatt; *Language as Gesture*, by R. P. Blackmur: *Sewanee Review*, vol. 63 (Summer), pp. 471–9.

The Way of Deliverance, by S. Hanayama: *New Statesman* (17 Sept.), pp. 337–8.

The Crowning Privilege, by Robert Graves: *New Statesman* (1 Oct.), pp. 400–2.

Speculative Instruments, by I. A. Richards; *Interpretations*, ed. John Wain: *New Statesman* (10 Dec.), pp. 799–800.

LETTERS

On Hopkins' 'Windhover', *Times Literary Supplement* (20 May), p. 269.
On Masques, *The Times* (13 June), p. 9.

1956

POETRY

Collected Poems (second impression with a supplementary prefatory note), Chatto & Windus.

CRITICISM

'The Theme of *Ulysses*' (includes text of BBC talk, 'Bloomsday, 1954'), *Kenyon Review*, vol. 18 (Winter), pp. 26–52.
'*The Spanish Tragedy*', *Nimbus*, vol. 3, no. 3 (Summer), pp. 16–29.
'Mr Empson and the Fire Sermon' (reply to A. E. Rodway's review of *CP* 1955), *Essays in Criticism*, vol. 6, no. 4 (Oct.), pp. 481–2.

REVIEWS

Dublin's Joyce, by Hugh Kenner: *New Statesman* (11 Aug.), pp. 163–4.

LETTERS

Reply to Geoffrey Strickland's article on 'Empson's Criticism', *Mandrake*, vol. 2, no. 11 (Autumn and Winter 1955–6), pp. 447–8.
On *Waiting for Godot*, *Times Literary Supplement* (30 Mar.), p. 195.

1957

CRITICISM

'Restoration Comedy Again' (contribution to 'The Critical Forum'), *Essays in Criticism*, vol. 7, no. 3 (July), p. 318.
'Donne the Space Man', *Kenyon Review*, vol. 19 (Summer), pp. 337–99.
'*Alice in Wonderland*', *Art and Psychoanalysis*, ed. William Phillips, pp. 185–217.

REVIEW

Return to China, by James Bertram; *The Blue Ants*, by Robert Guillain: *New Statesman* (2 Nov.), pp. 573–4.

MISCELLANEOUS

On the 'Fire Sermon', *Arrows* (Sheffield University student magazine), New Year edition, pp. 5–6.

1958

CRITICISM

'Great Writers Rediscovered. The Grandeur of Fielding's *Tom Jones*', *Sunday Times* (30 Mar.), p. 13.
'*Tom Jones*', *Kenyon Review*, vol. 20 (Spring), pp. 217–49.
'*The Spanish Tragedy*', *English Critical Essays, The Twentieth Century*, second series, ed. Derek Hudson, pp. 215–35. (Reprint. Correction added in a subsequent reprinting.)

LETTER

On *Paradise Lost* (reply to F. R. Leavis), *Times Literary Supplement* (3 Oct.), p. 561.

1959

REVIEWS

The Critical Writings of James Joyce, ed. Ellsworth Mason and Richard Ellmann: *New Statesman* (20 June), p. 868.
James Joyce, by Richard Ellmann: *New Statesman* (31 Oct.), pp. 585–6.

LETTERS

On *1984*, by George Orwell, *Critical Quarterly*, vol. 1, no. 2 (Summer), pp. 157–9.
'Christianity and *1984*', *Critical Quarterly*, vol. 1, no. 4 (Winter), p. 352.

MISCELLANEOUS

Listen, LPV 3, *William Empson reading Selected Poems* (a gramophone record). With sleeve notes on the poems by W.E., Marvell Press.

1960

CRITICISM

'A Defense of Delilah' (on 'Samson Agonistes'), *Sewanee Review*, vol. 68 (Spring), pp. 240–55.
'The Satan of Milton', *Hudson Review*, vol. 13 (Spring), pp. 33–59.
'Satan Argues his Case' (broadcast talk), *Listener* (7 July), pp. 11–13.
'Adam and Eve' (broadcast talk), *Listener* (14 July), pp. 64–5.
'Heaven's Awful Monarch' (broadcast talk), *Listener* (21 July), pp. 111–14.

REVIEWS

Shakespeare's Wooden O, by Leslie Hotson: *New Statesman* (13 Feb.), pp. 224–5.
W. B. Yeats and the Tradition, by F. A. C. Wilson: *Review of English Literature*, vol. 1, no. 3 (July), pp. 51–6.
Some Graver Subject: An Essay on 'Paradise Lost', by J. B. Broadbent: *Listener* (4 Aug.), p. 196.
Studies in Words, by C. S. Lewis: *Times Literary Supplement* (30 Sept.), p. 627 (anonymous).
A Critique of 'Paradise Lost', by John Peter: *Listener* (27 Oct.), pp. 750–3.

LETTERS

Concerning broadcasts on *Milton's God*, *Listener* (28 July), p. 157.
'The Muse in Chains', *Times Literary Supplement* (5 Aug.), p. 497.

1961

CRITICISM

Milton's God, Chatto & Windus.
Seven Types of Ambiguity (paperback edition), Penguin Books.
Collected Poems (second American edition), Harcourt Brace.

REVIEW

The Lotus and the Robot, by Arthur Koestler: *New Statesman* (6 Jan.), pp. 21–2.

LETTERS

'Academic Caste', *Times Literary Supplement* (28 April), p. 263.
On *King Lear*, *Critical Quarterly*, vol. 3, no. 1 (Spring), pp. 67–8.
On R. L. Brett's review of *Milton's God*, *Critical Quarterly*, vol. 3, no. 4 (Winter), p. 368.
On a review of *Milton's God*, *Times Literary Supplement* (6 Oct.), p. 663.

MISCELLANEOUS

'Pei-Ta before the siege', *Arrows* (1959–61), pp. 6–8.

1962

POETRY

'Bacchus' (reprint with a new note), *Poet's Choice*, ed. Paul Engle and Joseph Langland, pp. 85–6.

CRITICISM

'Rhythm and Imagery in English Poetry', *British Journal of Aesthetics*, vol. 2, no. 1 (Jan.), pp. 36–54.
Milton's God (American edition), New Directions.
'The Theme of *Ulysses*' (reprint with final paragraph dated 1962), *A James Joyce Miscellany*, third series, ed. Marvin Magalaner, pp. 127–54.
'The Symbolism of Dickens', contribution to *Dickens and the Twentieth Century*, ed. John Gross and Gabriel Pearson, pp. 13–15.
'Tom Jones' (reprint), *Henry Fielding 'Tom Jones': A Casebook*, ed. Neil Compton, pp. 139–72.
'Tom Jones' (reprint, revised), *Fielding: A Collection of Critical Essays*, ed. Ronald Paulson (Twentieth Century Views), pp. 123–45.

REVIEW

Shakespeare's Happy Comedies, by J. Dover Wilson: *New Statesman* (7 Dec.), pp. 827–8.

LETTERS

Controversy arising from *Milton's God* concerning Milton's *Eikonoclastes* (mainly with Professor P. Alexander), *Times Literary Supplement* (2 Mar.), p. 137; (23 Mar.), p. 201; (27 April), p. 281; (25 May), p. 380. (See Appendix to revised edition of *Milton's God* (1965).)

1963

CRITICISM

'Lady Chatterley Again' (contribution to 'The Critical Forum'), *Essays in Criticism*, vol. 13, no. 1 (Jan.), pp. 101–4.
'Early Auden' (broadcast talk), *the Review*, no. 5 (Feb.), pp. 32–4.
'Dylan Thomas' (contribution to 'The Critical Forum'), *Essays in Criticism*, vol. 13, no. 2 (April), pp. 205–7.
'Argufying in Poetry', *Listener* (22 Aug.), pp. 277–90.
Seven Types of Ambiguity (third edition, revised), Chatto & Windus.

REVIEWS

George Herbert, by T. S. Eliot: *New Statesman* (4 Jan.), p. 18.
The Gutenberg Galaxy, by Marshall McLuhan: *Universities Quarterly*, vol. 17, no. 2 (Mar.), pp. 203–4.
The Dyer's Hand, by W. H. Auden: *New Statesman* (19 April), pp. 592–5.
Milton's Grand Style, by Christopher Ricks: *New Statesman* (23 Aug.), p. 230.
Shakespeare's Sonnets, ed. Martin Seymour-Smith; *William Shakespeare*, by A. L. Rowse; *Shakespeare*, by Peter Quennell: *New Statesman* (4 Oct.), pp. 447–8.
The Active Universe, by H. W. Piper: *Critical Quarterly*, vol. 5, no. 3, pp. 267–71.

MISCELLANEOUS

'William Empson in conversation with Christopher Ricks', *the Review*, nos 6 and 7 (June), pp. 26–35.

1964

CRITICISM

'The Ancient Mariner', *Critical Quarterly*, vol. 6, no. 4, pp. 298–319.

'Hunt the Symbol' (on Shakespearean criticism), *Times Literary Supplement* (23 April), pp. 339–41.

The Structure of Complex Words (second edition).

REVIEWS

The Duchess of Malfi, by Clifford Leech: *Essays in Criticism*, vol. XIV, no. 1, pp. 80–6.

Shakespeare's Sonnets, by J. Dover Wilson: *New Statesman* (7 Feb.), pp. 216–17.

The Secret History of the Mongols, by Arthur Waley: *New Statesman* (13 Mar.), p. 410.

Mr W.H., by Leslie Hotson: *New Statesman* (24 April), p. 642.

The Decline of Hell, by D. P. Walker: *New Statesman* (21 Aug.), p. 248.

LETTERS

'Resurrection' (reply to John Wren-Lewis, 'The passing of Puritanism'), *Critical Quarterly*, vol. 6, no. 1, p. 83.

'Resurrection' (comment on John Wren-Lewis's reply to the above), *Critical Quarterly*, vol. 6, no. 2, p. 178.

On 'Hunt the Symbol', *Times Literary Supplement* (7 May), p. 395.

MISCELLANEOUS

'The Ogden Portrait of Shakespeare', *New Statesman* (9 Oct.), p. 550.

1965

CRITICISM

Milton's God (revised edition corrected with notes and an appendix on Milton's *Eikonoclastes*; see 'Letters' 1962).

'The Variants for the Byzantium Poems', in *Essays Presented to Amy G. Stock*, ed. R. K. Kaul, University of Rajasthan Press, Jaipur, pp. 111–36. (Also in special number of *Phoenix*, published by the English Literature Society of Korea University, pp. 1–26.)

REVIEWS

The Shakespeare Inset, by Francis Berry: *New Statesman* (18 June), pp. 966–7.

In Excited Reverie, ed. A. Norman Jeffares and K. E. W. Cross; *W. B. Yeats: The Later Poetry*, by Thomas Parkinson; *Yeats and the Easter Rising*, by E. Malins: *New Statesman* (23 July), pp. 123–4.

The Life of Dylan Thomas, by Constantine Fitzgibbon: *New Statesman* (29 Oct.), pp. 647–8.

A Reading of Paradise Lost, by Helen Gardner: *New Statesman* (24 Dec.), p. 1004.

LETTER

'Shakespeare's Characters', *Critical Quarterly*, vol. 7, no. 3, p. 285.

MISCELLANEOUS

Comments on the Symposium, 'The Living Language', *Times Literary Supplement* (14 Jan.), p. 32; (27 May), p. 437.

1966

CRITICISM

Preface to J. R. Harrison, *The Reactionaries*, Gollancz.

'The Phoenix and the Turtle', *Essays in Criticism*, vol. 16, no. 2, pp. 147–53.

Empson's reply to James Jensen's 'The Construction of *Seven Types of Ambiguity*', *Modern Language Quarterly*, vol. 27, pp. 257–8.

Some Versions of Pastoral (paperback edition, revised, with new preface), Penguin Books.

'*The Spanish Tragedy*' (reprint, with correction), *Elizabethan Drama: Modern Essays in Criticism*, ed. Ralph J. Kaufmann, pp. 60–80.

'Literary Criticism and the Christian Revival', *The Rationalist Annual*, pp. 25–30.

REVIEWS

Five Essays on Milton's Epics, by Northrop Frye: *Listener* (28 July), p. 137.

Collected Poems and *Under Milk Wood* by Dylan Thomas (reprint); *Dylan Thomas: A Collection of Critical Essays*, ed. C. B. Cox (Twentieth Century Views), pp. 84–8.

John Donne: The Elegies, and the Songs and Sonnets, ed. Helen Gardner: *Critical Quarterly*, vol. 8, no. 3, pp. 255–80.

LETTERS

Reply to W. W. Robson's review of *Milton's God*, *Oxford Review*, no. 3 (Michaelmas), pp. 77–9.

On the historical interpretation of *Macbeth*, *The Times* (25 Oct.), p. 13.

1967

CRITICISM

'Basstards and Barstards' (contribution to 'The Critical Forum'), *Essays in Criticism*, vol. 17, no. 3, pp. 407–10.

'Donne and the Rhetorical Tradition' (reprint), *Elizabethan Poetry: Modern Essays in Criticism*, ed. Paul J. Alpers, pp. 63–77.

The Structure of Complex Words (American edition), University of Michigan Press.

REVIEWS

'*King Lear*' in our Time, by Maynard Mack: *Essays in Criticism*, vol. 17, no. 1, p. 95.

The Judgement of the Dead, by S. G. F. Brandon: *Listener* (30 Nov.), p. 709.

LETTERS

'Donne', *Critical Quarterly*, vol. 9, no. 1, p. 89.
'On *Troilus and Cressida*', *Times Literary Supplement* (2 Mar.), p. 167; (6 April), p. 296; (20 April), p. 340.
Comment on 'The achievement of William Empson' by Roger Sale, *Hudson Review*, vol. 20, no. 4, pp. 534–8.

MISCELLANEOUS

Portrait of J. B. S. Haldane narrated by Lord Ritchie-Calder; contributions by W.E. (broadcast talk), *Listener* (2 Nov.), pp. 565–8.
Interview with Empson, *The Star* (Sheffield), (31 Mar.), p. 64.

1968

CRITICISM

Introduction to *Poems* (Signet edition of Shakespeare's poems).
'*Tom Jones*' (reprint), *Twentieth Century Interpretations of 'Tom Jones*', ed. Martin Battestin.
'Basstards and Barstards' (contribution to 'The Critical Forum'), *Essays in Criticism*, vol. 18, no. 1, pp. 236–7.
'To Understand a Modern Poem' (reprint), *Modern Poetry: Essays in Criticism*, ed. John Hollander, pp. 243–8.
'Literary Criticism and the Christian Revival' (reprint), *Writing in England Today: the Last Fifteen Years*, ed. Karl Miller, pp. 168–74.

REVIEWS

Black and White: A Study of Aubrey Beardsley, by Brigid Brophy: *Listener* (28 Nov.), pp. 721–2.
The Duchess of Malfi, by Clifford Leech (reprint): *Twentieth Century Interpretations of 'The Duchess of Malfi*', ed. Norman Rabkin.

MISCELLANEOUS

'William Empson in conversation with Christopher Ricks' (reprint), *The Modern Poet: Essays from 'the Review'*, ed. Ian Hamilton, pp. 177–87.

1969

CRITICISM

'*Volpone*', *Hudson Review*, vol. 21, no. 4 (Winter), pp. 651–66.
'The Theme of *Ulysses*', *Twentieth Century Studies* (Nov.), pp, 39–41.

REVIEW

The Duchess of Malfi, by Clifford Leech (reprint): *John Webster: A Critical Anthology*, ed. G. K. and S. K. Hunter.

LETTER

'Swinburne and D. H. Lawrence', *Times Literary Supplement* (20 Feb.), p. 185.

1970

CRITICISM

'*The Alchemist*', *Hudson Review*, vol. 22, no. 4, pp. 595–608.
'Dryden's Apparent Scepticism', *Essays in Criticism*, vol. 20, no. 2, pp. 172–81.
'Falstaff and Mr. Dover Wilson' (excerpted reprint), *Shakespeare, Henry IV, Parts I and II: A Casebook*, ed. G. K. Hunter.
'Joyce's Intentions', *Twentieth Century Studies*, no. 4 (4 Nov.), pp. 26–36.

1971

CRITICISM

Comment on Harth's reply to 'Dryden's Apparent Scepticism' (contribution to 'The Critical Forum'), *Essays in Criticism*, vol. 21, no. 1, pp. 111–15.

REVIEW

Dylan Thomas: Early Prose Writings, ed. Walford Davies; *Dylan Thomas: The Poems*, ed. Daniel Jones: *Listener* (28 Oct.), pp. 588–90.

MISCELLANEOUS

'Old Men Remember with Advantages', *Arrows*, no. 102 (June), pp. 8–10.
'Orwell at the BBC', *Listener* (4 Feb.), pp. 129–31. (Reprinted in *The World of George Orwell*, ed. Miriam Gross (1971), pp. 93–9.)
Foreword to *Peking Cookery* by K. H. C. Lo.

1972

CRITICISM

'Rescuing Donne', *Just So Much Honor*, ed. P. A. Fiore, pp. 95–148 (inaccurately printed).
On 'Alice' (reprint from *Some Versions of Pastoral*), *Aspects of Alice*, ed. Robert Phillips.

REVIEW

T. S. Eliot: The Waste Land: A Facsimile and Transcript of the Original Drafts Including the Annotations of Ezra Pound, ed. Valerie Eliot: *Essays in Criticism*, vol. 22, no. 4, pp. 417–29.

LETTER

On *Mansfield Park*, *Times Literary Supplement* (14 July), p. 819.

MISCELLANEOUS

Coleridge's Verse: A Selection, chosen and edited by William Empson and David Pirie.
W.E. on the Japanese (Broadcast talk, 1942) included in 'Voices from the Archives', *Listener* (2 Nov.), pp. 593–4.

CRITICISM

'The Intentional Fallacy Again' (Contribution to 'The Critical Forum'), *Essays in Criticism*, vol. 23, no. 4, p. 435.

'The Hammer's Ring' in *I. A. Richards: Essays in his Honor*, ed. Reuben Brower, Helen Vendler, and John Hollander, OUP, New York, pp. 73–83.

'Yeats and the Spirits', *New York Review of Books* (13 Dec.), pp. 43–5.

1973

MISCELLANEOUS

'The Gifts of China', *Sunday Times* (30 Sept.). A description of the Chinese Exhibition at the Royal Academy.